September Sundays

SEPTEMBER SUNDAYS

CLÍODHNA NÍ ANLUAIN

NEW ISLAND

SETPEMBER SUNDAYS
First published 2013 by
New Island
2 Brookside
Dundrum Road
Dublin 14

www.newisland.ie

P/B   ISBN 978-1-84840-278-2
ePub   ISBN 978-1-84840-279-9
mobi   ISBN 978-1-84840-280-5

Copyright CD Recordings © - RTÉ
Internal Images - see index on page 320
Cover design by Mariel Deegan
Typeset by JVR Creative India.
Printed by ScandBook AB, Falun, Sweden 2013

New Island received financial assistance from
The Arts Council (An Comhairle Ealaíon), Dublin, Ireland

10 9 8 7 6 5 4 3 2 1

Contents

Introduction by Clíodhna Ní Anluain   1

1. The Hurler's Seat by Cathy Power*   5

2. Tears of All-Ireland Sunday by Joe Kearney*   8

3. V.S. Naipaul and D.J. Carey by Louis Brennan   11

4. Existentialist Dog by Leo Cullen   14

5. Croke Park: A Tribute by Tim Carey*   17

6. This Morning in the Half-Light by Cyril Kelly   21

7. Mayo: 107 Years of the Green Above
   the Red by Art Ó Súilleabháin   24

8. Another Anniversary by Peter Fallon   27

9. The Moonlight in Mayo by Dan O'Neill   28

10. The Hurler by John Conroy   32

11. My Father by Theo Dorgan   34

12. Trasna na Sionainne by Bernie Ní Fhlatharta   38

13. Don't Hit the Ref if you're Winning
    by Tommy McKearney   41

14. The Star-Spangled Final by Josephine McArdle   45

15. Come Home, Sam, Come Home by Cyril Kelly   48

16. My First All-Ireland by Tom Seaver 51
17. The Day Kerry Beat Cavan in Ward's Meda by Pádraig McGinn 56
18. In Memory of Tim Kennelly by Cyril Kelly 58
19. Alternate Lives by Joe Kane 61
20. A Sense of Home by Mary Folan 62
21. The Princess and the Final by Alan Titley 65
22. Reservoir Dogs by Joe Kearney 69
23. Cast in Bronze by Josephine McArdle 72
24. From Mortal to Myth by Cyril Kelly 75
25. The Final Beginning by Art Ó Súílleabháin 79
26. Mayo Memories by Liam Horan 82
27. Religious Persuasion by Tommy Sands 85
28. Thunder and Lightning Final by Leo Cullen 88
29. The Scrapbook by Mae Leonard* 91
30. See Ye in another Thirty-Three Years by John Downing 94
31. Home by the Lee by John Conroy 96
32. The Beijing Banshees by Josephine McArdle 98
33. Listening to the All-Ireland of 1957 in Chittagong by Norman Freeman 101
34. Changing Times by Tommy Sands 105
35. Up the Déise by Lynn Cahill 109
36. A Panellist with Feeling by Gerry Moran 111
37. The Black and Amber Waistcoat by Cathy Power 114
38. The Mullinahone Boot by Leo Cullen 117
39. Dan Shanahan by Catherine Foley* 120

40. Alone, All Alone by Colbert Kearney 123

41. Heraclitus, Home and Hurling by Joe Kearney 126

42. The Sweetest Thing by Josephine McArdle 129

43. Speckled Cow by Joe Ó Muircheartaigh 133

44. The Day Kerry Cheered on the Red and
White of Cork by Joe O'Toole 137

45. Croke Park Under Dalkey Hill by Tim Carey 140

46. The Night Before by John O'Donnell 143

47. Deep Wells and All-Irelands by Leo Cullen 144

48. Kilkenny's Martial Arts by Joe Kearney 147

49. Team Photo by John O'Donnell 150

50. Elizabeth the First Hadn't a Clue by Cyril Kelly 151

51. Ghost Journeys by Joe Ó Muircheartaigh 154

52. We Shudda Won! by Larry McCluskey* 157

53. Like a Bat Out of Hell by Theresa Farrell 161

54. Daisy-Chain by Noel Duffy 163

55. Uisce Faoi Thalamh / Undercurrents
by Leo Cullen 165

56. Trapped in Amber by Joe Kearney 167

57. The Moon Behind The Hill: Kilkenny's
Real Anthem by Gerry Moran 170

58. I Never Saw My Da Hurl by Cathy Power 173

59. It's Only A Game by Theresa McKenna 176

60. I Can't Wait Till Next Year by Noel Ellis 179

61. The Oath by Bairbre O'Hogan 182

62. Moore Street Man by Joe Ó Muircheartaigh 185

63. Up Down by Conor O'Callaghan* 189

64. Sam Maguire and The Russian Connection
    by Nicky Barry   192

65. The Commentator by Joe Ó Muircheartaigh   195

66. Cat Fight in Croker by Gerry Moran   199

67. Lory Meaghar's Swallow by Joe Kearney   202

68. Ollie Walsh: Hurling Hero by Cathy Power   205

69. The First Sub by Leo Cullen   208

70. Hurling Final Girl by Mary Ledwidge   211

71. The Bus Journey by John Allen   214

72. All-Ireland Sunday by Josephine McArdle   217

73. Mick Carolan by John MacKenna*   221

74. In The Beginning There Were Rumours
    by Cyril Kelly*   224

75. Sky Blue by Colbert Kearney   227

76. Best of Times, Worst of Times
    by Joe Ó Muircheartaigh   231

77. Gaillimh Abú by Mary O'Malley*   234

78. Hurling Chose Me by Eamon O'Shea   238

79. The Hunger Games by Gerry Moran   241

80. Dreams of a Raggedy Bush by Joe Kearney   244

81. Michael Walsh: A Hurling Life by Patrick E. Walsh   247

82. A Journey Not a Route by Cathy Power   251

83. My Mother's County by Leo Cullen*   254

84. House of Pain by Tom Rowley   257

85. Con Houlihan by Cyril Kelly   260

86. Jimmy's Winning Matches by Denise Blake*   263

87. My First All-Ireland by Pat Coleman   266

88. Banquet of Dreams by Joe Ó Muircheartaigh   269

89. Yerra by Maurice Cashell   273

90. Dublin's Last Senior Hurling All-Ireland
     In 1938 by William Nolan   276

91. Father, Son and Slievenamon by William J. Smyth   280

92. How to Score in Hotpants by Martina Devlin   283

93. September 1982 by Paul Rouse   287

94. Wearing the Blue of Dublin by Tim Carey   290

95. Rebels at the Double by Bert Wright   294

96. Ye'll Make it to Croker Yet by Joe Ó Muircheartaigh 298

97. Only a Game by Maurice Cashell   301

98. Lining Out by Pat Boran   304

99. Over the Bar by Mary O'Malley   306

100. The Match by John O'Donnell   310

Author Biographical Notes   312

Photo Credits   320

Acknowledgements   323

(* indicates that this piece is included in the accompanying CD.)

To the memory of my father,
who lifted me up and over the turnstiles.

Ní fhacas riamh radharc ba ghile
Ná ceathrar óigfhear ag bualadh sliotar
A chamán féin i láimh gach duine
Fuaim a ngleo an ceol ba bhinne

(Eoghan Ó hAnluain, 1938–2012)

Introduction

RTÉ's *Sunday Miscellany* is one of the longest running and popular programmes on Irish Radio. Its successful formula continues, as it started out in 1968, to broadcast new short essays, read by their authors, interspersed with music. The selection of the weekly content comes from open submissions, as well as commissioned writing from well-known and new voices, covering a breadth of subjects and styles, recorded in studios, and sometimes at specially produced occasions with an audience.

Some books are already written before they've even been thought about. Such was the pleasant case with so much of the content of this book. As summertime receded during the year I started as producer of *Sunday Miscellany*, and it became clear which teams would line out for the All-Ireland Championship Finals, I started to receive submissions for consideration for those Sundays in September. The collective anticipation these matches had fuelled in the imagination struck me. So I was delighted when, having broadcast a selection of them on the appropriate dates, there was such an immediate, passionate and demonstrative response from listeners. Ever since, this annual experience has become an unbroken pattern of *Sunday Miscellany*'s output. Looking over the programme's archive, I am reminded that contributions on these Sundays reference matches stretching across the hundred years of championship finals played in Croke Park, and that the people, places and experiences captured in them are so much more expansive than the particular stories of the specific teams, supporters and matches of any given period.

Each of the book's contributions, its memory and its emotions, become those of us all. This is because aspects of the recollections of others echo our own. It is how, in compiling this book, my own first time in Croke Park has come back to me, or perhaps, over time, has been re-imagined from many different Sundays. I was reminded of why going to Croke Park is so much more than simply a physical journey to a particular place. Going to Croke Park bridges generations, fills in gaps in time and the unspoken and makes sense of why being part of something bigger than each of us matters.

The day I was first brought to Croke Park, my father parked the car somewhere between Parnell Square and the North Circular Road. We would walk the remainder of the way. He was assisted with the parking by a man in a hat, who told us he'd be keeping an eye on the car for us. My father had grown up within a twenty minutes' stroll of Croke Park and was instinctively familiar with and at home in the geography of the shortcuts he steered us children through that day: the narrow streets lined with closely knit rows of little houses and cottages behind and between the wider thoroughfares and squares that showed off far more substantial but nevertheless rundown buildings. This is where, as a boy, he had practised hurling a ball from one side of Parnell Square to the other while attending Coláiste Mhuire before graduating on to the Phoenix Park's Fifteen Acres, playing for Eoghan Ruadh and for the Dublin minor team. Here, he told us as we walked along, was where he saw and heard people from other counties meet and converse on All-Ireland Sundays, and where he gathered autographs. Once, he told us, he was lucky enough to get the signature of Christy Ring outside on the footpath between Barry's and The Castle Hotel on Great Denmark Street, where so many of the iconic players and former players could be spotted on big match days. He shared these stories with us in a way that made them vital as we walked along, pointing out to us landmarks that worked as prompts for the next instalment of some great narrative.

His stories connected me with those streets, and started a personal association with something vast that was 'just around another few corners,' he told us, if only we kept on walking. I took in colours and flag sellers, fruit and chocolate sellers, and the sense of a crowd building, of people gathering. Somewhere along here my grandfather comes into the picture, and joined us, and maybe my uncle, and some cousins, before the great colossus of Croke Park eventually appeared before us and we children were each lifted up and over the turnstiles. We had entered into the dark, overwhelming underbelly of the vast Cusack Stand on Jones's Road before re-emerging up into daylight again to take our place at one of the leaning crowd barriers along the sloping Canal End terraces. Those bars were of little use to me for leaning on as I was just tall enough to occasionally reach up and swing out of them during the course of the match. I spent as much time taking in the complete focus, the emotion and ways of talking of the people around me as the match progressed as I did, being intrigued by as much of the action as I could see on the pitch below me. The crowds around me wore a nod of colour towards the purple and gold of Wexford and the black and amber of Kilkenny in a crêpe paper hat or a rosette. It was a hurling match. By the end of it, I was hooked.

These days, as I bring my children to Croke Park and make it our own, it is me who does the pointing, who is passing on to them the likes of what my father showed and told me, and his father shared with him as they headed to Croke Park on so many long-ago Sundays. In years to come it will be my children recalling these present days, and adding on memories of their own.

Contributions in this collection also recall experiencing Croke Park through matches broadcast on the radio and on television around the country in Kilkenny, Armagh, Tipperary and Mayo, in London, New York and Chittagong.

The book includes contributions about great playing heroes such as Kevin Heffernan, Ollie Walsh, Lory Meaghar, Mick Carolan, Kevin Moran and Tim Kennelly. There are contributions too from people who played for their counties, as well as from some current managers, amongst them Dan O'Neill, Larry McCluskey, William J. Smyth, Nicky Barry and Maurice Cashell, Eamon O'Shea and John Allen.

Writers and commentators such as Con Houlihan, Breandán Ó hEithir, Micheál O'Hehir and Micheál Ó Muircheartaigh are celebrated. Authorities on the GAA such as Paul Rouse, Tim Carey, Joe Ó Muircheartaigh, William Nolan and Liam Horan make their own contributions.

Club matches, club county finals and provincial finals are included in other contributions. The GAA beyond Ireland, Ladies' Gaelic football and the Artane Band have their appearances, as well as the dreams of achievement and participation instilled by Cumann na mBunscol. There is poetry and prose amongst the contributions, as well as an accompanying CD that includes recordings of some of the original RTÉ broadcasts, read by their authors.

This year, 2013, marks a hundred years since Croke Park became the venue for September All-Ireland Finals. By way of this collection of a hundred contributions, *Sunday Miscellany* salutes those many magical days, and the way in which they have lifted us up and out of ourselves across a century of Sundays.

Clíodhna Ní Anluain
Editor and Producer
Sunday Miscellany
RTÉ Radio 1

THE HURLER'S SEAT
Cathy Power

I recently heard Seamus Heaney read his poem about a garden seat, and as usual it touched me. Perhaps it's because I have a project of my own that involves a garden seat.

There was a seat that stood outside the house where I was born: 23 Gardiner Place, Dublin. My parents were from Kilkenny, and so was the culture of that household. It was called Kilkenny House, although by rights it should have been called Kilkenny Hurling House, and it sat in the middle of the capital like a Kilkenny embassy, a little bit of that county's soil in a foreign place.

The seat never rested in a leafy bower or shady nook; it was naked and exposed there on the steps of that Georgian house. It was where we sat, in the evening sun, to watch the world go by in the time between clearing up after middle-of-the-day dinners and before the lodgers came home for tea.

On that seat we chatted to neighbours and watched the goings-on of the street. It was where a million moves on the hurling field were discussed and argued over, and where the wood became shiny from use by hurlers' and former hurlers' backsides.

It had an ornate skeleton of wrought iron, with fancy ends on it. The seat and back were made of wood, and it was an annual project to paint it, and so protect it from the weather it endured all year round, for it was never moved from that step.

My father often painted it, and my childhood memory pictures it in a pale green and then a dark red, but once I remember the job being done by a famous Kilkenny hurler, Tommy Leahy from Urlingford, who won All-Irelands with my father in 1932, 33 and 35.

A painter by trade, he grained it, using an elaborate process of stain, rollers and combs, with much talk of getting various stages of the task done before the rain came, because it was all done out on the step of the house.

In Kilkenny House, the day of a hurling All-Ireland, no matter who was playing, was bigger than Christmas, back when going to an All-Ireland Final was not something done after breakfast and before your evening meal.

People travelled the day before, or came on trains and buses that began their journeys in the middle of the night. Working men who had gone to make their living in England would come home for the All-Ireland. Arriving a few days beforehand, they would be welcomed into the house like family, invited down to the basement kitchen to chat and drink tea or large bottles of stout and small whiskeys at all hours of the day and night. This was their annual holiday, and they were determined to make the most of it. They could rely, of course, on the full co-operation of Kilkenny House. Regulars would know to book their bed well in advance for that first weekend in September. As a small child, I would be stationed, weather permitting, outside on that seat on the Saturday evening before the match, to tell people that we had no room and to redirect them to neighbouring guest-houses. No matter how many we had staying in the house, though, it was a dead cert that my father, having spent the evening in Tommy Moore's of Cathedral Street or Club na nGael in North Great George's Street, would come home with some poor auld divil that hadn't a bed and sure you couldn't leave him out. On many the morning of a match, we found someone stretched out on that seat on the step, having failed to find a bed elsewhere.

By lunchtime on match day, the house would be full of huge countrymen eating plates of cold ham, spuds and mushy peas, followed by jelly and cream and cups of tea to fortify them.

And amid it all there was the hunt for tickets, the swapping and bartering, buying and selling, the begging and pleading. If you had a spare ticket it was the place to come to sell it or swap it or even give it away. What mattered was to find a good home for it before the throw-in.

This was before the fans in Croke Park were called 'patrons,' and no one was telling them not to enter the 'playing area.' We called it 'the pitch,' and we had many ecstatic moments swarming onto it to watch trophies being lifted in the Hogan Stand by men in black and amber. Then we would rush back to Gardiner Place, to sit on that same seat and watch the huge stream of supporters moving down Gardiner Place on their way home again, many stopping for a quick post mortem of the match, heading for pints and more food at the Castle Hotel or Barry's before boarding buses and trains again.

A year or so after my father's death in 1965, we moved to Phibsborough, leaving a lot behind us in that house. But my mother took the seat, and so it rested in a garden for nearly 40 years.

When my mother died in 2003, I took it to Kilkenny, from where, for all I know, my grandparents brought it when they moved to Dublin at the start of the last century. It is sitting in my back garden in Thomastown and, if truth be known, needs a coat of paint and a few repairs.

All going well, it will be a resting-place for hurlers' backsides for another hundred years or so.

(first broadcast on RTÉ Radio in 2004)

TEARS OF ALL-IRELAND SUNDAY
Joe Kearney

We must have seemed an odd pairing on that Sunday afternoon. Myself, the fledgling hippy and the man in the blue suit huddled against a telephone pole in Dollis Hill Park, North London. I had drifted into the tired acres of beaten grass and gaunt shrubbery with a melancholic indifference that can only be provoked by empty pockets. The park was cheating autumn on that September day in 1967 by delivering a display of hot, sunny defiance.

I observed the man in the blue suit, saw him press a small transistor radio against the pole, and would have sauntered past him had my ears not been arrested by a familiar voice: the unmistakable singsong chant ebbing and flowing from the tinny speaker. The man in the blue suit was using the telephone pole as a conduit to enhance his radio reception. Its own aerial, even fully extended, was as useless as a polished broken tine on a hayfork.

The voice on the radio was the voice of my childhood Sundays, from a place I thought I'd lost and a self I thought had vanished.

I gestured to the man in the blue suit. Was it okay if I joined him to listen? He responded with an indifferent 'Suit yourself.'

I watched him appraise my appearance, saw him take in the tie-dyed, beaded, long-haired creature that was the opposite to his white drip-dry nylon conservative self as one could imagine.

The National Anthem followed the county anthems. Emotion built in incremental steps. The hair stood on my arms and on the back of my neck. The water level built up behind the fragility of the dam. I defied the overspill with sheer will-power and self-control for as long as I could. That was until Micheál O'Hehir extended a welcome to all those listening in Boston, New York, Chicago… London. The Croke Park roar reached us in waves like the phantom seas in a shell held to the ear of memory. It was then that the tears found the line of least resistance and coursed down my embarrassed cheeks.

The man in the blue suit observed all.

'It's times like this that you'd miss the auld place,' he said, offering me a cigarette from the fresh packet of Major.

The softness of his lilt hinted his origins.

'You're from Cork?' I asked.

His eyes crinkled with mischief. He trotted out his icebreaker, his party piece:

'Cork me hole!' he shouted, 'I'm from Mallow!'

Seeing my reaction, he crumpled under the power of his own wit, and was overtaken by a spasm that was part laughter, part cough, until the tears that sprung to his own eyes matched mine.

'What county man are you yourself?' he enquired. I hesitated before replying, for I had grown up in a divided household where the waspish black and amber jostled with the banner of the red and white 'blood and bandage.' I could assume either allegiance. On this afternoon, however, county loyalty was unimportant. What was important was the reawakening of memories of previous All-Ireland Sundays and all that they meant; the end of summer and the return to school – pencils in their wooden case, pointed and sharp, schoolbooks that would leak knowledge from the wallpapered protection of their covers. Copybooks with pictures of round towers also pointed and sharp; as sharp as the attention we promised to pay to our teachers, as sharp as the bittersweet blackberries of the hedgerow. As sharp as the crack of tar bubbles when they burst beneath bicycle tyres in potholed country lanes, as sharp as the memories flowing down the tarred pole and out of the radio.

When finally the 'Hip, hips' were counted out we shook hands and parted. Back home, soda bread was being cut for tea.

Ash plants were being picked up, Wellingtons pulled on and cows collected for milking.

We left the park and returned, not to the small fields of our origins, but to the bedsits of Cricklewood and Kilburn.

I will remember the man in the blue suit today as I do on all other All-Ireland Sundays when I renew my vow. When Micheál Ó Muircheartaigh welcomes those listening in Sydney, New York, Brazil… London, and the roar goes up, I will not cry; this year I swear I will not cry.

(first broadcast on RTÉ Radio in 2004)

V.S. NAIPAUL AND D.J. CAREY
Louis Brennan

On All-Ireland Sunday in 1987, I relaxed in Port of Spain during an island-hopping tour of the West Indies, time off from the milk round of Caribbean electricity companies that might buy my Irish transformers. Trinidad is the biggest of these islands, and it seemed a logical place to rest up for the weekend.

Sport was prominent that day in the Sunday *Guardian*: the local Brown Jack had won the big one at the Santa Rosa track, beating the foreign-bred colts for only the second time in thirty years. The cricket correspondent pondered the forthcoming World Cup. The West Indies were favourites, and already the calypso writers were weaving rhythms in celebration. Croke Park and Kilkenny were far away, but excellence in other disciplines was all around.

Across from the racing results lay the book page, and another dominant name: V.S. Naipaul gazed tolerantly out beneath a bold headline: *The Enigma of Arrival*. The great man had written a new book, and the paper had given it half a page. I had already read this novel with enormous pleasure, so I approached the review with unusual interest. I knew that V.S. Naipaul, of Indian extraction, had grown up in Trinidad beside the sugar cane, the chattel houses and the palm. His father had been a writer, indeed his brother Shiva had followed V.S. between the covers before dying young of a tropical disease. V.S. Naipaul himself had made his way to England on a scholarship and, after an uncertain start, found his literary niche there in the evocation of the eclectic sounds and stories of his youth. V.S. Naipaul became 'VS.' Like the DJ in D.J. Carey, V.S. became a patent on an acronym for excellence.

His new book, *The Enigma of Arrival,* was a moving account of the rites of passage endured by people undergoing change. The novel, set on Salisbury Plain near Stonehenge, charted the slow and painful development of a writer's way of looking at life. V.S. wrote with a tenderness that belied his occasional public persona of arrogance. Great subjects are illuminated best by small dramas. He demonstrated a compassion for the ordinary, both in the colonial tropics of his youth and in his later pastoral world of Middle England. The *Enigma* was a fanfare for the common man.

The literary critic in the Sunday *Guardian,* however, disagreed: twenty-five years after Independence, VS, he thundered, was still trapped in the colonial genre, and had been bypassed by the creolisation or regeneration of the new creativity. The book was a return to, and an acceptance of, the degeneration from which he had fled.

Serves me right, a hurler on the ditch, for what do I know? How could I enjoy something so much, unaware of the sentiments of this carnival land? Could I not have anticipated the reaction of the literati of this island of music, colour and scent?

I wondered at first, knowing VS's penchant for conflict, whether he and his reviewer many years ago had competed for the same gymslipped spice girl as they walked home from school. Or was it that VS, when playing at home, only a few decades after independence, had to be both VS and DJ, and represent something wider than literature? So I wrote to the critic of the *Guardian.*

I wrote that VS was an artist, that he had his own playing-field and that he should be read. *The Enigma of Arrival* was not VS striding out to bat, with pads, gloves and pencil behind the ear, in a crisis on Sabina Park with West Indies twenty-one for four wickets down. His critic's reaction was, however, understandable:

at a similar stage in our own history, it was thought that our writers had to be banned lest we got the wrong end of the stick.

Monday, after the football final, with insufficient stamps, brought the following Sunday's *Guardian*. Naipaul should be read, said the heading over my letter, and a new photo showed a more cheerful VS.

Recently, an old newspaper cutting brought back the memory. Now perhaps I would add a rider: VS and DJ – what would happen if DJ also wrote poetry?

(first broadcast on RTÉ Radio in 2004)

EXISTENTIALIST DOG
Leo Cullen

The dog walks freely towards the turnstiles. Freely, he lives in the small streets behind the stadium and falls in step with the pair of feet he thinks he recognises but ultimately doesn't. The feet go through the stiles; he follows. Black and white dog, small, but it doesn't matter what size or colour, because he is just a dog like any other, curious. He walks between legs, now there are more and more legs. He sniffs the ground, free dog, he sniffs the steps leading up to the terrace. He doesn't sniff anything he knows – things that smell something like him. Small boy drops packet of crisps before him. Can dog believe his eyes? He doesn't have to; dog is not interested in belief, only freedom. He munches crisps, he licks crisps; he licks the bag until it is see-through cellophane. Then he ambles along. He looks up at all the faces. Nobody has any time for dog. Everybody hurries, everybody walking in the same direction. Dog follows. Sniffs the virgin concrete. Everybody sits, he sits too for a moment. Does he consider why everybody is seated and talking, all talking, about the same thing? Dog doesn't consider. Only thing dog ever does consider is Mr Buckley, the butcher who lives down his street. Butcher Buckley isn't here. Or at least he hasn't spotted Butcher Buckley. Or smelled Butcher Buckley, who he can smell a dog mile away.

Dog considers the field below him. Big spaces, running spaces, are things a dog, a free dog like he, does consider. If his path goes by that way at some stage, he might just pop into that field.

Everybody sits down; dog sits down. Then everybody stands up; dog stands up. It gets noisy. They are shouting all around him. Swelled chests and tonsils. First one big shout, accompanied by waving of cloths. Then another big shout, accompanied by waving of other cloths. Dog doesn't consider colour. He doesn't differentiate red and white from black and amber. He doesn't consider that they are all shouting at him, all waving their cloths at him. Only Butcher Buckley shouts, only Butcher Buckley waves his cloth at him.

Dog grows bored. Ambles back down towards where he came from. Now there is nobody down there. He squints out at the street he knows. Nothing out there on which a dog like he, an athletic dog like he, might achieve his potential. He licks another crisp bag. He licks melted chocolate and ice cream. He licks a burst peach, but he doesn't like peach. He licks his lips and returns to the fray, this time through a new entrance, through a tunnel! Dog likes tunnels. He catches a glimpse of the field. Men in there, with sticks! Dog likes to run after men with sticks. Then he can't help doing just that, because he is in there too.

He runs across the field. Noisy on that side also. Runs right across the field again. Whom to follow? This one with socks down around his ankles? This one with the ball? Now he hasn't got it any more! Confusion for dog? Dogs don't get confused. Dogs run, stop and sniff.

Dog likes to lie and scratch his back on grass. He does just that. On his back, he scratches his paws against the sky. The noise up there is like black thunder. Dog doesn't think that. Dog feels it. Who cares what a dog thinks? He licks a burst bottle. Now he stands in the very centre of the field. A man with his hand out to him, a whistle in his mouth. The man is not Butcher Buckley. Dog knows that much. But still he runs away from him. Now dog runs, not across the field, because across the field leads to nowhere, as he knows, but runs along the length of the field. Dog runs into a net. Man with wide stick tries to jump on him. Dog escapes. Oh, great roar goes up when dog does that. 'Goalie, you can't even block a shaggy dog?!' Come to think of it, everybody now is trying to block him. 'Here dog. Dog, dog. Get off the god-damned field, dog!'

Does dog hear things properly? Do the massive roars and laughs, and even screams he hears on the stands, happen to coincide with each time somebody makes a lunge for him and misses? Man in white coat lunges; dog sidesteps. 'Run, funny dog, run!' The stands erupt with gleeful laughter. Is Dog enjoying it? – Dog running so fast his ears lift in the wind? – No, Dog is just there, just playing the game of his life. Life is a dog's game.

(first broadcast on RTÉ Radio in 2004)

SPORTSFILE | 27 August 2005; Referee Gerry Kinneavy removes a dog from the pitch. Bank of Ireland All-Ireland Senior Football Championship Quarter-Final Replay, Dublin v Tyrone, Croke Park, Dublin. Picture credit: Damien Eagers / SPORTSFILE

CROKE PARK: A TRIBUTE
Tim Carey

The earliest known published account at a match day of what is now known as Croke Park was written in 1896 about a football match between Tipperary's Arravale Rovers and Young Irelands of Dublin. In many ways, the scene described is utterly recognisable. The article begins:

> All bets on bad weather being called off at dawn, and if we failed to discern the sun coming over those eastern hilltops and a heavy, murky atmosphere precluded a sky of blue, still the day ripened out into a proverbial summer's one, rather oppressive to the players, but delightful from a spectator's point of view. Long before the scheduled time for starting, streams of spectators were seen wending their way towards Jones's Road.

The writer continues, and tells of a Tipperary father bringing his Dublin-born children to see the team of his native county play, of the people who gather at the Canal Bridge before the match, of the proverbial Gaelic man, the clerk, the artisan, and now and again an outsider.

Then, with the streets deserted, the tense seconds before the match starts:

... when the last buzz of excitement dwindled down, and each one held his breath. A shrill blow of [the referee's] whistle announced the advent of the fray, in goes the leather, and the spectators giving vent to their pent-up feelings, a roar awoke the surrounding echoes, which never ceased throughout the hour.

When the article was written, Croke Park was the City and Suburban Sports Ground owned by Maurice Butterly – the Gaelic Athletic Association would not purchase it for another seventeen years – and it was used for everything from pony racing to Gaelic games.

The only facility for spectators was the now long gone Pavilion Stand. Most people stood, unimpeded, at the edge of the pitch. The venue has certainly been transformed beyond recognition – there is the Hogan Stand, the Cusack Stand and Hill 16, each of which is freighted with their own history. Today, in the region of 80,000 will pack into what is the third-largest sports stadium in Europe, with its spectacular, sweeping stands, corporate boxes and hi-tech pitch.

Croke Park on All-Ireland day is a communal experience – families, villages, counties on the move. It is also one that is intensely personal – that sick feeling in your stomach, the beating heart, the sweaty palms. A cocktail of emotions is shaken by anticipation and distilled by memory.

Places and buildings possess their own autobiographies and guard their own memories. Croke Park is as much about memory as it is about live action. It is memory that gives it its resonance. The memories of past victories and defeats. The memories that make countless connections between ostensible strangers.

I have my own memories of Croke Park. The 'Twelve Apostles' or 'The Dirty Dozen' of the Dublin football team who defeated Galway in the 1983 All-Ireland Final – one of the most bad-tempered finals on record, hence the reduced numbers. The agony of the defeat to Meath in the epic encounters of 1991. But my own personal favourite memory of All-Ireland day comes from the time when I worked in Croke Park.

It was the morning of the 2001 All-Ireland Football Final between Meath and Galway. I arrived just after sun-up, and went up into the vast bowl of seats, with the field of green in the centre. The silence of the empty cauldron was almost overpowering in its intensity. It was the silence of 80,000 voices yet to arrive. Every door unlocked echoing, every cough amplified. As the match day staff started to arrive, we congregated together, almost nervous, though most of the staff had done this many times before. At their head was Pat Guthrie who, though he had attended every All-Ireland since 1980, had watched none. Then came the first ritual of the day: morning Mass. Only in Ireland.

I am a devout agnostic – if such a thing is possible – but was intent on attending the Mass, which was held in one of the rooms under the Cusack Stand. Sitting on an improvised altar, decked out in the county colours of the day, stood the Sam Maguire trophy that would be contested for that afternoon. During the Mass, there is a brief well-wishing for the teams.

After Mass, the day gradually builds up to its climax and, like in 1896, in the seconds before the throw-in there was a hush in the crowd, and then the release of pent-up emotion.

Today's All-Ireland football final will trigger off a whole host of memories and create new ones. At 3.30 p.m., when, when Kerry and Mayo fight it out, millions of people, both in Ireland and abroad, will for the duration take part in the common experience of All-Ireland day at Croke Park. The only thing is I just wish Dublin were playing.

(first broadcast on RTÉ Radio in 2004)

THIS MORNING IN THE HALF-LIGHT

Cyril Kelly

This morning, in the half-light, they set out, bound for the pale. Cramped cars and sleeping-coaches slipping from Bun na hAbhann and Belturbet, slán go fóil le Dún Chaoin agus Portmagee. In the gloaming of rear-view mirrors, Blasket and Achill Sounds receding, filigree of white Atlantic foam soundless. Eager flags aflutter, advancing into the silence of the morning, along the estuaries of the Owenmore and the Moy. Red and green flapping curlews awake, green and gold startling seal pups around Slea Head. Wisps of hope dawning, these colours rolling into the brightening day ahead are heading for Drumcondra. Ceann scríbe? Páirc an Chrócaigh. Croke Park. For this, the third Sunday of September, is All-Ireland day, the great and final gathering of the year for Gaelic Football.

And on this very morning, a Diaspora of backpackers in the Antipodes, already facing into Monday, have earmarked Irish pubs where they'll congregate to watch the midnight match. In the Philippines, marooned on rainy season sugar plantations, Columban Fathers are testing internet radio reception. Holy Ghost Fathers, plateaued in Kenya, are ready to swap Swahili for seventy impassioned bilingual minutes of Micheál Ó Muircheartaigh. Still sleeping enclaves in Hartford and Boston, dreaming through Eastern time, hear golden plover cries on the blanket bog above

Pontoon, watch foxes loping on the lower slopes of Brandon. But alarms are set, 3.30 GAT: Gaelic Athletic Time.

From Crossmolina and Castlebar, secondary roads, like rivers in spate, converge at Knock for early Mass at the Basilica. While they are praying for Maughan and Mayo, a hooting cavalcade from the Kingdom is charging through Limerick, the vanquished neighbour. Windows wound down, there is a mayhem of yodelling and giuhooing whirling into the morning air. Men from Bally and Listowel, erstwhile sworn enemies, are exchanging V signs of mutual admiration and invincibility.

Preparing to forge the pale ring of the M50, men and women of Mayo will pull in for one last pow-wow at Leixlip. The Kerry contingent will muster at Kill. In a throwback to days in the bog, flasks of tea and wedges of home-made loaf will appear. Some seanóir or spritely granddad will reminisce; finals of the past, wet-and-dry batteries spared for the broadcast, crowding into any house that had a wireless, the windows thrown open for latecomers standing outside. And for those lucky enough to be on it, the ghost train, whistling through the night.

Each tribe has its own pantheon of heroes. The early 1950s was the golden age of Mayo football. Paddy Prendergast, swashbuckling full back, the flying doctor, Pádraig Carney, and staunch as Nephin at corner back, Seán Flanagan, later selected on the team of the century. The Kerry crowd will salute its own: Paddy Bawn, peerless high fielder O'Connell, Aeroplane O'Shea. And from the Barony of Fitzmaurice, the parish of Beale: Bomber Liston.

The River Tolka and the Royal Canal are a mile apart. On this football-final Sunday, Drumcondra Road, between Tolka Bridge and Binn's Bridge, will be a magic mile, a jostling sea of colour, swirls of red, eddies of green, surges of gold, all swashing and backwashing beneath the arching, autumnal sycamores. Cries at every corner; 'Hats, flags or colours.' Like ventriloquists, burly touts pitch voices amid the throngs; 'Anyone buyin' or sellin' tickets?' Burgers sizzling. Bartering culchies annoying Brendan Behan's statue; 'Three Cusacks for two Hogans together.'

Outside each of the four pubs, a promontory of people like a longshore drift, talk of the voyage so far. Kerry steady as she goes. Mayo's moments under full sail. The Mortimers, McDonald, Gooch, the O'Sheas. This afternoon a sidestep, the bounce of a ball, a gust of wind or a glorious goal could make a prince of one, a pauper of another.

And then, out at the back end of the year, young lads and lassies lashing a ball near Dún Chaoin or into the wild wind outside Belmullet, will recall this day.

(first broadcast on RTÉ Radio in 2004)

MAYO: 107 YEARS OF THE GREEN ABOVE THE RED

Art Ó Súilleabháin

The little village of Carnacon is situated near the shores of Lough Carra, about ten miles south of Castlebar in the heart of County Mayo. The village has a population of about two hundred, and boasts a church, a school, a shop, two pubs… and a place in history inconsistent with its size. The first Republican President of Connaught came from Carnacon. He was John Moore, of the Moores of Moore Hall. This Irish Catholic landlord family returned to their native Mayo from Alicante in Spain in 1790, after the easing of the Penal Laws. With 200,000 pounds, they bought a vast estate around Carnacon. John Moore was appointed President of Connaught in 1798 by General Humbert in that ill-fated 'Year of the French.'

George Henry Moore was a founder of the Home Rule Party as MP for Mayo during the Great Famine, and is remembered in Mayo and beyond as a courageous and generous famine ameliorator. His portrait still hangs over the back door of the church in Carnacon. George Augustus Moore was a distinguished novelist at the turn of the twentieth century, with books like *Hail and Farewell, Esther Waters* and *The Lake*, and he was involved with Yeats in the establishing of the Abbey Theatre. Senator Colonel Maurice Moore was the Irish envoy to South Africa appointed by the first Dáil in 1920, and later served in the Seanad under Éamon de Valera.

On the other side of this pleasant village of Carnacon, the Blakes of Towerhill were also Catholic landlords. In 1849 they built the local school, and were its admirable managers and patrons until 1946, when they handed it over to the church. The Blake family was often involved with the Moores at the horse-racing and hunting events, but the Blakes also had a liking for other sports. A handball alley was built on the estate in the 1880s, and thus they continued another long sporting history.

Football, however, held pride of place in the village. In 1885, the first reported game of football in Mayo was played at Towerhill. There, the *Connaught Telegraph* reported, the 'boys of Carnacon and Ballyglass met in this manly sport.' This match was won by the Carnacon boys, and after the game Colonel Blake and his lady ordered a barrel of beer from his cellar to refresh the victors and the vanquished – some things never change.

It seems that the game quickly became very popular with a huge following, and the Carnacon and Ballyglass boys came together to form one team. Sponsorship seems to have actually begun right here, because it is reported that the Carnacon team henceforth took to the field with pretty, light blue caps (from the racing blue of the Towerhill Blakes).

However, politics and sport were destined even then to be inextricably linked. Colonel Blake, being a Catholic landlord, wanted to make a statement when his team took to the field in 1887 against the Belcarra boys from the Protestant estate of the Browne family. The green was better than the red and, to prove a point, Colonel Blake dressed his team in a jersey with a green band above a red band. It seems that the point was well noted by his opponents, and the match ended in some kind of a shemozzle. Carnacon won the rematch, with the Belcarra boys now wearing green and gold.

The Green above the Red was later adopted by the county team, and is still sported by the men from Mayo a hundred years later. The little village is still producing heroes – Cora Staunton, the brilliant and gifted ladies football star, hails from Carnacon.

On All-Ireland Sunday, the proud men from Mayo with the Green above the Red have another point to prove against a team wearing green and gold: Kerry. Over a hundred years later, can that green above the red overcome another green and gold and bring the Sam Maguire Cup to Mayo for the first time in over half a century? We'll know in a few short hours.

(first broadcast on RTÉ Radio in 2004)

ANOTHER ANNIVERSARY
Peter Fallon

You turn
hearing the joy
of football
In the yard.
You yearn
for that football
of the lost,
the scarred.

Again, and again
and again
you feel the sten-
gun attack
of that 'What if?'
and that 'What then?'
Well, then
he'd be a boy

who's ten.

(first broadcast on RTÉ Radio in 2004)

THE MOONLIGHT IN MAYO
Dan O'Neill

From the 1930s to the 1950s, Mayo enjoyed three decades of glorious football fame. They won their first All-Ireland in 1936, when Henry Kenny, father of present-day leader of Fine Gael, Enda Kenny, was at midfield, to beat the might of Laois powered by Tommy Murphy, after whom the GAA's newest competition was named, and won recently by County Clare.

Mayo came to Croke Park again to take on the men from Breffni in the All-Ireland of 1948. Cavan were champions, having beaten Kerry the previous year in the Polo Grounds in New York in what was the only All-Ireland ever played outside the country.

There was no television in Ireland then, and people who did not travel to matches depended on the golden voice of Micheál O'Hehir on Radió Éireann. He captured every move, every kick of the ball, and gave the precise distance the player was from goal when taking a shot or a placed kick. Taking that kick was a daunting task, and no one could move, cough or sneeze until that free was taken.

Within two years, Mayo were back again in Croke Park to win two All-Irelands back to back led by their captain, the versatile Sean Flanagan. This was a team of classic styles, and every young boy in the country wanted to play the game like it was played in Mayo.

Sean Wynne in goal was the first keeper to hurl himself into the air like we saw Johnny Geraghty of Galway do later in the 1960s. The high fielding, majestic Paddy Prendergast at full back, the stout-hearted defence of Flanagan John Ford, Henry Dixon, Joe Staunton and Fr Peter Quinn.

I was a student in St Gerald's College in my home town of Castlebar, and those of us in the college team tried to emulate the brilliance of the athletic Eamon Mongey at midfield, the goal-scoring Peter Solan, Sean Mulderrig, Joe Gilvarry and Tom Langan. As we practised taking frees, we called to mind the great Pádraig Carney.

Louth people will never forget the fleet of foot Mick Flanagan, who scored that all-important goal that brought the Sam Maguire Cup to the western county for the second time in 1950. Five years later, the Meath supporters would not want to remember the shot that went by Kevin Smith to the roof of the net from the peerless full-forward Tom Largan. The following year was another great year for Mayo football. The county was back in Croke Park to defend the title and retain the Sam Maguire Cup against the mighty men from Royal Meath.

This they did in fine style, and they prevented the Boynesiders from adding to their first and only title in 1949.

Kerry had their legion of stars in these years. Dan O'Keeffe, Paddy Kennedy, Joe Keohane, Paddy Ban Brosnan, Jackie Lyon, Seán Murphy, Tadhg Lyne and Paudie Sheehy, and that great dynamo at corner-forward Dr Jim Brosnan.

It had to follow that the boys throughout the kingdom were inspired by the great tradition of so many wonderful players of the past. And with Mick O'Connell and Mick O'Dwyer following in their footsteps, the teams of the 1970s of Jack O'Shea, Páidí Ó Sé, Ogie Moran, Pat Spillane, Bomber Liston and Mickey Sheehy will also never be forgotten.

Mayo won another National League title in 1954, and saw new blood introduced: Frank Fleming, John Nallen – uncle of the present-day star James Nallen – and two other young players: Seamie O'Donnell of Ballaghaderreen and myself from Castlebar.

The semi-final against Dublin was a cliffhanger. This was my first game in Croke Park. To come out of the tunnel to a sea of faces and to hear the roar of the crowd was a daunting experience.

The Dublin team was powered by such famous players as Dan O'Mahony, Mick Moylan, the longest kicker of a dead ball in the country, Jim Crowley, Ollie Freaney, Snitchie Ferguson and Kevin Heffernan.

Andy Murphy, Brendan Hayden and Ned Doogue were stalwarts throughout that League Final between us and Carlow. By winning that national league title, it earned for us and Cork, who were the hurling league champions, a trip to New York to inaugurate the St Brendan Cup games.

Fifty years ago it was a dream come true for us young lads to go to America and play football or hurling in the Polo Grounds and in John Kerry O'Donnell's Gaelic Park in the Bronx.

That same year, 1954, I joined An Garda Síochána and was stationed at Drogheda, County Louth. Three years later I experienced the thrill of playing in an All-Ireland Final when I lined out at midfield for the wee county against Cork in a most exciting encounter. We won by just two points, and brought the Sam Maguire Cup across the Boyne at Drogheda for the very first time.

Any player who has been in a dressing-room in Croke Park on All-Ireland day knows full well what those lads from Mayo and Kerry will be going through today. The tension and the excitement in the dressing-room were at fever pitch, everyone trying to remain calm. Some were taking deep breaths. Others were standing up and sitting down again, pulling up socks, then pulling them down again; tightening their laces and then loosening them. Each one was dealing with his own nervous tension. The stifling smell of winter green and olive oil penetrated through every inch of the room, and to add to the stuffiness of the room, all windows were closed tightly to cushion against eavesdropping by the opposition.

Rhetorical questions were asked. 'Has it rained?' 'Will we need gloves?' 'How strong is the wind?' All that remained then was to hear the loud, hard knock on the door from the steward, whose job it was to get the teams out onto the pitch on time.

I can remember Kevin Behan standing to take a sideline free about twenty yards in from the end line, with the silhouette of the pillars of the then new Hogan Stand upright and custodial as sentries within the fenced building site.

With about nine minutes to go, Behan, as cool and as accurate as ever, kicked the ball towards the goals. All hands reached high in the square, but highest of all went corner-forward Seán Cunningham, who fisted the ball to the net to give Louth the lead, which we never lost.

We had played the entire game without introducing a substitute, and when Jimmy Magee, the well-known sports commentator, and himself a Louth man, on his *Question Time* radio programme, asks his pet question: 'Who were the last two Mayo men to win senior All-Ireland football medals?' I hope after today the answer will not be Seamie O'Donnell and Dan O'Neill.

It is my fervent wish that John Maughan, the only manager who has brought Mayo teams to three senior All-Ireland Finals, will be rewarded today with an impressive victory over Kerry, and that when we welcome home him and his heroes back to McHale Park in Castlebar on Monday evening, the celebrations will continue into the night, and that the glittering silver of the Sam Maguire Cup will be reflected in the moonlight in Mayo.

(first broadcast on RTÉ Radio in 2004)

THE HURLER
John Conroy

He told us there was no place for fear.
He told us that a scar
from the eyebrow to the lip tip
might come, a chance for a cosmetic smile
or a slow walk under gazing eyes,
he wouldn't mind, he said, but go now

if your stomach will quease from battle heat
or from freshly stitched skin,
we didn't, we were boys waiting to be men,
as we jostled and clipped dandelions
to the wind, seeds scattered carelessly
that brought ash sticks to life again.

He told us the game was about passion,
who we were and wanted to be,
we'd find in the game our ancestors played,
And we'd find ourselves too,
in aching wrist play and wild pulls
across purpled shins, coloured in
fields of play.

But skill always won out.
After all the scrapes and swollen hands

tightening on the sliotar, it was the lithe muscle
that made the grade, bending with the ash stick,
graceful movements and clipped sound breaks,
recorded on summer Sundays.

(first broadcast on RTÉ Radio in 2005)

MY FATHER

Theo Dorgan

My father was a quiet and undemonstrative man, soft spoken and not given to showing his emotions. A hurler in his youth, and for a brief while an amateur boxer, he valued a kind of stoicism that would have had English army officers or cricket commentators queuing up for lessons in understatement.

Not the lantern-jawed, strong, silent type, you understand, just an ordinary man who valued a certain kind of grace under pressure – well, most of the time. Put him on the grass bank at Ballinlough on a midge-filled Sunday evening when his beloved Na Piarsaigh were up against an inexplicably unformed Glen Rovers aided and abetted by a blind and partisan referee, and this air of Ciceronian detachment would melt before your very eyes. I would stand there fascinated watching his eyes bulge, his face twist and spasm, his shoulders bunch, his fists clench and unclench, as he all but levitated at whatever injustice was making a purgatory of that particular moment.

He loved hurling as a game. He was a connoisseur of the finer points of skill. He could sometimes manage a detached murmur of admiration when someone on the opposing side did something elegant or stylish. But far more than this, he loved his team, whether Na Piarsaigh, which he helped to found, or the blood and bandaged warriors of our beloved Cork. Never mind the gentlemanly guff about playing the game for its own sake; what he desired above all else was the sweet, thirst-slaking cup of victory.

Partisan to the backbone, he knew that victory for our team depended on the implacable will and unswerving determination, not just of the players on the field of battle, but of each and every supporter. A moment's loss of concentration, the tiniest wavering of belief in our team, and whatever dark powers held victory in the balance would turn their backs on us. I never got to stand with him at an All-Ireland Final. I would give a great deal to be in Croke Park today with that man beside me, revelling in the drama the thunder and glory of it all. I've inherited his tribal lust for victory, his naked vulnerability to the lightning flashes of fear and delight and exultation that a great game of hurling will wake in the soul and show in even the most disciplined face. He was, as I have said, a founder member of Na Piarsaigh. Today I will be remembering not just my father, but John Gardener, who was his friend who stood shoulder to shoulder with him in many a heroic and forgotten battle. I will have a special place in my heart and hopes today for a younger John Gardener, and for his comrade Na Piarsaigh man Seán Óg Ó hAilpín. Some years ago I was asked to write a poem for Na Piarsaigh on their fiftieth anniversary. The match I wrote about never took place. It's a compound of many matches that lit up my childhood like torches on a dark path. It was all the matches I ever went to with my father, and it is the one eternal match that is never over until someone steps up to strike the heroic blow that claims victory for us all.

And here is the poem – 'The Match down the Park' – for Na Piarsaigh on their fiftieth anniversary:

Tom Knott comes bulling out, his shoulder down
bringing weight to bear on the sliotar dropping
from his hand. The crack of ash on leather echoes
the length of the Park.

Like a new evening star, the ball
climbs the November air, a clean,
white flash in the cold and cloud.

All of the faces around me turn
like plates to the sky, tracking the rising arc.
Over the halfway line now, and dropping into
a clash of hurleys, forward shouldering back.

Our jerseys are brighter than theirs
in this eerie light, the black and amber
fanning out into a line, a berserk charge.

My face is jammed through the flat bars
of the gate, the goalposts make me dizzy
leaning back to look up. The goalie is jittery,
the chocolate melts in my fist, I hear myself

howling from a great distance
Come on Piarsaigh, come on, face up, face up . . .
Sound stops in a smell of mud and oranges.

I can feel the weight of them bearing down on goal,
I can't see, Mr Connery is roaring and Johnny Parker,
I bet even my Dad is roaring, back there in the crowd
but I can't leave the gate to go see, I can't –

a high ball, a real high one, oh God
higher than the moon over the fence towards Blackrock,
it's dropping in, they're up for it, Pat Kelleher's fist

closes on leather, knuckles suddenly badged with blood
in the overhead clash; he steadies, digs in his heel,
he turns, shoots from the 21 –
the whole field explodes in my face.

A goal! A goal! Their keeper stretched across the line,
his mouth filled with mud, the sliothar feet from my face,
a white bullet bulging the net.

Everything stops.

A ship comes gliding on the high tide, her hull
floating through the elms over the rust-red stand.
A man on the flying-bridge looks down to us.

I race back to my father, threading the crowd,
watching for heavy boots, neck twisting back
to the net still bulging, the ship still coming on,
the green flag stabbed aloft, the final whistle.

Sixpence today for the bikeminder under his elm.
Men in dark overcoats greeting my Dad
Well done Bert, ye deserved it. And
A great game, haw? Ah dear God what a goal!

I'm introduced as the eldest fella. Great man yourself.
Men anxious to be home, plucking at bikes, pushing away.
The slope to the river, the freighter drawing upstream.

And then the long, slow pedal home,
weaving between the cars on Centre Park Road,
leaning back into the cradle of his arms.

That was some goal, wasn't it, Dad?
It was indeed, it was. His breath warm on my neck;
a wave for the man on Dunlop's gate,
we'll pass the ship tied up near City Hall.

He's a knacky hurler, Pat Kelleher.
He is, Dad, ah jay he is.
By God, that was the way to win.
It was, Dad, it was.

(first broadcast on RTÉ Radio in 2005)

TRASNA NA SIONAINNE
Bernie Ní Fhlatharta

It's hard to ignore the excitement of today's All-Ireland Hurling Final. Even for someone like me, who would normally not be seen dead on a sports field, or even in a room where there's a match on the telly. But today is different.

Today our team is going to make Galwegians everywhere proud. Fair play do mhuintir na Gaillimhe. Tá súil agam go n-éireoidh linn inniu. There's no question of Cork beating us. I can't even think it, let alone say it. I'm not even thinking it in case any negativity flows into the atmosphere and, God forbid, lands on the shoulder of a Galway player.

The excitement started this summer for us when my fifteen-year-old son Seán got his first taste of Páirc an Chrócaigh for the quarter-finals. That's when Galway beat Tipp. What luck that he experienced a win at his first outing to Croke Park.

And then, a few weeks later, it was pure magic when Galway won against Kilkenny, the giants of hurling, in the semi-final.

That night, Seán could hardly speak because his voice was spent shouting for Galway. His father wasn't much better.

I had watched on the telly at home and, being an Irish mother, I was thrilled that Seán had experienced his second win, so to speak. Bhí mé chomh bródúil. Cheapfá go raibh mo mhac féin ar fhoireann na Gaillimhe agus b'fhéidir go mbeidh le cúnamh Dé. Bhí mé ag screachaíl agus ag béiceadh ós comhar an bhosca le gliondar. Ní raibh sé deacair a shamhlú cén sort screachaíl abhí thuas i bPáirc an Chrócaigh. Like most Galway people, plans were laid immediately in our house for the next stage, the Big Day, the All-Ireland. And of course the usual scramble for tickets meant that these plans were made in the absence of tickets.

Train tickets were bought, and arrangements were made to meet friends outside McGraths, all in the expectation that the tickets would materialise.

Of course there was the usual begrudgery about those who would jump on the bandwagon, only getting tickets now that the team had reached the All-Ireland. What about the supporters who had filled the stands when Galway hadn't even been in the reckoning?

The scramble for All-Ireland tickets is a mystery to me, but in our house the excitement of not knowing if the tickets were coming or not certainly added to the excitement in a perverse way. It also made the tickets priceless, and it's no wonder people are willing to pay anything to touts on the day just to get inside the stadium.

As one of those supporters who will be watching on the television, who can blame them? I got caught up in the excitement and I wasn't even there. Just watching the looks on the faces of supporters on the stands said it all. It was good to be a Galway man, woman or child on the last two occasions.

The success of the Galway hurlers has made a huge difference in our house. There's a feeling of well-being, of contentment, of pride and of expectancy. It's a good feeling. Multiply that by thousands of homes around the county – and indeed further afield, not only in this country but among the ex-pat supporters all over the world – and you've got a solidarity that's unique.

There are pubs and houses in Galway that have redecorated their exteriors in the maroon and white colours. There are flags, buntings and banners. The one wishing Galway Good Luck hanging outside Supermacs in Eyre Square caused a bit of a flutter, but thankfully the Council weren't spoilsports and it's still there.

In fact, there's a bit of divide between city and county on this one. There appears to be much more excitement outside the city, even though four of the players represent city clubs.

I wonder, has the city really become so metropolitan that they have lost touch with the GAA? Ach is cuma faoi sin uilig. Ní fiú a bheith ag smaoineamh ar a leithéid seafóide. Is cuma ach an corn sin a ardú inniu agus é a thabhairt trasna na Sionainne. Caithfear muintir Chorcaigh a bhualadh inniu!

(first broadcast on RTÉ Radio in 2005)

DON'T HIT THE REF IF YOU'RE WINNING

Tommy McKearney

Ignoring the sniggers of better-off neighbours in Dungannon and Coalisland, our manager Michael John always insisted that buying the old freight container to serve as a dressing-room had contributed greatly to our team's rise from obscurity. For a small Tyrone club in the mid 1960s, having a dedicated changing-area was real progress. Nevertheless, the accommodation was so basic that it would make contemporary minimalism seem cluttered. We had nothing in that container except somewhere dry to leave our clothes, and a degree of privacy to plan what passed for tactics in those distant days before 'total-football' GAA style was born on the exacting training grounds of the Moy, Omagh, Carrickmore and Errigal Chiaráin.

Michael John and his advisors always struggled to have their advice heard in that excited, pre-match period. A handicap they faced in their efforts to gain attention was the ongoing, semi-acrimonious scuffle that invariably accompanied the distribution of the team strip. We had bright red football shirts that looked remarkably like those worn by the then all-conquering Manchester United, and every player wanted one. This was the era before anybody at our level in the GAA dreamed of sending players onto a football field wearing matching pants and socks as well.

Unfortunately, we no longer had a complete set of twenty football shirts, since eight fine, bright red jerseys had been lost one ill-fated evening the previous year.

Hurrying to attend a post-match altercation at an away fixture, Michael John had left one pillowcase full of *geansies* on top of his car. Unusually for a GAA setting at the time, somebody (or bodies) stole the eight tops. Had the lot been taken we would have been forced to buy another set. The club committee, however, decided that since they were still paying for the pavilion – as they called the container – the minor team would have to supplement the deficit from the remnants of a set recently discarded by our senior side.

The club had bought new jerseys for the senior team after they had reached the final of the County Championship, and the ragged, old strip – with its unlovely navy-blue stripes – was now surplus to requirements. Nevertheless, none of us minors wanted these hand-me-downs. Not that we hadn't pride in the jersey, but for many of us they were too big, too baggy and simply too old-fashioned for dedicated followers of the then-essential George Best look. So instead of listening intently to our mentor's plan of campaign, there was always a scramble for what remained of the newer, trendier kit.

Had I not followed Michael John so closely into the dressing-room one evening we were due to play Eglish, and dived immediately into the kitbag, I too might have been part of the broader mêlée struggling for a fashionable jersey, and would consequently have missed out on one of the classic dressing-room moments.

Our manager was demanding self-discipline. He reminded us of the calamity that had befallen our senior side at the County Final in Clonoe a few weeks previously. Coasting to a comfortable victory over a fancied side from the shores of Lough Neagh, and with only minutes left on the clock, one of our players succumbed to a fit of gross indiscipline. Irritated by a refereeing decision, he attacked the unfortunate official, causing the game to be abandoned. The County Board met in Pomeroy for an emergency investigation, and ruled against us. The trophy was awarded to the Lough shore men, and our senior side was suspended for the rest of the year.

As a result of stupid, inexcusable indiscipline, the parish had missed its first taste of football glory, Michael John told us. A new and tighter regime would rule over his charges. Our club would not see silverware snatched from its grasp because some idiot couldn't control his temper. Banging his fist off the container side, he shouted that there would be no toleration for the miscreant who would thus rob us of greatness.

'Now,' asked Michael John, turning to the minor team captain who had just wrestled a bright red jersey from his younger brother, 'What is the golden rule about raising your fist on a football field?'

'Don't hit the ref if we're winning, Michael John,' our captain answered.

(first broadcast on RTÉ Radio in 2005)

GAELIC ATHLETIC ASSOCIATION

FOUNDED 1884

OFFICIAL SOUVENIR PROGRAMME

ALL IRELAND FOOTBALL CHAMPIONSHIP FINAL

at

POLO GROUNDS, NEW YORK

SEPTEMBER 14th, 1947

SUBSCRIPTION 50c

THE STAR-SPANGLED FINAL
Josephine McArdle

Europe was recovering from the trauma of World War II. It was the year that Big Jim Larkin died, Al Capone too, and Ireland was commemorating the centenary of the Famine.

Kerry were due to play Roscommon in the All-Ireland Football Championship Final. Since the harvest was so bad, though, the game had been delayed until October. Many an emigrant was returning to his adopted country deeply disappointed, among them John Kerry O'Donnell, a prominent official of the GAA in New York, himself 'home for the final.'

All was not yet lost, and when the game ended in a draw, O'Donnell contacted his good friend Michael 'The Canon' Hamilton, a parish priest in Newmarket-on-Fergus, to enquire about the possibility of having the replay in New York. Unfortunately, arrangements had already been made, with the venue and date for the match decided. But the seed had been sown, and what was to follow was undoubtedly the greatest and most impressive achievement of the GAA in living memory, when the 1947 All-Ireland Football Championship Final was played in the Polo Grounds in New York. An unusual and unique occasion, and the only All-Ireland Final ever to be played outside of Ireland, immortalised by the late Mick Dunne as 'The Star-Spangled Final.'

At the GAA General Congress on Easter Sunday in April 1947, Canon Michael Hamilton had proposed the Clare motion that New York be the venue for that year's All-Ireland Final. His proposal was greeted with incredulity, and a marked lack of enthusiasm, by the delegates present.

Because of the absence of so many young Irish and Irish–Americans, who were serving with the US forces, and also the total ban on emigration from Ireland during the war years, there had been a drastic slump in Gaelic games across America. The Canon put his case to Congress on behalf of all the Irish emigrants in the US. The final would also bring about a much needed revival of interest in hurling and football, he argued. His greatest plea was on behalf of the exiles themselves: 'Strong hearts will throb with emotion,' he said, 'an emotion that only those who have been in exile can appreciate or understand.'

Following a very emotive speech to Congress, Canon Hamilton's motion was passed, and another extraordinary chapter in the history of the GAA was written.

The decision made, primary concerns were focused now on two issues.

Firstly, how would they get there? With civil aviation in its infancy, and the jet age years away, there was a great ocean to be crossed. Secondly, what about the average Gaelic supporter in Ireland? Could a transatlantic radio broadcast be arranged? Radió Éireann had not yet aired a live programme from across the Atlantic on any subject, sport or otherwise and broadcasting was very unsophisticated and basic in contrast to the satellite technology of today.

These difficulties, which at first seemed insurmountable, did not phase the officials and the organisers. John Kerry O'Donnell and his team of volunteers worked alongside GAA officials like Paddy O'Keeffe and Tom Kilcoyne to set up the event and ensure its success. The venue selected as the most suitable was in the Bronx suburb of New York: the Polo Grounds, home of the Giants.

There was tremendous excitement built up that summer as huge crowds turned up at all the championship games, the teams buoyed up of course by the promise of a trip to America. Many fans waved not only their county colours but the Stars and

Stripes also. It was a colourful season, and Kerry had been more determined than ever to qualify for their New York appearance against Cavan. The mood was set.

While the preferred mode of transport for most of the team members and the officials would have been the steamboat from Cork to New York Harbour, the steamship company could only offer accommodation to a limited number of passengers, since they were still heavily booked out transporting the military and their families back to the US after the war. In the end, nine members of the party set sail aboard the RMS *Mauretania* from Cobh on 3 September, and the rest, forty in all, flew out from Shannon on 8 September.

Unlike the luxury of the Airbus 320 or the Boeing 777 seven-hour flights enjoyed by today's transatlantic passengers, only lumbering, propeller-driven aircraft were available. But it was an exciting if lengthy adventure, a thirty-nine-hour journey in total, the airplane making two stops *en route*: one in the Azores and another in Newfoundland.

Finally, on that very special, unique Sunday in September 1947, a young twenty-nine-year-old Micheál O'Hehir relayed the entire scene of splendour with his groundbreaking, live, transatlantic broadcast commentary.

The men of Erin gave a thrilling, pulsating exhibition of Gaelic football before a crowd of 40,000, and Cavan triumphed at the Polo Grounds.

Just as Canon Hamilton had predicted, when the strains of 'Amhrán na bhFiann' wafted across the stadium, chords were touched in the hearts of that Irish throng that nothing else in this whole world could touch. Tears of joy glistened in the eyes of thousands of men and women.

Some things never change.

(first broadcast on RTÉ Radio in 2005)

COME HOME, SAM, COME HOME
Cyril Kelly

One of the wisecracks doing the rounds that year in Kerry was to ask whether the last person leaving the county would please turn off the lights. Ever since the semi-final win against Armagh, history's tantalising finger beckoned that fantastic Kerry team. In fact, the annals of history seemed to beckon the whole county. The entire population of the Kingdom was making plans to witness – as Seamus Heaney, in another context, put it – 'hope and history rhyme.' The only thing that could stop Sam Maguire coming home for a record-breaking fifth year in a row was under-dogs Offaly.

Supporters began to leave Kerry the week before the match. From every town and townland in the county, impatient dreamers and passionate drinkers set out. They left Lislaughtin, Lisselton, Listowel. Bye-bye to Ballydonoghue, Ballyduff and Ballylongford. As that week counted down the days, all that was left in every 'lios' was a fairy host, and the 'baile' in every Bally grew more and more deserted.

Such a splendour of silence remained behind that the whirring wings and gurgling voices of sea birds could be heard coming ashore. From the Blaskets, petrel and puffin cries scattered in along the craggy coast of Comeenole and Dún an Óir. A lonesome chorus of seals sang Port na bPúcaí to deserted headlands in Iveragh and Corca Dhuibhne. In ancient cathedrals of oak woods around Killarney, slanting spears of autumn light were impaled in the quivering stillness as moss-covered boulders kept vigil. Out at Muckross, spritely doe and antlered sika stag roamed at will among scots pines.

Throughout that week, the Kerry contingent converged on the capital. By the time they arrived, many looked the worse for wear. Already they bore signs of solid, serious celebration. During the pilgrimage to the Pale, some had paid their respects to turf accountants along the way. Although Kerry were odds-on, there was no shortage of shekels for a bet in those cash-strapped days of 1982.

On the morning of the match, the pubs around Croke Park were packed. But even with drink on board, the Offaly supporters were slow to voice any rash predictions. Ironically, some of those followers from The Faithful County would only hazard a guess as to the likely margin of Kerry's victory. With the modesty of champions, the magnanimity of the truly great, Kerrymen drank deep and were silent.

Nelligan, The Bomber, Jacko, Mikey Sheehy… the names of that Kerry team were listed like a roll-call of honour by those Offaly supporters. Most Kerry people were hard pressed to name half a dozen Offaly players that day. Martin Furlong in goal might have got a mention, mercurial full forward Matt Connor. But certainly, a name down among the Offaly subs, a name destined to enter the folklore of Kerry football, would not have figured in any analysis.

In the final minutes of a fabulous game, with Kerry leading by two points and poised on the brink of their place in history, a man called Seamus Darby sprinted onto the field. He hardly took time to thrust his scrap of paper at the ref. Almost immediately, as if there were signs and portents in the sky, he stood staring into the heavens, barely twenty paces from the Kerry goal. Like a man who could read his name among the stars, he stood resolute, his gaze unflinching. The ball, that perverse pig's bladder of a ball, looped from on high like a gift from the fickle deities of destiny, right into his outstretched arms. With one diabolical turn, with one lethal, left-footed shot, he blew our fervent aspirations to Kingdom come.

So the people of Kerry began the long trek back. Back to the majestic McGillycuddy Reeks, back to the tranquil banks of the River Feale. The legends of generations grew in their minds as they took the last familiar twist of a byroad that led to a place called home. And what is home but a refuge, a sanctuary? It is a place where the injured and the maimed can shelter. It is a place where fickle fortune can be forgotten, where the body can regain its strength, the mind re-new its wisdom, where the soul can refresh its fervour all over again.

(first broadcast on RTÉ Radio in 2005)

MY FIRST ALL-IRELAND

Tom Seaver

The excitement is always the same in Dublin on the day of an All-Ireland Football Final. Croke Park is Mecca, as the crowds descend from all quarters on the entrances to the stadium. From the centre of the city, up Parnell Square as far as Findlater's Church, then the turn into Denmark Street, past Barry's Hotel and straight on by Mountjoy Square until you cross the North Circular Road into Jones's Road itself. This is what might be called 'The Pilgrim Way.' The groups of supporters sporting their team's colours walking along regardless of traffic, the rosette and flag sellers displaying their wares, the touts slyly asking for, if you don't mind, 'any tickets' – all contribute to the heady atmosphere of the great day.

It seems like only yesterday that my father took me to see my first All-Ireland. I had just started school at the Brothers in Synge Street at the time, and Gaelic Football had taken a firm grip on my imagination.

The previous year, Dublin were All-Ireland champions. Sure hadn't I even seen the Sam Maguire cup on display, accompanied by a picture of the team in Clery's window in O'Connell Street. Every time I passed there, I stopped to admire it. At night, I dreamt about it. A pride in my county seemed to envelop me, and I longed for the day on the following September when I could see Dublin playing in the final in Croke Park. I was convinced that they were invincible, and knew they would be in the next final for sure. All I had to do was to wait.

However, I was in for a big disappointment. The following year, Dublin were beaten in the first round of the championship. I was left flabbergasted. I wouldn't, after all, be going to Croke Park that September. But something happened in the meantime that was to change the course of events.

My father, you see, was an Old IRA man. He had fought with Thomas Ashe at the Battle of Ashbourne in Easter Week 1916, and just at this time there was a plan to raise money for a memorial to Ashe and the Fingal Brigade at the site of the battle. All the old comrades were roped in to help with a public collection for the purpose, and what better time to hold it than on the day of the All-Ireland Football Final! My spirits rose. There was a good chance now that I would see the match, and what matter if Dublin weren't playing!

We set off early in the afternoon on the Sunday of the big game, my father and myself, and took up position near the canal bridge on Jones's Road. The crowds were milling all around us. The colours of the teams were everywhere: the primrose and blue of Roscommon, the royal blue of Cavan.

Dad had the collection box, and was shaking it vigorously. 'Help the Thomas Ashe Memorial Fund,' he called out over the shouting of the touts and street-vendors. The fans, on their way into the grounds, were chipping in generously. The box was filling up, and I could judge by the expression on Dad's face that he was very happy.

But time was moving on, and soon it was half-past three. I knew by the cheering that the game was on. There was deafening roar. Someone had scored. After a few minutes, there was another roar. My patience was giving out. 'Dad!' I pleaded, 'Can we go now? The match is on.'

'We're nearly there,' he replied, as he buttonholed a few latecomers for the last of the donations. But there was further delay. He had to return his box to the treasurer's office on Clonliffe Road, where the inevitable queue of collectors handing back their boxes had formed. I was beginning to think I would never see the game at all.

It was nearing half-time when we finally made it into the ground. What a thrill! The stadium was jam-packed, and Dad tried to elbow his way in among the crowd standing on the terraces in front of the Hogan Stand. (Needless to say, we had no stand tickets.) I was small, and couldn't see anything except the backs of the spectators in front of me. I stood on my tippy-toes. Still no view of the pitch, but I could see people sitting precariously on the wall behind the railway goal. It would be terrific, I thought, to be perched up there.

Dad saw my dilemma, and hoisted me onto his shoulders. That was great. Now, I could see all that was happening. The scoreboard read: An Cábhán, 1–4; Ros Comáin 0–3. The half-time whistle blew then, and Dad left me down again. 'Did you see the scoreboard?' he asked me.

'I did.'

'Cavan have it won,' he said. 'They're four points up.'

I thought about it. Up to this I had been neutral. Now my mind was made up.

'I'm up for Roscommon!' I declared.

'No, you're wrong there,' he countered. 'Wait till you see!'

I was up on his back again to watch the second half. I began to join in the cheering. Whenever Roscommon got the ball, I shouted 'Come on, Roscommon!'

I listened to the names of the players as supporters called out to them.

'Put that one over, Murray!' Or, 'Get rid of it, Carlos!'

They were shouting to Jimmy Murray, the Roscommon captain, who wore the No. 11 jersey. Bill Carlos played at centre half-back and wore No. 6. Cavan supporters were appealing to Big Tom Reilly, or Benson in goals, to clear their lines, because Roscommon had come more into the game and were pressing hard to get the equalising scores.

Dad had got tired at that stage and had put me down again. Cavan were still ahead, and he was convinced that they couldn't be beaten. I could hear the crowd roaring, but could see none of the play. After a few minutes, I pleaded with him to let me have one last look. He hoisted me up, but I sensed his reluctance. Now

I could see the Roscommon forwards bearing down on the Cavan goal. Suddenly, the shout went up. Goal! The ball was in the back of the Cavan net! The stadium erupted. So did I.

Dad shifted my weight on his shoulders and told me to be quiet. I couldn't.

The game was entering its final phase, and Roscommon were now ahead. I looked down at my father's head and felt sorry for him, but he had the last laugh. Soon after, Cavan got the point that levelled the match. When the final whistle blew, and the crowds began to disperse, there was no one more relieved than him. He had got me off his back in more ways than one.

Cavan hadn't won, but neither had they lost. His mind, I suspect, was more on the amount of money he had collected for the Thomas Ashe Memorial Fund than on the result of the match.

He never lived to see the unveiling of the monument at The Rath Cross – or The Rath Roundabout, as they call it now – the scene of the Fingal Brigade's victory near the village of Ashbourne. Whenever I pass the spot, I think not only of the part he played in that triumph, but of the sacrifices he made for me on the day I attended my first All-Ireland Final.

Today, many youngsters from Kerry, Tyrone, Mayo and Down – and from other counties too – will see Croke Park for the first time and savour the excitement of their first big day there. The magic moments they take away with them will be etched on their memories for many years to come. The ones I took away from the drawn final of 1943 are still the stuff of dreams for me.

(first broadcast on RTÉ Radio in 2005)

Clár Oifigeamail

i bpáirc an Chrócaiġ, 26-9-'43
ar a 3.15 p.m.

Craob peile na h-Éireann

Cabán
— CAVAN —

v.

Roscomáin
— ROSCOMMON —

✠

LEINSTER MINOR FOOTBALL FINAL

Cill Dara v. Luġḃaḋ ar a 1.45 p.m.

luaċ 3p.

Ar Aġaiḋ linn

THE DAY KERRY BEAT CAVAN IN WARD'S MEDA
Pádraig McGinn

The toughest boy in our street was the Boxty Malone. He was a year or two older than any of us, and he was built square, like a tank. When we played football on the street or in Ward's 'Meda,' Boxty's team was always Cavan and he was always 'Big Tom,' the captain of the Cavan team. As well as being the Captain of the Cavan team, he always gave a running commentary on the match as he soloed up the field, side-stepping opponents or shouldering men out of his way, before scoring a goal. Sometimes a newcomer might object that Boxty had taken too many steps or handled the ball on the ground, but as the self-appointed referee, Boxty overruled these objections. If the opposition did score a goal, he might rule that it was a square ball and disallow the score. We didn't know what the square ball was, but we got to know that it was no use arguing unless you wanted a bloody nose, and it was no surprise that Cavan, captained by Boxty, always won. As there was no crossbar, and only two coats or jerseys for goalposts, the difference between goal and points was often a matter of opinion. It was Boxty's opinion that counted, so most of Cavan's scores were goals and Kerry's were usually points.

We played with an old leather ball, stuffed with hay, for it was wartime, and rubber balls could not be got. But one day we had a real ball, an inflated leather one. Wee Mickey's aunt came on holidays from England and brought him a real ball, as well as a football jersey, shorts, socks and football boots. Wee Mickey's mother never let him play on the street with the rest of us, but this day, as he had a new ball and a complete football rig-out, she accompanied him to Ward's Meda, and watched him from the sideline.

Wee Mickey was the only player who had proper football gear. The rest of us played in our everyday street clothes. As usual, Boxty said that his team was Cavan and he was Big Tom, but Wee Mickey claimed that, since he owned the ball, he was entitled to be Big Tom. Boxty got very red in the face, and he was about to settle matters in the usual way when he saw that Mickey's mother was taking a keen interest from the sideline. He then announced that he was Joe Keoghan, who side-stepped his way to scoring goal after goal for Kerry, and he seemed to take a a special delight in scattering the bogus Big Tom out of his way every time he got near him. As he did so, his commentary was reminiscent of Micheál O'Hehir at his most exciting moments. 'Joe Keoghane has the ball. He shakes off the man. He shakes off two.' And every time Joe Keoghane 'shook off one man,' a player bit the dust. Only it was muck rather than dust. Time after time, Wee Mickey had to pick himself up off the ground until the new football jersey and the clean, elegant white togs were covered in muck, and the rest of us were wondering how long it would be until his mother intervened. When Kerry were leading Cavan by ten goals, Wee Mickey's mother called full time and took Mickey and his ball home. That was the only time we played with a real ball during the war years, and that was the only time that Kerry ever beat Cavan in Ward's Meda.

(first broadcast on RTÉ Radio in 2005)

IN MEMORY OF TIM KENNELLY
Cyril Kelly

Plough and spade and seineboat shaped them for the deeds they were to do,
Street and school and mountains heard their victory cry,
Now their memories arch like rainbows o'er the meadows of the mind,
The Alive who'll live forever and the Dead who'll never die.

With days descending fast into December, with darkness cockily cock-stepping earlier every afternoon to a man's window-sill, he could do with being spellbound by a few arching rainbows of memory. With songbirds silent in stark winter hedges, with mallard below on the Royal Canal, their blue and bottle-green heads already tucked under the quilt of their wings, a man sitting by the light of a table lamp, a man gazing out through his reflection in the glass, listening to wars and rumours of wars from the radio on the shelf beside him, such a man could do with memories arching *like rainbows o'er the meadows of his mind.*

And then Brian Carthy, GAA correspondent, comes on to relay the tragic news: Tim Kennelly, renowned Kerry footballer, famed centre half-back during the golden Kingdom years, has died suddenly. So if the listening ear just so happens to be listening within a fifty yard free of Croke Park, it is easy to hear the hoarse roar of the crowd swelling, rising, tumbling through the tunnel of thirty years. Here they come, those memories, and never was their colour more needed, their sparkling showers more welcome, arching like rainbows o'er the meadows of my smitten mind.

Ague of age falling from my shoulders, I am standing on the Canal End. Waiting for the two teams to sprint onto the hallowed turf, excitement is arcing like bolts of electricity through the crowd. It is 1975, and it's twenty years since Kerry and Dublin have met in an All-Ireland Final. During the preceding weeks, there has been saturation coverage. Were the Blues going to do what the sky blues, Heffo, Freaney and Co. had failed to do in 1955, namely shut the Green and Gold Kingdom up?

Suddenly, the Kerry team, the youngest ever sent out, raced onto the pitch. The crowds, like the swash and backwash of the tide, swayed ominously down the terracing towards the pitch, paused precariously, righted itself again and heaved back towards the Royal Canal once more. I had heard about this team's redoubtable march to the final. Cork dispatched in Munster, Sligo in the semi-final, but this was my first time seeing them in the flesh. My friend Pat was with me. He could name them all. In a true display of jingoistic fervour, the only one I knew was fellow Listowel man Tim Kennelly. What delight and vicarious pride I got from watching the exploits of that prodigious horse of a man.

That day was the first of his heroic tussles with Tony Hanahoe. Like two warriors of old, like Cúchulann and Ferdia, prey and predator, at times so tigerishly brawn to brawn the terraces trembled, at times almost balletic, almost slow motion, brain throwing down gauntlet to brain; athlete to athlete, instinct covering instinct; a feint, almost counter; a shimmy, a shoulder; a fetch dispossessed by a block.

Watching Tim, his stamina, his strength, his resolve – to paraphrase Hanahoe's famous admonition – I never lost the faith. 'Cos I knew they made them tough out in Coolaclarig, where he was born and reared. Out there, a few miles outside Listowel, you can be sure that you won't get things easy from the Cloonmacon lads, or the lads from Cloontubrid and Kylebwee. And any young lad who played in the Listowel Town league, as Tim did for the Boro, knows what its like to be forged in the intimate, white, defining heat of adversity.

And I see Tim now, his fleet-footed shade on a solo run this misty morning, solo runs he often did in The Cork Athletic Grounds, or bursting up along the wing below the Hogan Stand, only now he's a legend, a winged Pegasus, like a thunderbolt, thundering over stretches of bogland in Bedford or Curraghatoosane. And there he is, borne shoulder high once more, a cavalcade over Gale Bridge. It is 1979 and, captain of that fabled team of all the talents, he is holding the Sam Maguire aloft in triumph. And Sigerson Clifford's lines take up their elegiac refrain once more:

Plough and spade and seineboat shaped them for the deeds they were to do,
Street and school and mountain heard their victory cry,
Memories arch like rainbows o'er the meadows of the mind,
The Alive who'll live forever and the Dead who'll never die.

(first broadcast on RTÉ Radio in 2005)

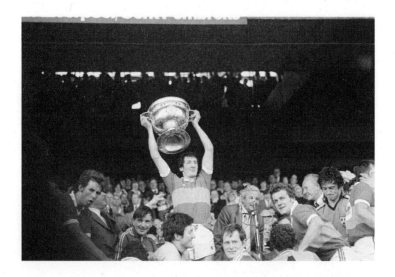

ALTERNATE LIVES
Joe Kane

Took your time, there was no rush,
young sapling in the photograph, 1887.
Bending and swaying with the northwesterly.
Today, stiff and broken-limbed,
rot set in your heart. Now,
the last to wake up in spring,
first to sleep in autumn. Your doom
held in the trough of some future storm,
bringing you to ground to complete the cycle.
Good only for the kitchen range.

But you could've been a contender:
Taken down in your prime
waxed and left to dry slowly
rimmed and dressed,
ready for the workshop:
the right hands would have found
the fruit within, dense, flexible, responsive,
spoke-shaved to its final shape,
sanded for the hand of a virtuoso.
The first puck of the sliotar would have told all.

(first broadcast on RTÉ Radio in 2006)

A SENSE OF HOME
Mary Folan

'Look out for the two ugly guys in the white van!' he said. 'Hmm, surprise me,' I muttered, as I dashed across town to Blackhall Place. 24 April was my D-Day, delivery day – more to the point, the delivery of the designer shelving unit, that extravagant piece of furniture that I bought on a whim months previously when the frustration of ever getting the keys to my first home manifested itself in a mania for buying things I *definitely* couldn't afford! On that sunny Saturday morning, the delivery men in the white van, father-and-son team, Stephen and Darragh, of course turned out to be handsome, fun and curious, giving me an excuse to be giddy and relieving the slog and tedium of turning house into home.

Finding a home of my own began the previous September in my pal Marguerite's Ford car. I was what you could call a more discerning first-time buyer since I had delayed it for so long. I didn't dare tell Marguerite that I hadn't a clue where I wanted to live, but would *know* when I found it. Instead, with notebook and pen in hand, we toured the neighbourhoods of Dublin city – Harold's Cross, The Coombe, Meath Street, Dunore Avenue, Rialto, the South Circular, Crumlin, finishing up in Stoneybatter at dusk. Little did I know that evening, while staring into the window of an estate agents in Manor Street, that I had come home.

Seven months later, I was a proud denizen of one of Dublin's oldest and most vibrant neighbourhoods: Stoneybatter.

Well, almost. I set up home at the junction of Stoneybatter and Blackhall Place, in a building that once housed a clothing factory and more recently a pharmaceutical depot.

Up to then, that indefinable thing, 'a sense of home,' had sort of eluded me since childhood. I had felt it as a teenager, stretched out on the big rock, behind the family home in Spiddal, holding host to the cormorants on sunny afternoons or swanning around the medieval city of Galway – a place that always allows me to be myself. Or when I lived in Triana in Seville – a neighbourhood populated in previous generations by sailors and gypsies and exuding a carefree, spontaneous feeling of being part of something vital and vibrant. Was it instinct or just serendipity then that, in such a historic and colourful part of my own capital city, I would find home again?

Dealing with the cut and thrust of setting up home didn't come as instinctively. People kept telling me that they found moving house a stressful life event. I thought smugly that they were just disorganised. After all, with six weeks to go, Peter, the architect and I had gone through the snag list to our hearts' content, until the affable foreman showed signs of losing his temper; I had washed and ironed everything in sight; boxed and labelled all my treasures and, with military precision, had begun the process of moving in. Why then, with ten days to go, were things suddenly out of sync – *with the plumbing,* that is?! Noises similar to Air Force One taking off in water tank; water gushing from spout underneath sink; light bulb going 'bing' in bathroom – water in light-bulb – yet not enough in toilet cistern. Was this a nightmare or the never ending snag list all over again?

Thanks to the three Cs, I finally set up home: coffee, Coca-Cola and *Carmina Burana.* Yes, when things got really tough, Carl Orff's insistent rhythms and raunchy lyrics never failed to rouse me as I dragged my tired body on to the next 'to do' list.

These days, to put me in a calmer mood, I stand under the canopy of the majestic oak, overhanging the pavement, from The Law Society's front lawn, a stone's throw from my new home. After all, *it* spent 300 years a-growing, and is now 300 years a-living, so maybe it has some wisdom to impart.

My father has this endearing habit of *always* greeting me with a welcome and a sunny smile, no matter what the circumstances of my arrival at *his* home in Spiddal. Now when he – a fanatical follower of Galway football and hurling – comes up to Dublin to cheer on the Tribesmen in Croke Park, it will give me great pleasure to say 'Fáilte abhaile, a Shéamais, go Baile na gCloch!'

(first broadcast on RTÉ Radio in 2006)

THE PRINCESS AND THE FINAL
Alan Titley

Your first All-Ireland Hurling Final is a kind of an initiation rite, like your first day at school. You are initiated into a culture, which stays with you for the rest of your life. Like all culture, it is a mixture of glory and of pain, of clarity and confusion. There was a reason why I had never been at an All-Ireland Hurling Final until I was in my early teens. Growing up in Cork, we knew we were the greatest, but in my time, unfortunately, we didn't have any evidence for it. The greatness of Cork hurling was merely folklore to us, something we had heard about, like the emergency, or rationing, or the distant guns of the civil war. Because I came to hurling knowledge in the shadow of that monstrous Tipperary hurling team who beat seven kinds of trash out of everybody they met, and since it seemed that I was never destined to see Cork in an All-Ireland Final anyway, I resolved to go to Croke Park, just, as they say, for the experience.

It didn't matter to us that it was Waterford and Kilkenny in the senior final, and Wexford and Limerick in the minor, with ne'er a smell of either Cork or Tipperary. If Genghis Khan and his Mongols were playing the hordes of hell, we would have gone anyway, Gerry my pal and I. On the morning of the match, something strange happened. There in our letter-box, certainly unusual for a Sunday morning, was an envelope. In the envelope there were two tickets for the Hogan Stand. I had no idea how they had got there, or who had put them there, as out of the darkness of the night they had simply appeared. It was like Santa Claus had arrived on the first Sunday of September.

It didn't matter. We took the tickets, and the train, and arrived in Dublin, a city that spoke a different language, which we only ever heard on Tolka Row, or in ads for sausages. Dublin was big. In Cork, if you walked far enough there was a chance that you might, if you were unlucky, see a field in the distance. In Dublin, it was all smoke and clangour. And Croke Park was big, much bigger than it is now – a giant waving its arms, or a cave of wonders that drew everybody in. We milled around with everyone else, not quite knowing what to do. Then we spotted an official-looking man with an armband that had 'Maor' written on it, and seemed to be ushering people towards the turnstiles. We approached him diffidently, two youngfellas, lost to the world, and to Croke Park.

He snorted at us at first when we asked him the way, but when he saw our tickets a transfiguration came over him. He drooled a bit and smiled and even giggled. He took us by the arm and led us to another 'Maor' of at least equal authority, and instructed him: 'Will yez look after these two youngfellas, please?' then leaving us with this official, who led us through the labyrinthine passages of Croke Park, all the way to our seats.

The only unusual thing about our seats was that they were a different colour from everybody else's. They were a bright cardinal red, and the reason became quickly clear: we were plonked smack bang in the middle of the VIP special guests' corral. There we were, two snotty-nosed youngfellas, barely out of short pants, surrounded by serried ranks of ring-kissed bishops and archbishops and monsignors and priests flushed with wine and the non-joys of life, the smell of succulent roast beef on their breath; they in their turn were surrounded by a clatter of politicians determinedly decked out in Sunday grey, wearing their importance in the middle of the action.

The hush about the place where we were sitting had nothing to do with us being in the midst of these dignitaries, but with the two guests who happened to be sitting a few short rows in front of us, and over whom the press had been salivating these last few days. They were Prince Ranier of Monaco, and his newish wife Grace Kelly, who had made the extraordinary sacrifice of giving up a glittering Hollywood career just to become a princess. There they were, almost touchable – the supreme ideal of many people, the magic of, the splendour of, the wonder of, the unattainability of royalty itself, with blue blood coursing in their veins. As we didn't have any ourselves, sure, Grace Kelly was the next best thing.

I was watching the hurling, of course. It was a wonderful game of ten goals and twenty-five points. Waterford scored the magnificent total of six goals and eight points, but were still barbed by the wasp sting of Kilkenny. But from time to time my gaze would wander to the special guests, as I knew I would be questioned about them by inquisitive aunts and relations when we got home. The questioning would be especially rigorous because, as I had learned, just as we were about to leave for Dublin, the tickets had been bequeathed to an American friend of my mother's, who had been given them by none other than Pádraig Ó Caoimh, after whom Páirc Uí Chaoimh is named, and who had given them to us when he learned that we were going, as they say, 'up for the match.'

But just for a moment, I thought I saw, even fleetingly, white flecks of dandruff on the black collar of Prince Ranier Grimaldi's coat. They may have spread from the head of an adjacent bishop, of course, or just have been bits of talcum powder blowing in the wind. Or it may just have been the vagaries of my own imagination, which doesn't have much time for kings or queens, or princes or princesses, or dukes or duchesses, or tsars or tsarinas, or barons, or counts or viscounts or orders of the lesser garter, or any of that ridiculous paraphernalia of mediaeval and primitive superstition that civil society was supposed to have banished.

Maybe the point was that he was human, very human indeed, just as she was, just another Kelly. Like all the Kellys of the most common surname in Ireland.

But down there on earth, down on the field where the hurlers were, there were gods. Up where we were, up in the stands, there were only mortals. It will be the same today.

(first broadcast on RTÉ Radio in 2006)

RESERVOIR DOGS
Joe Kearney

All week they had been showing *Cheyenne Autumn*, featuring Richard Widmark and Carroll Baker. It caused us to imagine our mongrel bicycles were mustangs and broncos and that the dust of open prairies clung to our lips rather than that blowing from the Fair Green. We even transformed distant Slievenamon into the foothills of the Sierras. It was in the time before the cinema burned down and we would find ourselves forced to endure the ten-mile bone-shake into Kilkenny in the back of Jacky Nolan's bus if we wished to see the pictures.

But all that was in the future; for now all we cared about was holding on to the last days of freedom. You see, all summer long our gang had hung out together. Sure, we had bickered and battled, but now, at the onset of the return to school, we were united as one in our impending misery. What we needed was one last adventure before surrendering up to autumn's anguish.

Sunday afternoons in Callan could be slow, but All-Ireland Final Sundays turned the place into something resembling a ghost town of the Mohave, where both time and luck have run out. I think it was Spider's idea that we should go to Mullinahone. He suggested a raiding party deep into enemy territory. For this was not just any All-Ireland Hurling Final, it was the grand final battle in a war that was waged far away in Croke Park. On this September Sunday in 1964, Kilkenny hurlers were facing their nemesis... Tipperary. Borderlands are dangerous places in times of war, and we were within a decent sliotar-strike of the county boundary.

In early afternoon we rounded up our cabal. There were six of us, if you counted John Joe's dog. Saddling up, we whooped and hollered up Green Street and out past the cemetery in Kilbride. Hot tar bubbled below a branding-iron sun. It popped like bubblegum under the wobble of our front tyres. The roads were empty. Each house we passed seemed to have its windows thrown open so that the singsong chant of Micheál O'Hehir could escape out into the ripening yellow fields.

We crossed the bridge that marked the border into County Tipperary, and we could gauge the score by the roars from cottages and farmhouses alike. The Kilkenny boys were struggling.

Hot and thirsty we galloped into Mullinahone. If anywhere could be imagined more desolate than Callan then this was it. A solitary cat spat defiance at John Joe's dog as we rode up and down the street. There was no one else to challenge. A sign advertising Palm Grove ice-cream flapped a limp greeting to us, but when we reigned in our mounts we found the shop shut in our faces. It resembled a scene from *High Noon*. Nothing except pistol-shot cheers burst out from lace-curtained windows, and ricocheted about our ears. It was all one-way traffic at Croke Park.

We were hungry, thirsty and at a loss... that was until Spider suggested that we raid the orchard in the walled garden at the back of Killahy castle. The plan restored our spirits. Were we not a bold raiding party after all, and were we not in the heart of the enemy camp?

It was decided that Spider and I would do the deed while the rest of the gang kept watch. We circled the orchard until we spotted a rusty ladder attached to a giant water tank beside the wall. Overhanging dangles of Beauty of Bath apples that carried rosy blushes on their ripening cheeks enticed us in. Up the ladder, over the wall, we filled our pockets with red apples, green apples, hard apples. We were sorted in jig time.

But back on the sag of the ladder, disaster struck. We were circled by a pack of mixed hounds that leaped, snapped and snarled at our sandaled toes. Chucking apples only made them worse, and the remainder of the gang had vamoosed.

We were finally set free by the owner, who, when he learned we were from Callan, laughed that knowing the final score in Croke Park should be punishment enough... Tipperary 5 goals and 13 points, Kilkenny 2–8.

The journey back seemed longer. Farmers hunting in cows for milking roared 'Up Tipp!' as we cycled past. The thought that tomorrow represented the first day back at school had combined with the green apples to turn our stomachs sour, and if that wasn't bad enough, our final summer adventure had been spoiled by the reservoir dogs of Mullinahone.

(first broadcast on RTÉ Radio in 2006)

CAST IN BRONZE

Josephine McArdle

The sun had burned off the early morning mist as I left Neidín behind and headed for Kilgarvan. Turning off to my right from the main road at Morley's Bridge, I drove through a blazing trail of Monbretia. With cries of 'No Surrender' from the hedgerows, September was holding fast to summer and the third Sunday was fast approaching.

Snaking across the county border, I slipped a CD into the player and rolled down the window. Enormous outcrops of rock rose up on either side of me. Nanci Griffith sang about her *Lone Star State of Mind*, and I sang along. Soon, red and white chequered flags appeared on the gateposts urging The Rebels on to victory. I remembered the old Kerry aspiration of having the hay saved and Cork beaten before the start of September and I cringed.

Yet both the Hurling and the football championship trophies are named after Corkmen, one of whose ghosts I was chasing today.

I overshot my turn off, and had to double back and follow the narrow road into Mallabracca.

'Is this the homeplace of Sam Maguire?' I enquired of the friendly, dreadlocked young man who approached me when I drove onto the building site.

He directed me on further, where I met a man with the curiously familiar name of Pat Spillane, the person who is driving the project to restore the dwelling-house, stables and outhouses where the Maguire family was born and reared. I met Sam himself in the centre of Dunmanway, cast in bronze. What is that he's holding in his hands, I wondered, and I moved in closer. Are they letters... or could they be... All-Ireland Final tickets!

At the early age of twenty, Sam Maguire seized a golden opportunity and took the boat to England, where he began working in the London General Post Office. A new millennium was dawning, and Irishmen everywhere were bracing themselves for an independent republic.

Educated in the Model School in Dunmanway, and later schooled by Master Madden, Sam had successfully passed the exams for the British Civil Service.

The young Corkman worked diligently, concealing his allegiance to the Irish Republican Brotherhood. Few of his superiors would have suspected that a Church of Ireland son of wealthy landowners would harbour anything but unquestionable loyalty to the Crown.

Two of his four brothers soon followed suit and joined Sam in London, leaving the eldest son to farm their 200 acres in the townland of Malabracca, four miles to the north of Dunmanway.

Fired up by the success of his local team the Doheneys when they reached the All-Ireland Clubs Final in 1897, Sam now joined the London Hibernians, and his long association with the GAA began.

His football career took off. In the space of four years he had captained the London Hibernians on three occasions in the All-Ireland Football Finals, albeit defeated dismally by Tipperary, Dublin and Kerry in 1900, 1901 and 1903 respectively.

Sam made another foray into the history books when he again led the London Hibernians onto the pitch at Jones's Road in 1906 in the early stages of the Croke Cup. He hung up his boots shortly afterwards, and went into the administration of the London GAA, becoming the Chairman of the London County Board in1907. Serving with him as Vice-Chairman of the Board during his tenure of office was one Liam McCarthy. Two sterling Irishmen, literally.

Meanwhile, in his role as employee of Her Majesty's Posts and Telegraphs, Sam Maguire was playing the game of his life intercepting official state documents relevant to British military and political intentions in Ireland, and passing on this valuable intelligence to his comrades in the IRB. This very same south of Ireland protestant swore into the IRB any young Irish post-office workers whom he deemed trustworthy. The cause of Ireland's freedom was well served by Maguire, who soon rose to the rank of Lieutenant-General of the IRB and director of Intelligence in Britain.

In 1909, another young Corkman from Clonakilty was sworn into the ranks by Maguire. Answering to the name of Michael Collins, Sam welcomed his former schoolmate, also tutored by Master Madden for the British Civil Service Exam, into the secret circle. Remaining above suspicion, Maguire continued to work in the London Post Office during and after the Easter Rising, passing on important information until after the assassination of Sir Henry Wilson. A retired Unionist MP for North Down, Sir Henry was shot dead outside his home in 1922. British Intelligence officials were closing in on the elusive 'S.M.'

It was time to run for cover and return home, but Maguire was deeply distressed by the divisions in post-civil-war Ireland. He chose to remain in Dublin, where he got employment with the newly formed Irish Civil Service, a career that was, alas, short-lived. Poor health forced him to return to Mallabracca, where he died of Tuberculosis on 6 February 1927. He was forty-eight years of age.

In 1928, a group of his friends formed a committee to raise funds for a commemoration of this formidable man.

Honoured today in his home town of Dunmanway, Sam Maguire is permanently cast in bronze, and is annually commemorated in silver when the winners of the All-Ireland Senior Football Championship hoist the GAA's most prestigious trophy.

(first broadcast on RTÉ Radio in 2006)

FROM MORTAL TO MYTH
Cyril Kelly

D id I realise, I wonder, on that September Sunday of 1962, that my last Listowel summer had just elapsed, that the final summer of my youth had just passed by? As I strolled around the streets of the town that morning, did I realise that life was about to change irrevocably? Within a year I would have done my Leaving Cert. I would be departing for Dublin, taking the first tentative steps towards adult life. Was it this twilight zone between Blake's *Songs of Innocence* and *Songs of Experience* that enabled me to turn a local mortal into myth in the space of forty seconds that very afternoon?

On that All-Ireland Sunday, when Kerry took to the field against Roscommon, a local lad, a lad who lived a few doors down from myself, made history. Within forty seconds of the throw-in, Gary McMahon had scored a goal, the fastest ever in All-Ireland annals.

For months the town had been preparing for the races, which took place on the week immediately after the All-Ireland. Known as 'The Harvest Festival,' the very name was redolent of a bountiful countryside; of tilled fields, of bog and meadowlands around North Kerry. Rails of turf trailed whiffs of darkness through the autumn town; stately domes of hay blessed streets with the scent of light. For months, Jackeen Godfrey, reeking of turps, gasping with painter's colic, had pumped his blowlamp from house front to house front. It was a dragon spitting hoarse lilac fire. But then, with oily linseed smells, he magiced in his wake a pristine town.

Night, noon and morning, Mosheen Carmody, ensconced on a cushion of straw at the front of his dray, bobbed from the railway yard. Half tierces of porter sloshed around him to the silvery tune of the chuckling harness. At the back gate of every pub, Mosheen toppled casks from the cart onto his cushion of straw. With a well-aimed boot he sent them barrelling in along the flagstoned yards, rumbling like thunder, disappearing one by one into the cockroach sheds.

Tadhg Brennan, long tongs in hand, is standing beside the fire at the back of the forge. On a plinth of blocks, the fire is level with his hip. Crunching another shoe into the black bed of slack, Tadhg reaches for the hickory bellows handle. In the darkness his face reflects gushes of firelight. His chomped lips are pink against his soot-grained skin. Roger True Blue totes another sack of sawdust from the mill. He's bound for John B. Keane's decent pub. And none better than J.B. himself – me oul segotia – to proffer a reward: one more creamy pint, Roger True Blue's elixir of life. And down by the river, a wagon train of tinkers is circling in primary colours. Canvas covers baskets of trinkets, holy pictures, miraculous medals and sheafs of ballads to sell and sing during race week.

And into our expectant town, a town stacked with crubeens and mutton pies, stroll the troupe of autumn players. The strong man gnawing six-inch nails; nifty chancers complete with butter box and three-card tricks, tic-tac men and the Pecker Dunne serenading the bebuntinged streets with 'The Moon Behind The Hill.'

Finally, McElligots of Castleisland come to erect loudspeakers on telegraph poles throughout the town, great, grey foghorns of speakers that will broadcast Radio Listowel for the week. But before Bridie Gallagher or 'The Gypsy Rover' or 'She Wore Red Feathers and a Hooly-Hooly Skirt' can come through those speakers, the All-Ireland Final of 1962 is relayed thoughout the town. Micheál O'Hehir's heroic tableau's pitched the length and breadth of each deserted street.

Standing that Sunday in wonder and awe, outside my own hall door, lace curtains ballooning softly through nearby windows, I saw Croke Park more clearly than if I were there. Echoes and reverberations had three or four simultaneous versions of the National Anthem pulsing in the air. And O'Hehir was welcoming Radio Brazzaville and immigrants from Boston to our town. Then, almost catching me off guard, the ball was thrown in. I could see it, could see it clearly, a dark orb rising in the sky. The blaring commentary bounced off John R's shop, ricocheted across the road to resonate from Farrell's wall, suspending the ball aloft interminably. At last it dropped into a thicket of grasping hands. Some giant in blue and saffron emerged, clutching it to his chest, booted it towards the Kerry goal. But a quick clearance landed it back outside John R's, where Kerry got a free.

From O'Connell's unerring boot, Micheál O'Hehir described the magnificent trajectory of the ball. It sailed over bunting and strings of coloured lights to land amid a cluster of players, on the edge of the Roscommon square. And there, it bobbled and it bounced and, at last, broke free, right into the path of a stalwart in green and gold. And he, delirium of deliriums, punched it straight into the net. Forty seconds since the game began, the fastest goal in history, by Gary McMahon.

While O'Hehir's voice was still ringing from the rooftops, I gazed at McMahon's house, a few doors down from my own, his brothers in school with me, taught by his father Bryan, The Master. But in that forty seconds, in that moment caught between a time of innocence and experience, a young man not much older than me, a man I'd seen playing for our street's Ashes, could, with one flick of the wrist, transform himself from ordinary mortal status to take on the mantle of myth.

(first broadcast on RTÉ Radio in 2006)

THE FINAL BEGINNING
Art Ó Súílleabháin

Mayo will be playing Kerry in the All-Ireland Final today, but my first real memories of Gaelic Football and of seeing television are inexorably linked. As a family we had returned from Boston in 1961 to live in the picturesque village of Corr na Móna, on the shores of Lough Corrib, in north-west County Galway. The nearest thing to a football pitch was the fifty yards or so of the school field. It ran at an incline of at least twenty-five degrees, but we kicked ball there with youthful gusto regardless – not that I was ever of any use at the game. There was no television there in 1961, so as children we had all the time in the world to discover those mountains and to explore the rivers that crowded our lives with fishing and nature.

The summer of 1966 changed some of that. I was ten, and my uncle Jack from Cong in County Mayo decided that I should be brought to experience the excitement of some football matches, and to dream with him of an up-and-coming Mayo team ending Galway's bid for three All-Irelands in a row. That summer I watched the said Galway football team at their majestic best. They beat a valiant Mayo by a single point in Castlebar at the Connaught Final, and I was hooked. There was no possible way, though, of seeing Galway progress through the later stages of the championship. They had beaten Kerry in the 1964 and 1965 finals, and they were now on the way to a possible historic treble. The feverish excitement all around the village was palpable.

In Corr na Móna our family lived with only the priest's house between us and the church. That summer saw a strange brown box arrive next door. It was a large, mahogany-cased, grey-screened piece of furniture that we saw vaguely glimmering through his living-room window. On a rare occasion we had been invited in to see the news, but it was a bit like being invited to the 'big house,' and was an uncomfortable setting for a ten-year-old.

Anyway, black and white distractions only vaguely interested me while so many river pools, hills and islands needed exploration in the colour-filled freedom of a balmy summer full of eels, wild mushrooms and boats.

In late September all that changed. The after-Mass talk was all about the final in Croke Park. How would we get to see the magical Colleran, Leyden or Purcell in action again? The local priest had a ticket to the match, and would be gone all that weekend. The thought of furtively accessing his living-room was tempting, but to my innocent mind was akin to breaking into some forbidden tabernacle.

However, on the Saturday before the match word spread like wildfire that the priest had given the sacristan permission to open the house for a few who wanted to see the game. Early on Sunday afternoon, a few began to gather at the church grounds, but by half-past two there were twenty people gathered to watch the game, and by three o'clock there must have been close to forty people there. The large window in the living-room was opened, and the television was carefully positioned on the broad limestone sill. I sat on the grass on the church lawn while what seemed to be half the village squatted or stood peering at the black and white drama unfolding in the curate's window, Micheál O'Hehir's familiar voice describing the action we could now see. The cheering of the locals echoed periodically around the churchyard like some exotic chant. Galway eventually won the day, beating Meath for that historic treble.

There will be millions of television viewers for the All-Ireland Football Final today, and the voice of Micheál Ó Muircheartaigh will enthral thousands of radio listeners. It will be no easier to get a ticket for Croke Park, but the excitement of the beginning of the final will be echoed in villages, streets and houses in Kerry and Mayo, just as it was on the church lawn in Corr na Móna in 1966. But just maybe this time Mayo will be celebrating, and my uncle Jack will be smiling from one of the best seats in Heaven.

(first broadcast on RTÉ Radio in 2006)

MAYO MEMORIES
Liam Horan

The poet Paul Durcan implored 'Daddy, Daddy' to 'pass out the moon' on a journey to Mayo.

We were nowhere near as demanding as children. For us, a Connacht final in Castlebar was the very peak of glamour, and even if Daddy had this annoying habit of abandoning the car at the faintest suggestion of a traffic jam, we could forgive anything on this day of days.

The four of us were arranged in random order in the back, arguing over who would hold the Mayo flag out the window, and making sweeping predictions about the day ahead. Invariably, in these circumstances, we seek reassurance from our elders: 'Daddy, who do YOU think will win?' but those were lean times for Mayo football, and he could never quite deceive his children with promises that might later be cruelly crushed.

On the outskirts of the county town, he would swing the car around on the road with an almost presidential flourish, and park it up on the grass verge. Face her for home. We would disembark and set off walking.

Eventually, other Mayo supporters would join us *en route*, eyes fixed on the road ahead: pilgrims on the Camino de Santiago, or, perhaps more appropriately, the Tóchar Phádraig just a few miles away.

It was here we first heard the phrase 'Hope Springs Eternal,' for, alas, that was the mantra with which followers of the green and red consoled themselves during those unrewarding days.

Up over the bridge at the railway station, down by the Breaffy Road junction, John Hanley's shop on the left, Coll's Garage in front of us; young and old scurrying towards the sacred field; the urgency of it all; the quickened steps and the hurried conversations, the need to press on and secure a well-appointed perch from where we could survey the unfolding drama.

Then up onto McHale Road itself. We felt that strange surge of emotion, maybe even a tear welling in our eye, as we admired the Mayo bunting draped artistically from every house on the road. Who, we asked ourselves, went to all the trouble? And we wondered what it must be like for the Mayo players – Tommy O'Malley and Martin Carney, Horse Sweeney and John P. – to walk down McHale Road on this day, beneath this *ad hoc* green and red sky, with the hopes of a county riding on your shoulders?

Then along by O'Malley's Shop on the left-hand side. Though we were riveted by the scene and the crowd, we would still request essential provisions such as choc-ices and bags of Tayto. 'No applications,' our father would have proclaimed on the car journey down, but he would always relent, and we would slip in to Mr O'Malley's and stock up.

Across the road then, and the ticket booth – not quite ticket booth, but a temporary structure crafted from beer barrels and long timber planks. Into McHale Park then, the most beautiful stadium in the world, stretching majestically out in front of us; all the way down to the Bacon Factory End, the entire scene alive with possibility.

Here, we were hermetically sealed off from life beyond the walls of the old venue. It was a parallel universe. There was the certainty of great drama on the field, and gripping entertainment off it. We children unfurled our Mayo flags and wondered if this would finally be THE day. Please God, just this once!

Mick Melodeon moving at funereal pace through the crowd, row by row, singing age-old ballads – '… Those homes are destroyed and our soil confiscated, The hand of the tyrant brought plunder and woe/The fires are now quenched and our hearts desolated, In our once happy homes in the County Mayo…'

Mick was older than time and wizened as an ancient cat. He wore the same dark coat year after year. We wondered where he slept at night, if he made a living from the busking, and we hoped he was doing okay. We were glad no one stopped him from coming in.

From his accordion hung a rough-and-ready tin can, and it did our heart good when someone threw a few coins into it. On and on he would shuffle, singing of blackbirds and spinning wheels, winking and nodding at the crowd, a timeless addendum to this mighty pageant.

'Ice-creams, anyone for the last few ice-creams?'

'Sit down, will you, we all paid to get in.'

Shouts of recognition pass between friends, as if they hadn't met for years. A nudge from my father: 'That's the great Seán Purcell there,' as a legend of far-off days quietly moves to his seat, thousands of eyes quietly studying his every movement.

Someone says they saw the Flying Doctor Pádraig Carney too, that he must be home from America for the match. The past and the present mingling together: all channelled into this one crowded hour.

As the minor match finishes, we squeeze together to make more room for the swelling crowd. There's the riot of noise as the teams emerge and the struggle to drink in every twist, turn and nuance of the warm-up. The rich, traditional green above the bold, unpredictable red: those colours that mean so much to Mayo people all over the world, from Clare Island to California, Murrisk to Melbourne.

And then there's the throw-in, and the always present possibility of a sensation.

Mick Melodeon won't be in Croke Park today, but hundreds of thousands of people who claim the western seaboard county of Mayo as their home, will be singing his song. '…so boys pull together, in all kinds of weather, don't show the white feather, wherever you go – be like a brother, and help one another, like true-hearted men from the county Mayo…'

(first broadcast on RTÉ Radio in 2006)

RELIGIOUS PERSUASION
Tommy Sands

There were no Protestants at Mayobridge School except Harry McGarry. He was different. He didn't come into the catechism class when the rest of us were learning about who made the world and who God is. Instead, Harry kicked a ball about the schoolyard on his own. While we were becoming good Christians, he was becoming a good footballer.

But he told me that he also believed in God, and that he even believed that it was God who made the world. I said I liked football too and we became good friends.

I noticed that he never touched the ball with his hands when he played.

'We're not allowed to,' he said.

'Is it a sin?' I asked.

'I suppose so,' he said.

What a strict religion, I thought.

Later that evening, my father explained that it wasn't really football he was playing, it was a game called soccer, and it came from England. Our football game was called Gaelic and it was Irish.

'Is it a sin for a Catholic to play soccer?' I asked.

'If you play for a Gaelic team, then you're not allowed to play for a soccer team,' he said. 'That's rule 27 in the official GAA guide.'

'Would you go to hell if you did?' I asked.

'Not necessarily.' He smiled. 'But you might be told to.'

He explained that all down the years England wanted Ireland to become English, but by playing their own games and singing their own songs, the people here were saying, 'We're Irish.' England didn't want Protestant people here playing Irish games either, in case they would become Irish, for then Ireland would not become English after all.

It all sounded very complicated to me, but I passed it on to Harry as best I could. And we played a mixture of Gaelic and soccer in the schoolyard.

The next day, Harry told me that his da had told him to tell me to tell my da that even if good Protestant policemen wanted to play Gaelic, which they didn't anyway, the narrow Gaelic rules would not allow it, and to 'put that in his pipe and smoke it.'

That night my father told me to tell Harry to tell his da that the rule only came about because the police force had made an earlier rule banning their own policemen from playing Gaelic games, and to put that in *his* pipe and do what he liked with it.

I don't think either of them even smoked pipes, but I knew they liked whiskey and I wondered why they didn't tell each other all those complicated things while they were drinking together in Hale's pub in Newry on a Saturday night.

Still, some of the messages rubbed off on the messengers and we learned a lot, Harry and me, in that playground of knowledge at the Bridge of Mayo. Sometimes Harry and I wondered why Catholics and Protestants didn't go to the same school in the first place.

'Tell young Sands to tell his da that Catholics won't go to state schools because the Church of Rome wants to keep control over them, and while he's at it, would he ask him if he could lend me the loan of the stirrup pump for a few days' whitewashing.'

'Tell young McGarry to tell Big Davy that for years England made it illegal for Catholics to receive any education at all and was it any wonder Catholics built their own schools, and what the hell stirrup pump is he talking about?'

'Tell that wee skitter's get to tell his oul' Fenian da that the Penal days were years ago and there are now lovely schools for everybody to learn in, and there would be one in Mayobridge too, but the Catholics wouldn't go to it, and the stirrup pump is the one he said was great for whitewashing with last Saturday night in Hale's pub.'

'Tell that black-mouthed son of a Presbyterian Orangeman that they can stick their state schools for those schools tell only an English view of Irish history and that I can't lend him the stirrup pump because I lent it to him last summer and he never gave it back, but if I had it, he would get it, for he's a decent man, and if he isn't doing anything next Monday, would he give me a day at the threshing?'

And so it went on until the seemingly insoluble conflicts would be shelved for the time being, for friendships were just as deep as differences and life went on from sowing to mowing and from mowing to threshing.

(first broadcast on RTÉ Radio in 2007)

THUNDER AND LIGHTNING FINAL
Leo Cullen

'The Thunder and Lightning Final of 1939,' my father would say. 'Cork versus Kilkenny, it rained and it rained.' He would shake imaginary rain off his shoulders for emphasis as he described that game to me, and I would picture him on the open expanses of the old Cusack Stand. 'Thunder and lightning,' he would say, 'but not a soul left the ground until the final whistle, so gripping was that game that Kilkenny in the end won by a single point.' And he would continue his reverie, falling into a sadder note: 'I remember walking up Grafton Street after that match. There were people standing in shop doorways, white faced with fear, cowering from the sound of that thunder. And do you know who they were?'

'Who were they, daddy?' I would ask.

'They were Poles. Polish people, airlifted to Dublin from Warsaw, escaping from the Nazi bombings. First casualties of war: the children looking up into the parents' faces for comfort, but all they saw was fear.'

Oh my father told important All-Ireland stories; he was important on atmosphere.

You were born on the early hours of a Sunday in 1948, he would tell me, in which Waterford, led by John Keane, brought home the McCarthy Cup across the Suir for the very first time.

Now, wasn't that a great thing for any young lad to know… on what day of the week he had been born! In that way my father unwittingly filled in a lot of my early details for me.

I don't know if it was that revelation that started my own fascination with All-Irelands and the teams that played them, but what I do know is that I can name the winners of every All-Ireland Final going back to the year of my birth: Waterford, 1948, Tipperary, 1949 and so on… phalanx after phalanx of heroic fifteens.

Some dates shine out above others: 1957 – a great new Waterford team had emerged on the scene. They were back in an All-Ireland Final again, facing the craft of Kilkenny. That date shone out, because on that year I had got something new. My mother had died a few years previously, and that year I had got a new mother. My Tipperary father had remarried. And she came from the county Kilkenny, rural Kilkenny, a rose of Mooncoin. And she had a sister living in Waterford, married to a townie, and that sister was loyal to her adopted town and to townie life. Waterford and Kilkenny: I had married into one of the great rivalries of hurling. Unmercifully, those two chided and teased one another over the fortunes of their favourites. The victorious one would crow and tease, the vanquished would be close to tears.

In 1957, they travelled to Dublin, those sisters, and it was the turn of my stepmother to tease. Unemotional woman as I had estimated her, she brought home to our house that night something of the atmosphere of Croke Park. Her hair stood wild, there was colour in her cheeks; her eyes danced. She filled our house with an afterglow, just as my father had done with talk of his Thunder and Lightning All-Ireland.

Then 1959 came, a hot summer in which the country's wells went dry, and my family went to the sea at Clonea into October days on which we came home to milk the cows in the dark. The blue and white flags fluttered in the Déise that year. The team of Tom Cheastey, God rest him, carried home the cup first carried home on the day of my birth. That year it was the turn of my stepmother to show her tears.

Came 1963, the third and last All-Ireland encounter between those two. The sisters travelled again, Waterford scored six goals, and from where I listened at our kitchen radio in neutral Tipperary, I heard the clash of each goal in Croke Park. I heard my Auntie Mary scream six times. Kilkenny did not score as many goals, but Eddie Keher scored the points, and I heard my mother's more muted exhortations high in the Hogan Stand. Her team prevailed that day. What a game.

And here we go again… well, not quite. And it is to my father I must return, to introduce the team who stand against Kilkenny this year – his most heroic phalanx of them all. He never tired talking of them, and of the man from Aghane. Mick Mackey, his own personal hero. He described him to me: 'Barrel-chested and fearless, he would go through anything. He would put his head where another man wouldn't put his hurley.' I wondered how a barrel could go through anything, but my father's enthusiasm carried my imagination. Munster hurling, he said, 'close, tight, pull on the ground and in the air – is best typified by Limerick. They were the team of the 1940s.'

Yes, and now Limerick are back again, with that blend of city grit and Golden Vale extravagance. They too have had their many clashes with lissom Kilkenny. Today begins a new era.

So let there be once again on the stands rivals shouting support: the heart in the mouth roars of Auntie Marys and the quieter exhortations of Mothers. I can hear them. It is happening again. And I can see them: The stories of my father – the Polish immigrants and their children who were with us then and now are again. The Thunder and Lightning Finals. Let this one begin!

(first broadcast on RTÉ Radio in 2007)

THE SCRAPBOOK
Mae Leonard

I didn't know him back then – when the Limerick Minor Team won the All-Ireland Hurling Championship in 1958 – in fact, I had never seen a hurling match in my life.

Coming from The Parish – the Isle – in Limerick City, I was heavily into swimming and rugby and rowing. Hurling didn't even enter the equation.

I didn't know him throughout the early years, when his hurling skills were developed to the point where he was one of the chosen few to wear the green and white of his county. But, thanks to my mother-in-law, I have been afforded the privilege of sharing her pride, excitement and devotion to his and Limerick's sporting career of some fifty years ago. I have inherited her scrapbook – a scrapbook of everything to do with the hurling career about which I really know very little.

It is not just the scrapbook itself; it is the way it is lovingly put together – or I should perhaps say *not* put together. Nothing is in proper sequence; there are no dates on the yellowed newspaper clippings, and there are reports of matches between teams from clubs that have long since faded away. There are action pictures that any press photographer would be proud to claim. There are home-made badges and paper hats all stuck between pages of the huge old diary of 1958.

Now leafing through it, some of the pasted-in items become dislodged, and in my mind's eye I can see her, his mother, mixing a bowl of flour-and-water paste. It is probably late at night when she has the eight of them asleep. Then she takes the most recent newspaper match reports and pictures, carefully cuts around them, applies the paste and smooths them onto the pages with her son's face scowling up at her. He never seemed to smile in those pictures.

The one I like best is a mid-air clash with a Waterford forward when he clears the sliotar away from the goalmouth. I've heard Limerick followers describe him as talented, strong, reliable, always first to the ball, solid and skilful in holding his half-back position. But I think the best description of him is in an article by An Mangaire Súgach – Manachín Seoighe – in the *Limerick Leader* sometime in the early 1950s. Manachin reports of attending a Limerick hurling match when he overheard a supporter remark, 'Boy! That Leonard is a quare hawk.' And, depending on the way you look at it, that's admiration indeed.

By the time I met him and we started to see each other regularly, he was playing on the Limerick Senior Team. And then came the time he had to meet my parents. My mother suggested that I bring him to tea one Sunday evening and, horror of horrors, he was late. When he finally arrived he had a black eye, three stitches over his right eyebrow and his knuckles were raw and bloodied.

He was welcomed, however, and over mother's high tea, my father, a rugby follower all his life, pulled out all the stops to discuss the greats of current-day hurling – Tom McGarry and Dermot Kelly of Limerick; Jimmy Smyth of Clare; Donie Nealon and Tony Wall of Tipperary; Pat Fitzgerald and Jimmy Brohan of Cork.

Things went just fine, and my father would joke about it afterwards in his father-of-the-bride speech – 'When this fellow came across the bridge into The Parish famed for rugby, carrying a hurley, everyone stared at it and asked – "What's that?"'

(first broadcast on RTÉ Radio in 2007)

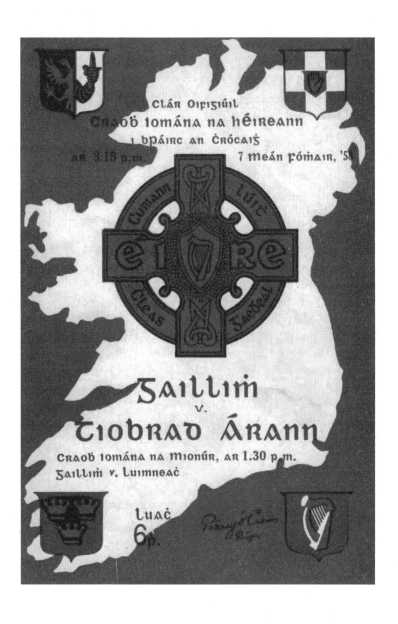

Clár Oifigiúil
Craob Iomána na hÉireann
i bPáirc an Chrócaig
ar 3.15 p.m.   7 Meán Fómhair, '58

Gaillim
v.
Tiobrad Árann

Craob Iomána na Mionúr, ar 1.30 p.m.
Gaillim v. Luimneach

Luach
6p.

SEE YE IN ANOTHER THIRTY-THREE YEARS

John Downing

We only realised how wet it was when we saw the streaks of black and amber smearing all the way down the old man's face. To us, the dance of the misty rain was irrelevant. My brother Joe and I were standing with a large group of elated friends on the canal end of Croke Park, witnessing something most die-hard Limerick fans never thought possible. It was the first Sunday in September 1973, and Limerick were about to beat Kilkenny by seven points in an All-Ireland Final and bridge a gap that dated back, Christlike, to 1940. I was sixteen years old at the time. The old man took off the Kilkenny paper hat with its running dye, and in disgust he threw it on the ground, taking care to stand on it before he made to move on. We jeered at him loudly. He turned back briefly and he eyeballed Joe before spitting, 'Ah, see ye in another thirty-three years!'

We can make two remarks about that old man. On a sad note, we must concede that he appears to have been was largely right, at first glance at least. But on a lighter note, unless there's absolutely no justice in this world at all, that old man is long gone to the great Hogan Stand in the sky by now.

Yep, Limerick's poor haul of just seven hurtling All-Irelands is well known to Irish people who have even a passing knowledge of the game. It is paltry when compared to that of the princes of hurling in Kilkenny, Cork and Tipperary. But that less-than-encouraging statistic hides a storehouse of the crucial facts about Limerick and hurling, and it is those hidden facts that have sustained my passion for Limerick hurling across four decades. Chief of these encouraging Limerick hurling facts is the passion of its supporters. Every year when I make the pilgrimage to Thurles, Páirc Uí Chaoimh or the Gaelic Grounds, I'm astounded to meet this legion of green and white fans. They come from Doon on the Tipperary boarder, Abbey Feale next door to Kerry, Kilfanane and other places too close to Cork for comfort, and all the places in between. They come in strong numbers from Limerick city, a place where rugby and soccer have long held a far longer sway over the dreams of youth.

I am part of what I have always thought of as that city sub-tribe of hurling. We're small in numbers, but we're never lacking in passion and commitment. Many years of living outside of Limerick have not dimmed my belief in membership of that tribe. It is an open group, which happily welcomes the rugby and soccer fraternity, which also temporarily but proudly supports the green and white. Though we've not won since 1973, we've had our big days in the sunshine. There were unsuccessful finals in 1974, 1980, 1994 and 1996. Each came with varying tales of heartbreak, with 1994 leaving scars still too tender to probe. We've had the glory of our under-twenty-one side, and their superb three back to back All-Irelands, and we depend so much on many of those lads this afternoon. We must also reflect on the harsh reality that once you take out the big three of Cork, Kilkenny and Tipperary, you realise that hurling really depends far more on Limerick, Wexford, Waterford, Dublin, Clare, Offaly and the others for its survival. But those thoughts are for another day. Today, let's just note that that old Kilkenny fan with the rain-soaked black and amber face and his injunction that he would see us again in another thirty-three years was not really that right after all. Damien Rail's men take to the field this afternoon well conscious of the tradition of pride and passion that drives Limerick hurling, and despite a Christlike-plus-one hope followed by deep disappointment, I believe they will win.

(first broadcast on RTÉ Radio in 2007)

HOME BY THE LEE
John Conroy

At best, it is my adopted county: I got my first proper job there, met my future wife in the shadow of Finbarr's Cathedral, willingly drank from the overflowing rivers of good humour and cockiness, the real Capital, Jack Lynch territory, the greatest Taoiseach we ever had, the spills and breaks of the blood and bandage and the peoples' Republic – CORK, home by the Lee, history and rebellion, the Barrs and the Glen, Nemo's imported kingpins with the swagger of Morgan at the helm, a hurling county at its core, but on its day big enough to have a compliment of footballers as good as any in the country.

Cork, its own place. I was three years there when I found myself in a garage, not more than ten miles outside the city, trapped in a conversation of nods and half-finished sentences, the mechanic in full flow, a vague idea of what we were supposedly agreeing on, words contorted to a multitude of meanings, an etymologist's dream-world of repeating vowels and missing consonants, French melodies meshed with Arabic guttural soundings – all married and mashed together in a stream of rippled resonance, a thunderous waterfall of energy and sound, indecipherable to the untutored ear.

But back to the main event: Football. In terms of All-Ireland successes, Cork come fifth with six All-Ireland wins behind Kerry who have thirty-four, Dublin with twenty-two, Galway nine, and Meath seven. As a Galway man, I like that statistic. It seems to reflect what we intuitively know about the game's traditions and the origin of the truly great players that have adorned the game down through the years. I would bet that most Cork people believe they are closer to Kerry in the honours list, certainly ahead of Dublin, and would probably nod suspiciously at Galway's lofty position, consulting further before believing the hard facts of events. It's the reason why Cork teams have won games before taking to the field at all, and why they have lost games too, games they should have won but for the skein of false assuredness.

So, Kerry and Cork in 2007. The first time the teams have met in an All-Ireland Final. A rivalry that equals, maybe even surpasses, that of Galway–Mayo, Meath–Dublin, Tyrone and Armagh. No place for the faint-hearted. A deep, searing line of revenge omnipresent, ready to surface with artesian exactitude, upwelling across mentors and players, never far from the surface – no better way to win an All-Ireland though, taking the glory with a heavy, delicious scalp, to be hung on every gatepost and outhouse, photographed and dispersed like the lightest bag of feathery down, everywhere falling for a full year, the sweetest victory of them all.

Both teams will expect to win. Both sets of supporters will demand it. In the boiling dressing-rooms, the condensate will smell of sweat and nerves, and most of all the fear of losing – not to Kerry above all else, never to Cork in football. And there the lines will be drawn.

Those of us with a love of the game will watch and wish our own county was there, basking in the low September sun, nervously surfing the rolling wave of noise and excitement that is Croke Park on judgement day. For those of us with an affiliation to Cork – its landmarks, the fond memories of a southern lowland awash with good-humoured character, a thriving people with dialects doused in lyrical simile – we will anxiously look on, inhaling from our memory banks the malted scent of the city, revisiting the majesty of the River Lee, the bustle of Patrick Street on a Saturday afternoon, urging on, nail biting our way to the final whistle.

(first broadcast on RTÉ Radio in 2006)

THE BEIJING BANSHEES

Josephine McArdle

The Asian Gaelic Games are the highlight of the GAA scene in Asia. It may surprise you to know that there are Seoul Gaels and Dubai Gaels, Shanghai and Korean Gaels.

Derek Brady and the Taiwan Celts formed a GAA Club in 1996, and many other groups from Shanghai to Singapore followed suit. Soon the concept of the Asian Games was born, and the first Games were held in Manilla in 1996. Indeed, out of nowhere Asia has become the fastest growing territory for GAA membership and club growth.

Phenonmenal economic growth in Asia has attracted large numbers of Irish expats to places that were hitherto only visited by missionaries and diplomats from Ireland.

After Derek Brady's tragic death, his family donated the Derek Brady Cup to commemorate their son. This cup is a replica of the Sam Maguire that is hoisted in Croke Park by the All-Ireland Senior Football Champions.

Gaelic football was first seen in Beijing back in April 2002, when the Irish contingent there was asked to play a friendly match against the lads in Shanghai, for the craic.

After a couple of hastily arranged training sessions, the game took place, and this is where Beijing Celtic had its its origins. In November 2003, a ladies gaelic team was formed in the city and, after a lengthy debate over the name, they decided on the Beijing Banshees.

Their finest moment to date was when they won the All-Asian Games in 2005 in Shanghai, capped only by marching behind the brass band of The People's Liberation Army to the strains of 'The Green Fields of France.'

Among the players marched Aoife O'Loughlin from Mountmellick, one of six daughters, three of whom have played county football for Laois.

Then there's Angela Keane from Lispole in the Kingdom, who'd just returned from Ireland after SARS in the late autumn of 2003, picked up a hairdresser's business card from the foyer of the Kempinski Hotel and went along to meet Jennifer Ullman to have her roots done. Jewish and from Chicago, Jennifer worked from home and was delighted to chat to another westerner, and the two were soon swapping stories about their lives in Beijing.

The greatest challenge for many young professionals in China is of course to maintain fitness in spite of the demands of their busy careers and the monotony of the gym.

Because work brings people to Beijing, it tends to rule life, and a conscious decision must be made to step away from the desk and onto the training pitch, usually the sports facility of the local international school.

Hearing from Jennifer about a newly formed group of women who were talking about coming together and playing Gaelic football, Angela was delighted to follow the trail and telephone… wait for it… Xanthe Visram.

She didn't sound too likely a contact for the GAA, but Xanthe managed the email distribution list for the Gaelic teams, as well as playing too. Daughter of an Indian father and an English mother, Xanthe gushed with enthusiasm, and before Angela could mumble *Confucious Says*, she was going to training regularly on a Saturday afternoon, and was soon togged out for the Banshees.

Unlike Hong Kong or Singapore, where they have a large contingent of expat Irish teachers and nurses, girls who have played since they were knee high to the Sam Maguire back home, Beijing is made up of other nationalities, and there are women of every origin wearing the Banshees' jersey.

This multicultural line-out has fielded Raewyn , former New Zealand gymnast, Brook, a PE teacher from Australia, Erica, a morman from Pennsylvania, Rhian from Britain, who boasted of having the genuine Irish Granny, Tammy from Canada and Lucy from Xian, who is very happy to be gaining insights into Ireland's most popular sport.

The Asian Games is a two-day event, with group games taking place on the Saturday followed by the knockout stages on the next day. It was as the result of two years of slogging it out on the playing field and learning the hard way that these ladies eventually found their rythym and made it to the final playoff in the late autumn of 2005, in a game that was described as the one of the best matches to have been played during the entire season. Down to the wire, and after extra time the Banshees held on to their lead. Having trained relentlessly throughout the polluted Beijing summer months, it had paid off in a wave of victory.

Nine hours ahead of us, they will be catching up on their beauty sleep when the ball is thrown onto the pitch in Croke Park.

Nevertheless, as Ireland continues to befriend China economically, it's not inconceivable that at some time in the not too distant future a team from Shanghai or Hong Kong will be playing in the All-Ireland Gaelic Football Championship in Croke Park. And who knows? Perhaps the Beijing Banshees may even take up the camán and sliotar and face those magnificent women of Wexford!

(first broadcast on RTÉ Radio in 2007)

LISTENING TO THE ALL-IRELAND OF 1957 IN CHITTAGONG

Norman Freeman

When the deck-passenger ship on which I was serving reached the port of Chittagong, at the top of the Bay of Bengal, there was a letter waiting for me. It was from my mother in Omeath, County Louth.

Among other things, she told me that there was a great stir in the village. The year was 1957, and the Louth Gaelic football team was training at St Michael's College there. The team was preparing to do battle with Cork in the All-Ireland Football Final at Croke Park on Sunday 22 September. One of them, Seamus O'Donnell, was a Garda stationed in Omeath.

I was on Eastern Service as a radio officer with the Marconi company on ships plying the Indian Ocean, and I hadn't been home for over a year. I badly wanted to hear the All-Ireland.

In 1957, long before the era of earth-girdling satellites and the internet, hearing the All-Ireland in far-flung places meant tuning in to Radio Brazzaville. Radió Éireann did not have a global short wave service; however, aware of how much hearing an All-Ireland meant to many Irish people in far-off lands, it arranged to have the match rebroadcast from the powerful transmitter in the then French Congo on the day following the big game.

So on this Monday night I went into the sweltering radio room of our ship, the *Aronda*, switched on one of the big marine receivers and connected it to the main aerial strung high between the fore and after masts.

All around me were voices talking in Bengali, Hindi and Pushtu, but the voice I most wanted to hear was that of Micheál O'Hehir. It's hard to describe the mixture of emotions that surged up on hearing the familiar tones coming from so far away. Not alone that, but he began by sending greetings and messages to many of the other Irish people listening to Brazzaville – missionaries in Nigeria and the Phillipines, the many who had emigrated to the US, Australasia and other places and for whom the All-Ireland was a strong link with home.

The game started. It was a neck and neck race, but gradually Louth went ahead by five points to three. I saw a Lascar seaman looking in the door curiously when he heard me shouting 'Come on, the Wee County!'

Then there were two setbacks. First of all, a ball lobbed in by the Cork player Neally Duggan found its way to the back of the Louth net. Next thing the radio room was lit up by lightning that seemed only metres away. A tropical thunderstorm was upon us, moving steadily over the wide, dark Karnaphuli River. There was no option but to earth the aerial, even if it meant losing the sound of the All-Ireland. I was afraid of lightning flashing down into the radio room, blowing fuses, damaging the equipment and perhaps doing some harm to me as well.

I walked up and down on the deck outside in the dank, tropical heat, wondering how the game was going, willing that storm to go away quickly.

It was at least twenty minutes before I felt it safe to resume listening to the All-Ireland. The second half was under way, and Louth were three points down. They battled back but, with only five minutes to go the Cork side, with 'Toots' Kelleher playing well, were still ahead by 1–7 to 9 points. Then a ball came floating in towards the Cork goal and was fisted to the net by Sean Cunningham to put Louth in the lead. They held out to win their third All-Ireland. The cup was accepted by their captain, the late Dermot O'Brien.

When I eventually got home to Omeath, I got chatting to my grandfather about the All-Ireland of 1957. He was full of praise for the Louth team.

'Ah they're brave fellows,' he said. 'It'll not be long before The Wee County wins the All-Ireland again.'

Sadly, that was Louth's last All-Ireland, and they never contested a final since. But they take to the field in hope each year, with the folk memory of that 1957 victory somewhere in the back of their minds.

(first broadcast on RTÉ Radio in 2007)

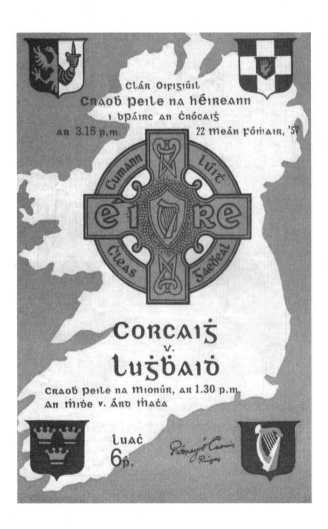

CHANGING TIMES
Tommy Sands

My Father was not, by any stretch of the imagination, a violent man. With some rare lapses, however, in 1960, he managed to cut off all relations between our house and the rest of the world.

In August 1960, he coolly picked up the biggest knife in the kitchen and stabbed or our old wet battery wireless in the speaker. He followed this by throwing a cup of tea in its face, soaking such far-flung stations as Stockholm, Oslo, Frankfurt and London with hot, wet tea-leaves. His general target on that oaccasion was Athlone, the headquarters of Ireland's national radio station, and Micheál O'Hehir, the brilliant sports communicator, in particular.

'Take that, ye karn ye,' he roared. 'And that, you knob-faced knur,' he shouted, delivering a bare-knuckled blow to its hitherto smiling dial.

It was because of a Gaelic football match. Down was trailing by two points against Offaly. It had been a bruising All-Ireland Senior Championship semi-final. There were just a few minutes left in the game, and James McCarten, the dynamic Down centre-half forward, had been downed in the square. Paddy Doherty was getting ready to take the penalty kick. All around Croke Park, you could cut the tension with the knife that was lying relaxed and innocent nearby, the knife that usually cut simple soda farls for quiet country people. O'Hehir was almost hoarse with excitement. 'Paddy Doherty is now standing back to take the penalty. His socks are down around his ankles. The crowd is hush…'

At that moment, the whole population of County Down, it seemed, was either in Croke Park or gathered around a wirelss like ours, teething prayers and threats alike to saints and other holy people who might have influence on Providence in such times as these.

'Can Doherty score this and save the day for Down and put them into their first ever All-Ireland Final in history?' O'Hehir went on breathlessly: 'He's placing the ball on the fourteen-yard line… this could be the most important kick of his life… the most important kick… holding their breath… here he comes…' O'Hehir lowered his voice to a whisper. 'He puts his head to one side in that familiar style… a hush has fallen over the crowd… here he comes…'

There was deathly silence. We stopped breathing, waiting for the kick. We waited and waited… and waited.

But Paddy Doherty never got the ball kicked in our house. Out wireless had stopped breathing too. The wet battery had run out. It needed to be charged again, but not in the manner in which it was bring charged, battered, butted and knifed by my father.

'You dirty, rotten, treacherous two-faced son of a bitch's ghost of an excuse for a wireless!' he roared, with lefts and rights to AFN Frankfurt and the BBC Home Service. 'If you were playing that pop rubbitch on Radio Luxembourg, you wouldn't break down. I houl ye, wouldn't ye not!'

Perhaps we had the volume turned up too loud. Liam Daly told us later that high volume could drain the power out of a battery. Others said that even a wireless could suffer the effects of tension, which, in turn, could have drained the battery. And then there was the weak signal from Radió Éireann. If the game had been broadcast on BBC Northern Ireland, it would have been clearer and less work for the old wireless, but the BBC never broadcast Gaelic games.

As it happened, Paddy Doherty scored that penalty and Down had qualified for its first ever All-Ireland Final, but we wouldn't know that until the next morning, when Jack Grant would come with the *Irish Press* and the groceries in Gorman's lorry.

We decided that we would go to Dublin for the final, just to be sure, and hopefully we'd see for the first time a team from the Six Counties with the All-Ireland Senior Championship.

It would be an unforgettable expedition. Josie Shevlin from Armagh said that she would take us in her car. We would all go, even my mother. With egg sandwiches, flasks of tea and a red and black flag we had sewn together from a dress belonging to my mother, and an old soutane belonging to Father Hugh, we headed for the border. All along the way, through the counties of Armagh, Louth, Meath and Dublin, Down flags hung from every tree, in support of the Wee North against the mighty Kingdom of Kerry. We went to the red church in Whitehall, near Dublin airport, for eight o'clock Mass. There were Kerry people in the congregation too, who would be expecting a different result from God. He had already delivered them nineteen All-Irelands. Down had been given none. 'Maybe,' I respectfully suggested to God, 'it is time for a change.'

We were waiting outside the gates of Croke Park from 9.30 a.m., along with thousands of others, singing and swapping sandwiches. At 1.30 p.m., we crushed in and got carried away with the crowd to a heavenly spot, right down beside the wire under the Cusack Stand, and there, in a kind of euphoric trance, we witnessed one of the most memorable spectacles in the history of Irish sport.

Through the two-inch mesh, twelve-foot-high wire fence, we roared, wailed, wept and cheered as these modern-day Cúchulainns leaped in the air like the very grass was on fire and swept up and down the field like waves of myth and magic. At the end, unable to hold back any longer, we scaled that fence like spiders and sped out onto the Croke Park grassland just to touch the hem of a red and black garment.

Down had beaten Kerry and, amidst unimaginable celebrations, Kevin Mussen, the captain, carried the Sam Maguire Cup across the border. For a long time, there was no work done on the farms around Ryan, and that victory united Catholic and

Protestant for many weeks and the whole of County Down walked on air.

My father's attack on the wireless that year cut us off from the outside world for many weeks, and until Hugh and I walked the battery two miles up the Crossan Road to Mrs Linden's shop to get it charged. More than thirty years later, her grandson Mickey Linden would lead Down to further All-Ireland victories, and I would write a song about with my son Fionán as we watched a new generation train in Kilbroney Park, Rostrevor, under the watchful eye of Peter McGrath. Every evening they ran up and down the side of Slieve Martin to Cloch Mór, the big stone thrown there by Fionn Mac Cumhaill to dislodge Benandonner, icy giant from the wintry north. They seemed to be suffering sweatfully for the very hills that were rising around them, to bring a sparkle of light to a loved homeland in a year of hate and a time of darkness.

> *The cheering like thunder rolled*
> *The flags they flew from every pole*
> *And we sang and danced the whole way home*
> *On the day we won the All-Ireland.*

When the wireless returned, it was never the same again. The newsreader, Charles Mitchell, seemed to be talking through his nose, or like a man who had been shocked by a sudden 'dig in the bake.' But he talked on regardless, and we heard news of John Fitzgerald Kennedy being elected President of the United States and scientists talking about exploring the moon. The whole world was changing.

(first broadcast on RTÉ Radio in 2007)

UP THE DÉISE
Lynn Cahill

My Dad is a Cork man. He was born and grew up on Bere Island in West Cork, but has spent much of his life living away from Cork in Canada, the UK and Dublin. If anyone asks him where he's from, he proudly says 'I'm a Cork man.' In recent years I've tried to pick this apart a bit. 'Dad,' I'll say, 'how do you know you're a true Cork man? I mean, how do you know your people were from Cork *originally*? What if they were Normans? That would make you a French man. Or maybe they were Vikings? Surely the Vikings made it as far as Cork? You could be a Norse man. Maybe that's where we got the blond hair from.' He's not a bit impressed with this line of questioning.

I envy my Dad and his certainty because I don't know where I come from. Well no, that's not quite true. I was born in Coventry in England, the child of Irish parents who had met and married in Newfoundland in Canada. I lived in an industrial area of the British Midlands until I was seven years old, then lived in my maternal grandmother's house near Fermoy for a year, and then spent the rest of my upbringing on a housing estate in Clondalkin in Dublin. I spent my twenties living in various parts of Dublin, my thirties living in Kilkenny, and now in my forties I am living in Waterford, the Déise, and it is here I intend to stay.

When people ask me where I'm from, I always hesitate. I don't quite know how to answer that question. I just know where I live now: Waterford. I've been here for two years, and I still don't know how to pronounce it properly. Is it Whatterford with a soft, Irish, buttery sound? Or is it the stretchy American version: Waaderfuurd? As in, Waaderfuurd Crystal.

And then there's the language barrier. Forget saying 'Hello' or 'Hi.' It's 'Well girl' to a female, and 'Well boy' to a male. It doesn't matter what age they are. At first I made the blow-in's mistake of answering with 'I'm very well thank you,' but now I know better. Now I know it's just a friendly greeting, not an enquiry after the state of your health.

A delicious powdery white roll for your lunch is a 'blaa.' This word is unique to Waterford, and the theory is that it came from the French Huguenot bakers in the city. Citizens of Waterford would buy their '*blanc pain*,' or white bread, which eventually got shortened to just 'blaa.'

But surely everyone in the country knows Waterford's battle cry 'Up the Déise!' It's as famous as Kilkenny's 'G'wan the Cats!' or the banner cry from Clare.

The Déise were an ancient tribe of people who lived here many years ago, and now, for the first time in forty-five years, the Waterford tribe are in the All-Ireland Hurling Final after a stomach-churning, nail-biting final against Tipperary.

Having lived in Kilkenny for fourteen years, I had grown complacent with the fighting Cats, and winning an All-Ireland Final was just another day at the office. But now it's Waterford versus Kilkenny in the big final. Neighbour against neighbour, the mighty Cats against the fierce men of the Déise.

There's no doubt that Kilkenny are the favourites to win and that Waterford are the underdogs. But sometimes the underdogs win, and what a wonderful, mouth-watering afternoon to look forward to. It's a proud day for any county to be up in Croke Park on the first Sunday in September.

I may be just a blow-in here, but already I can feel the roots beneath my feet. I'm on solid ground. And although I'll be in trouble with my friends in Kilkenny for saying this, I'll be hoping that the lads bring home the McCarthy cup to Waterford. And even my Dad, the proud Cork man, will be shouting 'Up the Déise!'

(first broadcast on RTÉ Radio in 2008)

A PANELLIST WITH FEELING
Gerry Moran

I want to be a hurling analyst on RTÉ Television's *The Sunday Game*. I want to be sitting there with Michael Lester and Cyril Farrell, Ger Loughnane and Tomás Mulcahy enriching the nation. That's my dream, and even though I'm a bit long in the tooth for dreams I'm a great believer in the old saying, 'you're never too old to become what you might have been.'

Not that I'm old – ancient maybe, or so my kids tell me, but what do they know and what do I know about hurling? To be honest, I know very little about the game. I know our team of course, the players' names, the positions they play in, but I have to confess that I don't actually know the game, don't know the subtleties, the intricacies, the moves behind the moves, the moves behind the moves behind the moves.

So why do I want to be a panellist on RTÉ's *The Sunday Game*? It's because I want to represent not so much the common man as the common fan. The common fan I believe is someone like me, someone who is not necessarily a connoisseur of hurling but who nevertheless loves the game, loves the tension, the excitement, the highs, the lows and above all, loves the clash of the ash. And that's why I want to be up there with Michael and the lads. I want to be telling the nation how I feel about the game. I'm sick to death of experts telling me what they think about the game. I want to be a hurling analyst for the ordinary Joe soap with high blood pressure, high cholesterol and high expectations. I want to be able to say to Michael Lester, 'See this bit, Michael, this is where I got so excited that I had to take three valium, three in a row, Michael, and see that dirty rotten pull on our man, that's a cardiac arrest pull, that's where I thought I'd have to call the paramedics. For me, not the player; the players are hardly boys and can look after themselves.'

And I want to be able to say to the nation, 'See that score, that brilliant goal, replay that, Michael, please, and again, and one more time, that goal is like gold dust to me, that goal will keep me going through the long, grey winter months.' See now the kind of hurling analyst I want to be? I want to be the feeling analyst. I want feelings, not thoughts. I want emotion. So maybe it's a hurling emotionalist I should be. A hurling therapist even, especially for the losing fans whose spirits are low, whose heads are bowed and whose hearts are like balls of lead in their chests. I want to reach out to those folks. I want to comfort them, console them. I want them to know that I too have been that supporter. I too have slumped away from Croke Park, my tail between my legs, the song of the victors ringing, stinging even, in my ears, my county colours burning into my flesh like stigmata, but colours I dare not, could not, would not remove. I want to sit there with Michael and the lads and talk about frustration, anger, angst and the cruelty of sport. Sympathy and empathy, that's what the losing fans need. Not more heartbreaking, soul-destroying detailed analysis of the winning team's superior tactics and goal-scoring prowess. That's the kind of hurling panellist, hurling therapist, I'd like to be.

The question is: is RTÉ ready for me? In the meantime, maybe, I'll keep sharing my opinions, my feelings, with the usual suspects: my fellow panellists in the local pub.

(first broadcast on RTÉ Radio in 2008)

THE BLACK AND AMBER WAISTCOAT
Cathy Power

If we don't go up the night before to stay with our friends who live in the shadow of Croke Park, we like to head out early. We have a good breakfast even though we're a bit nervous and excited and so the appetite is not so sharp.

We set off at about half-past eight, having first decorated the car, which has the major flaw of having a Waterford registration, and so it must be well distinguished.

There are two car flags – one in each side back window. There is a very large flag to be fastened to the lid of the boot and allowed to drape it, but not enough to cover the registration plate and risk being stopped by a garda who might not be a hurling fan.

A black and amber sash has to be placed across the top of the dashboard, visible through the windscreen, and lastly, a black and amber plait has to be run along the base of the rear window.

The kids have their Kilkenny jerseys on, and my daughter has a velvet jester's hat, which is huge and ridiculous and in which she still manages to look good. My son, who wouldn't dream of such a hat, wears the jersey and puts plaits around his wrists.

We're not flag-carrying people, but we usually have one, not on a pole, which one or another of them will wrap around themselves at some stage of the day.

In the belief that women of my age and size should not wear hurling jerseys, even on the day of an All-Ireland, I have made other arrangements. In what was then a pound shop I found a black and amber velvet, chequered waistcoat for sale in the week running up to an All-Ireland. It is a wonderful garment. It has two front pockets, perfectly sized to take my phone, a small purse and my ticket. For eleven years it has served me well, and still looks fine. This is because, of course, I only wear it a few times a year for Championship semi-finals and All-Ireland Finals and, even more importantly, win, lose or draw, to team home-comings.

It has been pulled and dragged and soaked on various occasions, but I have looked after it. Every year before the end of September, it is dry-cleaned and hung on its cleaner hanger under plastic in the back of my wardrobe, in hope and anticipation of its next outing. It's had a good run.

1998 was its début, and it was the first time I brought my then six-year-old son with me to an All-Ireland. It was my last time in the old Hogan Stand. He remembers it for the bitter disappointment of losing to Offaly, and for being on the pitch for the first time in his life, despite the loss.

In 1999, I wore it again. Despite begging and pleading for about a month beforehand, I did not manage to get a ticket. Holding both of my children by the hand, I had traipsed the pubs of Dublin that morning, but with Cork as opponents I was assured I hadn't a hope. Eventually, with no alternative, we retreated to a Kilkenny pub: The Bawn Rí on Dorset Street, to watch Cork beat us by a point.

In 2000, more in trepidation than hope, we travelled again. We were so scared of a third All-Ireland defeat that we hardly dared hope. This time holding my eight-year-old boy by the hand, I was there to see Willie O'Connor accept the Liam McCarthy Cup in the middle of the pitch. The Hogan Stand's reconstruction had begun, and he gave a great speech – too far away from the thousands who wanted to jump on top of him with the sheer relief of not losing three in a row.

In 2001, we didn't feature, but we took it from Clare in 2002. On the day of the 2003 All-Ireland, I was in San Cristobel de

Las Casas in Chiapas, Mexico, having made a long journey from Guatemala the day before. I woke up in our hotel room at about 8.20 a.m., and made a quick reckoning of time difference. In seconds, having calculated that the team must be parading behind the Artane Boys' Band by then, I was racing round the room throwing on clothes and waking my almost-twelve-year-old son.

Pathetically we raced around the central plaza looking for an internet café, but the technology then and in that place was not what it is today, and we managed only to get sporadic score updates from the RTÉ website.

At about 10 o'clock that morning, the locals were amused to see a mother and son, he in his Kilkenny jersey running and shouting around the square looking for the rest of the family to tell them that we'd won the senior and minor titles. I went straight out and bought myself an amber necklace with three sunbursts on it in celebrations.

In 2004, Cork beat us in a game without goals. In 2005, Cork won against Galway. In 2006, Kilkenny stopped Cork doing the three in a row, and when that final whistle blew it was one of those 'take me now, Lord, and I'll die happy' moments, as we dashed onto the pitch in delight to see Jackie Tyrell lift the silver.

In 2007, we saw an emotional Henry Sheflin take the Liam McCarthy cup and remember the tragic death of the Kilkenny goalkeeper's wife Vanessa McGarry, just weeks previously.

Last year, Cha Fitz took the cup and recalled the men who had achieved the three in a row in 1911, 1912 and 1913. As you're listening to this, this morning, we should be on the far side of Castledermot, travelling in hope.

(first broadcast in 2008)

THE MULLINAHONE BOOT
Leo Cullen

There was a saying once I knew:

> 'Nice and light, and high behind,
> Like the Mullinahone boot.'

Now was there such a thing as the Mullinahone boot? Was there a boot factory in Mullinahone, County Tipperary? I don't know.

For my purposes, growing up, the Mullinahone Boot spoke poetry about that place and about all around it. Here is how I read that saying:

Nice: yes it was nice; its people were always friendly, if given to slight flights of temper and imagination as befits people closely bordering rival counties, in this case Kilkenny and Waterford.

Light: It was light; when I was young I read Charles Kickham's *Knocknagow*, which was in reality Mullinahone, and that book let in a lot of light into my life, so that the town of Mullinahone seemed to shine with it.

The boot: I took it for a football boot – it wasn't lost on me that from up the road, in Grangemockler, had come the valiant footballer, Michael Hogan, the same man who had been shot in Croke Park on Bloody Sunday in 1920 while playing – as Matt the Thrasher said in *Knocknagow* – 'for the credit of the little village.'

Yes, and it was high behind; there was the mountain of Slievenamon there behind it – high and protective, with its comforting womanly presence.

Slievenamon was the mountain of the book, *Knocknagow*. So many times had my father told me about *Knocknagow*: 'The best book I ever read,' and about its great hero Matt the Thrasher, and Matt's famous words: 'for the credit of the little village,' that I too just had to get it from the library. A young lad, I carried it home. It was heavy, but it was like no other book I'd read before – I was walking through my own land. My own land, for a change. Not the land of Billy Bunter or *Just William* or Bertie Wooster or *Treasure Island*. And I was walking back in time. I was taking a horse and cart to Callan, I was taking tea at the Leahys' table; and the Kearneys brought me to Tramore and my girlfriends were Mary Kearney and Grace Kiely and Bessy Morris, and how I cried when the author let poor Nora Leahy die. There was light and shade from Slievenamon; there were evictions and heroism; the people spoke my language.

I went in my mind on holidays to Knocknagow. And in real life too I went on holidays to Mullinahone. I went to the house of a character who might well have stepped out of Knocknagow: he was a curate in Mullinahone once upon a time, a great horseman and sportsman.

Father Sweeney kept an open house. He was often late for his own Masses, but he kept a house of refuge. It was a shambling and rough and ready place, with armchairs that the stuffing was falling out of. Suffice to say of Father Sweeney, that while he may not exactly have been 'gospel greedy,' he always had an eye for down-and-outs. Principal among them were a small band of men, jockeys mostly, who we can describe as having a drink problem, and who moped about the house, but every now and then broke into mournful song, or even instructed young lads like me in the arts of riding ponies.

I remember a September Sunday of 1963, a year that started with record snowfalls, followed by flows of water and floods that lasted into summer. But all the flow was now in the excitement of a third Kilkenny–Waterford All-Ireland Final in the space of six years. All that Sunday I rode ponies with ex-jockeys at Fr

Sweeney's, while people of Kilkenny and Waterford processed to Croke Park, or to Tramore beach and listened to car radios and were cooled by the breeze, or stayed at home and sweated it out. That evening, the whispers came along the road, through the shadows of the sycamores, down from the village of Mullinahone, the fount of all knowledge. There was excitement and wonder in the whispers: they spoke of an All-Ireland Final in which one team scored six goals and still did not win the game. The score: Kilkenny 4–17, Waterford 6–8. The jockeys in the bunkhouse had plenty to talk about that night. It was like a bedtime story, like going back to Knocknagow.

Today brings another All-Ireland Final. It too has its origins within sight of Slievenamon – and of the Comeraghs – in case west Waterford men take exception to my geography. And I salute you all who partake in the contest. I salute you as Charles Kickham saluted his own hero, Matt 'the thrasher' Donovan. It was the day when Matt took on the great army man of the Empire, Captain French, in the sledge-throwing contest in a field below Slievenamon. French had landed a mighty throw. Bessie Morris, the little woman who loved Matt, was worried that, in trying to best it, Matt would break his heart. Kickham describes the contest: 'His breasts heaved, as with glistening eyes, and that soft, plaintive smile of his, he uttered the words "for the credit of the little village" in a tone of deepest tenderness.' And then Matt swung that sledge, a mighty swing, and the rest, as the fellow says, is history.

Today again history will be made: people of Kilkenny will look west at Slievenamon, from Mullinavat, from Mooncoin, from the Thomastown of Kilkenny goalie of 1963, Ollie Walsh. People of the Déise will look north at Sleivenamon, from Portlaw, from Kilmeadan, from the Ballyduff of Tom Cheasty who stuck many a sliotar in Ollie's net and sent shivers down Cats' spines. They will look today at the mountain and the words of Matt the thrasher will float above their heads and steady them – the humble but mighty aspiration 'for the credit of the little village.'

(first broadcast on RTÉ Radio in 2008)

DAN SHANAHAN
Catherine Foley

I'll never forget the morning Dan Shanahan came to our house in Ring to deliver the oil. Of course, my sister had hinted to the receptionist in Comeragh Oil that we'd especially love if the hurling hero were the one despatched from the depot to make the delivery.

The day was still fine, and the sun was making an early showing. RoseAnn raced up the stairs in a flurry of excitement to hurry me out. 'Dan Shanahan is here with the oil,' she shouted incredulously. It was better than having a film star or a pop star come to call. We were out the door like greyhounds.

In west Waterford, Dan Shanahan is revered. His prowess on the hurling field is undisputed. He is a gazelle on the pitch. He is grace and power, fire and skill, all rolled into one. He is a wizard with a hurl. He is the first player you will spot on the pitch. No one can score or ignite a crowd to greater levels of excitement than he. In Dungarvan town, middle-aged women smile with admiring nods when he passes. Men salute him with a congratulatory shake of the head and a comradely 'well, Dan the Man.' Young boys, and sometimes girls, nudge each other when he goes by. Simply put, he's a celebrity in the Déise.

My sister and I both ran up the road to the back of the house like mad women, hyperventilating and foolish. I patted down my uncombed hair and, with my bed socks, corduroy skirt and torn jumper, hoped I didn't look like a character out of *Dancing at*

Lughnasa. The giddy confusion I felt at the idea of meeting Dan Shanahan took me by surprise. Who knew I'd be so star struck, so like schoolgirls, but star struck we were: and there he was at our wall, standing tall by the lorry in all his handsome glory, the smile intact, the eyes full of vitality, the big hands hanging empty, as if ready to come to life when they took hold of a hurley.

We were hardly able to talk, such was our joy at meeting the man from Lismore. Over the years we've seen him play in Semple Stadium against Limerick, against Cork, against Clare. We've locked up and left parishes deserted in our wake to go and cheer for the men in blue and white. We've travelled with neighbours, bedecked in the Waterford colours, to away matches, when potential heartache battled it out with the sliver of the chance of victory. We've seen the team defeated in Croke Park when we stood in the rain, soaked and disbelieving, and we've hung our hopes on Dan.

Whatever the match, when Dan slips through the Cork defences and races up the field, it's time to jump to your feet and crane the neck, taut with tension. Pulses quicken when Dan moves like lightening. Voices galvanise and roar cheers of encouragement instinctively when he swings the hurley in a single, flowing swirl of force, and scores. It's like watching a great ballet when John Mullane, quick as a flash on thin, white legs that are going like pistons, gets possession of the sliotar and passes it seamlessly to Shanahan. Then the race to get another score quickens.

We've roared and cheered them on, Dan and the men. As he stood there on the road last month beside the oil lorry, unassuming and soft spoken, he chatted to us about Waterford's chances this year. At that stage, the team had yet to play Tipperary in the semi-final. 'Ye haven't peaked yet and that's good,' said I, knowledgably, like a seasoned commentator. He listened and nodded indulgently. Up close, he seemed so young and slight. Not the great beefy giant I had imagined. We swelled with pride as he chatted to us. 'Keep the prayers up,' he said. 'We will,' we assured him. And then, with a smile, he climbed into the cab of the lorry and he was gone.

That was a couple of weeks ago when our hopes were high, but caution and past defeats held our hearts in check. The heady excitement of playing in an All-Ireland Final, the first in forty-five years, had yet to lift us to new, dizzier heights. That was when the idea of winning the All-Ireland was still dream. Today, goals and points will, no doubt, rain thick and vast. The players will veer like greyhounds on a pinhead, and they'll send the ball flying under or over the goalposts.

Today my heart will rise up with pride when Dan lifts the sliotar onto his hurley. Time will slow down. All of us in the stands in Páirc an Chrócaigh will seem to breathe as one – exhaling as the ball flies over the bar, inhaling with terror when Kilkenny has possession. Time will seem to stand still. There will be great bursts of action as the seconds tick away. When the ball soars through the air, the day will quiver, as if nailed to a single moment of propulsion, and all of Waterford will hold its breath. With all the great Waterford men from all around the county, but especially with hurling star Dan Shanahan, on our side, the Déise is set to go all the way.

(first broadcast on RTÉ Radio in 2008)

ALONE, ALL ALONE
Colbert Kearney

When asked on a recent radio programme to choose a piece of music, a guest from Tipperary nominated Charles Kickham's 'Slievenamon,' adding that 'it's our song.' As Frank Patterson gave wings to the words – 'Alone, all alone on a wave-washed strand,' I was transported back the best part of half a century to a sunny All-Ireland Sunday afternoon in Croke Park, where Frank Patterson's tenor solo was overwhelmed by a vast choir of mixed male voices joined in passion.

I'm there in short trousers, standing beside my father on the Hill. There are some familiar faces around us, but we are outnumbered by masses of strange men. So far they haven't really made their presence felt, but everything about them changes when they recognise what the Artane Boys' Band are about to play. The strange men stand to a kind of attention – half duty, half delight – as they launch into song and link up with their fellow-countymen in the stadium, producing a sound of such force that all of Croke Park, including the sky above it, sways in ecstatic allegiance to a sweet maiden they once met on the banks of some river long ago.

My father joins in because he likes singing and knows all the songs. I know them to hear because he takes me to Croker for all the big games, lifting me over the stile and staying behind me as I make my way up the endless steps behind Hill 16; my little legs shaking with the effort and with anticipation of the sudden, enormous panorama, the pitch below, supernaturally green, surrounded by stands and terraces already beginning to fill up and buzz with excitement.

We make our way down to 'our spot' at the wall on which my father will seat me — and god help anybody who objects. He exchanges nods with the regulars. Most of them are Dublin men – this is before they evolved into Dubs and began to bring their female friends – but on days like this the Hill is taken over by men from that other world we know as 'the country.'

I can't take my eyes off them, fascinated by the sunburned reds and browns of their faces. They couldn't be more exotic if their skin was black or if they sported feathers. Everything about them, from the tops of their heads – limp, flat caps athwart long, glistening locks – to their high-laced boots, from their crumpled, blue suits to the way they cup their cigarettes, tells me they belong to another tribe; and this even before they open their mouths and emit their high-pitched hoots and hollers.

We're in a different Ireland, a much bigger and more varied place. Television hasn't arrived to familiarise us with the other thirty-one counties. The cinema has made most of us better acquainted with California than with Kerry. Only the very rich have cars; for the rest a journey by train is an adventure. Donegal is further away than New Zealand is today. Ireland is still a confederation of counties, a united states. When the time comes, we will all face the tricolour and lose ourselves in the mysterious communion of 'Amhrán na bhFiann'; but meanwhile there is the matter of the local anthem.

Oddly enough, given our pre-eminence as capital city, we are confused when it comes to our song, caught between the political correctness of 'Twenty Men from Dublin Town,' which few people know well, and 'Molly Malone,' which everybody knows but which, because it's a music-hall song, seems out of place here in the temple of our national games. Unlike 'The West's Awake,' the most dramatically patriotic of them all, for when the men of Galway rise up in the final verse, it really is as if a voice 'like thunder spake.' But most of the county songs are soppy love songs.

I was amazed the first time I saw big burly Kerrymen groaning with love for their saintly Mary, 'The Rose of Tralee,' or the sinewy men of Kilkenny getting all misty-eyed about lovely Molly, 'The Rose of Mooncoin.' But sung in Croke Park these were no ordinary songs. When twenty thousand Corkmen reached for the top of their range to assert the loveliness of their Lee, even I understood that their pride didn't stop at that.

I remember beginning to suspect that it wasn't merely the story of the song, or even the music. There was something in the vast waves of sound that was drawing me into them, making the skin on my head tighten as I imagined myself in that other world where a man walked along a river remembering.

Oddly enough, not all the great sporting counties have a song with which they are instantly associated, Waterford, birthplace of William Balfe, being one such. Perhaps some of their supporters will try a blast of the 'The Fields of Athenry,' which is perhaps the nearest we have today to the old local anthems. It can certainly keep the heart up when Munster are in trouble or defending a slender lead in the final minutes; but I never hear it without hearing echoes of the old Croke Park resounding with the older county ballads. Maybe it's just nostalgia enhancing memories of childhood, but I can't help believing that those mysterious maidens took us all much further back, back beyond our Christian heritage and down into the pagan depths where the foundations of our sense of place were laid.

(first broadcast on RTÉ Radio in 2008)

HERACLITUS, HOME AND HURLING

Joe Kearney

'You can never step into the same river twice.' This is the contention of the Greek philosopher Heraclitus. If the water into which you step is continually changing, it can never be considered as the same river.

I attempt to debunk this theory when I roll up my pants-legs and walk into the shallows of the King's River at a place where it bends before entering the town of Callan, in County Kilkenny, at a bathing spot known locally as the Pauper's Hole. It is almost half a century since I last stepped into this river. This was the place we favoured in the dying days of summer, where we held on to freedom and kept at arm's length the dreaded return to school. In a midland community without a swimming bath we could never be described as water babies, but we tried our best in that pool of the King's River. Some had even attempted the instructions of an enthusiast on Radió Éireann's programmes for children. I mean, it could only happen in Ireland that you learn to swim by lying across two kitchen chairs and floundering your arms, following the advice from a radio set. However, remaining afloat was not hugely important at our swimming hole, but hanging out with style was. This was where we went to meet the girls, strut our stuff and ponder the future, because, as surely as the river flowed on into the arms of the mighty Nore, we would soon follow its exit from the town. For many, this would be our last year at school, and those closing days of summer our last at the swimming hole. Who knew where the waters of the world would carry us? The only certainty was that we would go.

In these latitudes, we drift into the changing seasons through a gentle osmosis; nature is kind. But in those days the exception was the change from summer to autumn. The fall season arrived, like a door clanging shut on the lazy, freewheeling hours by the river.

One day it was as if time stretched on regardless of the clock, and the next it was filled again with the smells of chalk-dust, Caesar's Gallic Wars, and dog-eared Virgil. One event signalled the full stop of summer: the All-Ireland Hurling Final. It represented the last hurrah of freedom. By the time the last dying notes had faded from the radio speaker it was time to open the discarded schoolbag; time to inhale once more the aromas of rancid butter, stale milk, spilt ink and pencil shavings; time to dump the battered spine-bent volumes and replace the entire kit and caboodle with new unbroken promises.

In that last year I never got back to the river. Like many of the town's sons and daughters, I moved on.

This is my return visit to the shallows of the King's River. My reflection is wobbly in the slow water; I think that's a good thing. It's like looking out of our kitchen window, as a child, through the imperfect panes of so-called 'war glass.' The world looked lopsided and somehow magical; perspective became distorted. It was a Lewis Carroll realm. Today I see evidence of beaten grass along the margins. The swimming hole is still in use. Now at the end of summer, the docks have gone to seed, rosebay willow herb sends feathery down riding upon the ripples. The burdened brambles trail arms into the cold stream. It's as if all of nature is leaning towards the river, casting seeds far and wide.

The town's diaspora will tune in, turn on, download, even stream today's game in whatever part of the world they have been washed up. In the midst of new lives far removed from this small Kilkenny town they will experience a lump in the throat when the band strikes up the 'Rose of Mooncoin.' They will remember again their home-place and their own river flowing through it.

The mass of water on our planet is an unchanging volume. Our tears evaporate, condense and fall to earth where they flow again into another river in another place.

Heraclitus was wrong: it is possible to walk in the same river twice, but you have to be patient and wait at least half a century to do so.

And back at the river I believe there is the laughter of lost days trapped in the water where it chuckles over worn stones.

How sweet is to roam by the sunny Shure stream
And hear her doves coo neath the morning sunbeam
Where the thrush and the robin their sweet notes entwine
On the banks of the Shure that flows down by Mooncoin

(first broadcast on RTÉ Radio in 2008)

THE SWEETEST THING
Josephine McArdle

It was ten past nine, and I was sorting the newspapers on the counter when he marched in and stood in the middle of the floor. I assumed my serving position behind the cash register and waited. 'I'm to ask for Mr Heavey,' he said.

And at that moment the shop owner pulled up in his Ford Escort Estate onto the footpath directly outside the front door. He came in and looked at the skinny, young teenager. 'You must be Michael.' They shook hands. 'Come and help me unload the order from the cash-and-carry.'

He threw an eye in my direction before walking obediently after his new boss.

I watched him carry the boxes and crates inside, and stack them neatly at the back of the shop. He brushed the dust off his clothes and waited for his instructions.

'Josie will give you the prices, and tell you where to pack them,' said Mr Heavey. 'I'm going to the bank. Keep busy. There's plenty to do.'

That was our introduction.

Michael didn't say a whole lot. He whistled and drummed his fingers along the counter when he walked by. He made me nervous.

He had a short-back-and-sides haircut, and his face was pale, almost white, so that his green eyes seemed all the more vivid and alert.

'What age are you?' he demanded, pulling a packet of cigarettes out of his jeans pocket.

We were drinking tea in the little kitchenette in the storeroom. 'You still go to school?'

I didn't ask any questions. I knew all I wanted to know about him. I'd heard Mrs Heavey tell one of the customers earlier that he was from Artane, and that the McGraths had taken him out for the summer. Michael McGraths was his name. No relation to his benefactors, she said.

I'd heard all about Artane too. It was an industrial school, a reformatory, like Daingean and Letterfrack. I knew about reform schools because my two younger brothers were forever being threatened with incarceration in one or other of them when their behavior crossed the line of sufferance and my mother's patience had expired.

It wasn't a good provenance. There was nothing nice about Artane, and Michael became more and more a curiosity for me as I got used to his presence about the place, and I gradually came to enjoy his tales of bravado and high drama about his Alma Mater.

He vowed he'd go back and burn the place down when he made his fortune. He was good at blowing his own trumpet. He was fourteen, and I was thirteen and a half. I told my mother about the Artane Boy in the shop.

'Watch out and don't let him cod you,' she warned. 'He's not in there for nothing.'

My fear was turning to fascination.

At lunchtime he'd wait until I was ten paces ahead of him and then leave the shop. He'd trail me up Garden Vale Terrace. I could sense him there behind me, but I wouldn't turn around because then I'd have to wait up and walk with him.

Then he began to wait for me at the junction where our paths converged, pretending to be having a casual smoke. There was no avoiding him.

We walked past the Brothers' House, and he spat his chewing-gum at their front door. I winced. The Adelphi Cinema was next.

'I love the pictures,' he said. 'Do you?'

The Adelphi was rough, I told him, and it was smelly. The Ritz is nicer.

'Oh!'

The summer was coming to a close when he made his move. I'd soon be finishing work in the shop and taking a week off before going back to school. I said nothing to Michael about my intentions.

It was a Wednesday, and I left the shop at two o'clock. It was my half day; a glorious afternoon in August.

'Get out in that sun and make the most of it,' Mrs Heavey called after me.

I was halfway up the street and just past Mc Grath's, safely as I thought, when he appeared, keeping in perfect step alongside me. I smiled nervously and quickened my pace. He ran ahead and stood in my path. I could smell the lifebuoy soap. I stopped. He stepped in close. My cheeks burned.

Oh no! I thought wildly. He's going to kiss me!

'I was just wondering...' he said, and I caught the tiniest hint of hesitation in his voice.

'... I was thinking that you might come to the pictures with me. Later on, I mean.'

'I can't,' I heard myself tell him. 'You see, I already have a boyfriend,' I lied.

He shoved his hands into his pockets and spun around, never said a word, never said another word to me.

'Where's Michael?' I casually asked Mrs Heavey when he failed to appear for the rest of the week.

'Gone back,' she said, matter-of-factly.

'Oh!'

'He has to rehearse. He's the drum major you know.'

I didn't know. I felt the queerest tightening sensation in my chest, and I took a deep breath, but my eyes were stinging. Then, without warning, I began to cry, thinking of my lie, that big, black lie.

On All-Ireland Sunday I watched the final, for the first time, in our front sitting-room. Kerry were playing Offaly, but that was of little interest to me. My attention was focused on the Artane

Boys' Band, and when they took to the pitch on that Sunday in September, there he was.

The Drum Major, in his majestic scarlet and blue uniform, was commanding the band with an air of authority that I recognised immediately.

He marches in and out of my dreams.

Michael McGrath, the first boyfriend that I never had.

Ain't love the sweetest thing!

(first broadcast on RTÉ Radio in 2008)

SPECKLED COW
Joe Ó Muircheartaigh

1 946 was the year of the Bad Harvest. Global warming wasn't the cause of all the rain back then like it was these past few summers, but some things were the same. 1946 was like any other year – there was always the football to get lost in. That meant another All-Ireland day in Croke Park; Kerry's sixteenth title, and surely the most remarkable.

The Master Bryan MacMahon penned a ballad about 1946 to the air of the 'Rising of the Moon,' got it printed on cut-offs from Robert Irvine Cuthberson's printing works in Listowel, from where copies were sold on for a penny to passers by.

A penny for the thoughts of those involved in that All-Ireland story. They're nearly all gone now – Paddy Kennedy, Jimmy Murray, Billy Casey, Paddy Bawn, Gega O'Connor, Bill Carlos and many more. Two still standing are Eddie Dowling and Gus Cremin, two Ballydonoghue men who captained Kerry in Croke Park that year.

Dowling was the first. He started his Kerry career in the spring of 1946, cycling the twenty miles in the road to Tralee for his first game. Then he brought the Munster Cup home to Ballydonoghue – next up in his meteoric rise to fame was surely the All-Ireland.

Gus Cremin, meanwhile, was too busy to be thinking about All-Irelands. He was battling to save the summer harvest when the call to arms came via a telegram from Din Joe Bailey on the county board. 'Take it easy for the rest of the week,' said Din Joe, 'you're going to Croke Park and may be playing in Sunday's All-Ireland Semi-Final.'

The roller-coaster was beginning to move.

Din Joe Bailey was true to his telegram. Cremin came on as a sub against Antrim, and held his place for the final against Roscommon. But Dowling was the man to lose out, dropped, with the captaincy also passing to Cremin. Dowling still played his part in the final, coming on as a sub and doing his bit to ensure Kerry lived to fight another day. For the replay, a recall beckoned, while Cremin fully expected to make the first fifteen also.

In the end, both were disappointed. Cremin was dropped, while Dowling broke his ankle the Tuesday before the match. Dowling was in Croke Park on crutches on All-Ireland day and received no All-Ireland medal; another Ballydonoghue man Mick Finucane was a sub, but on the drawing of lots lost out on a medal to Dingle's Tom Long; Cremin did win a medal when making a cameo appearance as a sub, but there was no cup coming to Ballydonoghue.

It was heading to Annascaul with Paddy Kennedy instead.

Kennedy was a superstar from the day of his first game ten years previously in a challenge game in Tipperary Town. It had a novel start when the ball was dropped on to the field by an over-flying plane. Kennedy caught it, and so began one of the greatest of all careers in green and gold.

He did more than anyone else to win Kerry's sixteenth All-Ireland. There were twelve minutes left in the drawn game when Roscommon captain Jimmy Murray left the field nursing a bloody face after clashing with Paddy Bawn. Jimmy was smiling though as Roscommon led by 1–7 to 0–4. 'I'd better wipe the blood from your face so you'll look presentable when you receive the cup,' said a first-aid man, while another combed Murray's hair ahead of the presentation. At the same time, Roscommon's president of the GAA Dan O'Rourke was making his way to the presentation area. The highlight of his presidency would be to present Sam Maguire to Jimmy Murray.

It never happened, because Paddy Kennedy took over the management of the Kerry team out on the field. 'Come out of the corner, Gega,' he roared. 'Play centre-forward, I'll go midfield, we'll get a goal and make it respectable.'

They got two; Kerry drew, and came back to Croke Park a few weeks later to win the replay with Kennedy as captain.

Sam Maguire headed for Annascaul the following Tuesday night, while Ballydonoghue reflected on what might have been.

It was some night back west though. Bonfires blazed from the gateway to west Kerry at Blennerville. There were more in Derrymore, Lower Camp, Upper Camp and Gleann na nGealt. The biggest one of all burned beside Tom Crean's South Pole Inn in Annascaul. These days Paddy Kennedy Memorial Park in the village is the monument to one of Kerry's greatest, and one of the best to grace Croke Park. It was opened back in 1984 thanks to a local man Fr James Curtin. He was a contemporary of Kennedy's growing up in Annascaul, but left home to minister parishes in England for most of his life. For fun at weekends he filled pools coupons until one day his luck finally came in. Part of his windfall bought land and built Paddy Kennedy Memorial Park.

The field is in an area of Annascaul called Breach Luan – the Speckled Meadow. Paddy Kennedy's place.

(first broadcast on RTÉ Radio in 2008)

Cumann Lúit-Cleas Gaedeal

Official Programme

24 - 9 - 39

Páirc an Crócaiġ

Senior Football Championship Final

Miḋe

v.

Ciarraiḋe

An 2.30

Minor Football Championship Final

Muineacáin *v.* Roscomáin

An 1.15

Luaċ 2ṗ.

Pádraig Ó Caoiṁ

Rúnaiḋe.

Cló-Oifig Uí Caoilte, Tta., Sráid Staford, Baile Áta Cliaċ

THE DAY KERRY CHEERED ON THE RED AND WHITE OF CORK
Joe O'Toole

It's one of the great inter-county rivalries in Gaelic games: the Green and Gold of Kerry against the Blood and Bandages of Cork; the Kingdom versus the Rebel County.

That great surge of pride felt when pulling on the county colours to face the ancient foe spurred on by the primeval roar as that first flash of the beloved colours signals their heroes' arrival on the pitch. Yes!

But there was one time too when the masses of Kerry supporters, unbeknownst to themselves, cheered on the Red and White of Cork.

Oh but how history smiles as she weaves her own surprises, and this one begins in a Dingle Drapery shop, a family business: McKenna's of Dykegate Street.

When I was growing up, Jimmy McKenna was the boss. A good advert for his trade, Jimmy always dressed immaculately and managed a well-run operation. I would see him at the shop door or through the window and, just as a medical doctor might proclaim his trade with a stethoscope necklaced around his neck, Jimmy's measuring-tape would be draped from his neck and shoulders.

I remember a day, while still in primary school, being in the shop with Pat Neligan and asking about the team photograph hanging proudly behind the counter.

'That's the Dingle Football team, county champions 1938,' he told us. 'You young lads should never forget them.' He intoned that familiar Litany of the Greats: Paddy Bawn, Timneen Deas, Billimite, Tom Long, Billy Casey, Gerald Fox, Mikey Callaghan, Danny McCarthy, Paddy Barrett and more, 'Laochra! Legends! Princes all.'

Modestly, he hadn't mentioned the captain holding the cup.

'Is that you, Mr McKenna?'

'Indeed it is, and that's my brother Jackie sitting in front with Mossy Moore and Tommy Devane.'

Jimmy was the heart and soul of the Dingle club, and a lifelong trustee. He lived and loved Gaelic football. As a young man in the mid 1930s, after completing his formal education but before he was given any responsibility in the family enterprise, Jimmy had been indentured to a major wholesale and retail drapery business housed in the Queen's Old Castle in Cork City, there to serve his time studying the fundamentals of the drapery business and learning the tricks of the rag trade.

Cork County Board did business with Queen's Old Castle, and had ordered a new set of county jerseys. Jimmy was handling the order and, despite the purest of Kerry blood flowing through his veins, he could feel the power of those blood red jerseys, and mused on the great Munster or All-Ireland clashes where they might grace the stage.

The jerseys were carefully prepared and duly delivered on time to the County Board, who, even in those times, had a pernickety tendency. They were displeased with the jerseys.

Now I have never been able to discover whether the argument was to do with the pattern of the jerseys, the shade of red or the price, but for whatever reason the Cork County Board rejected the entire lot and returned them to Queen's Old Castle.

There, amid concern about ever finding a customer for them, Jimmy was given responsibility for repacking the Cork jerseys and putting them into storage.

Returning home after finishing his time, Jimmy, educated and organised, was press-ganged as secretary of the Dingle football club. This was a divisional club combining all the local

Corca Dhuibhne clubs, and under whose banner the County Championship was contested. There was no set colour for the Dingle club at the time, but Jimmy managed to convince them to settle on Red and White, and it was the simplest of tasks to negotiate a deal with his former employers in Queen's Old Castle to take the returned set of Cork County Jerseys off their hands.

They were lucky jerseys, because that year, 1938, Dingle won their first ever Kerry County Championship wearing the Cork county jerseys. And that's why, to this day, the colours of the Dingle football team are still the red and white of Cork.

But that was nothing to what happened a few months later.

It was 1939, and Kerry were to face Meath in the All-Ireland Final. Both counties play in Green and Gold, but Kerry lost the toss and had to wear a change strip. Kerry County Board met to decide on the colours. Dingle were the county champions, with more than eight players on the county team. Among them, as county captain, was my cousin Sean Brosnan. Jimmy Mc Kenna's proposal that, as a tribute to the club, Kerry would play in the Dingle jerseys was accepted by the County Board.

So on a September Sunday in 1939, Kerry ran on to Croke Park togged out in the jerseys rejected by the Cork County Board.

Because flu prevented Sean Brosnan leading his county to All-Ireland glory, it was Gega Connor, Jimmy Tom Dick's son from Barr na Sráide, wearing the red and white of the rebel county of Cork, who proudly lifted the Sam Maguire Cup for Kerry and brought it home to Dingle.

(first broadcast on RTÉ Radio in 2008)

CROKE PARK UNDER DALKEY HILL

Tim Carey

Studs click and scrape on concrete. Hurls skewered through helmets rest on shoulders, like weapons. The day has come. We pile into the car, and put on a CD of the Pogues singing 'The Rocky Road to Dublin.' It is our going-into-battle song. It is our going-to-Croke Park song, the one we put on when we approach the Liffey bridge on our way to see the Dubs. On the road I look in the mirror to the back seats where my six-year-old boy Aaron and seven-year-old girl Jennifer are preparing themselves for the fray. But today we are not going to Croke Park, because today it is the last day of the mini All-Ireland competition at the Cuala GAA club in Dalkey, south county Dublin.

This is certainly no staunch GAA area. It is no hotbed of gaelic games like Toomevara, or An Ghaeltacht in Kerry, or Crossmaglen. But you would not know that if you arrived at the grounds on Hyde Road on a Saturday morning. Cuala has the largest academy in the country, and between 9.30 a.m. and 10.45 a.m. on Saturday mornings hundreds, literally hundreds, of children between five and seven years are there in Cuala's red.

Cuala has ruined my Saturday mornings, morning which were once the preserve of things like bagels and coffee and newspapers.

Cones and posts demarcate the playing fields into stations where the children are put through various drills. I try to do my bit, but confess that sometimes I dodge the eyes of the coaches, like a coward, or a child not wanting to be asked a question by a teacher. Please don't ask me to do a station! My hope is that I can grab twenty precious minutes on my own in one of the village's coffee shops. But, often as not, I find myself with ten boys or girls on a drill.

Now, don't get me wrong with what I am about to say. Cuala is a highlight, indeed sometimes the highlight, of a weekend. But it can seem like a futile exercise. As one attempts to introduce these children to perform the basics of the games, a frequent look given back is that they have no idea what you are talking about. Some seem to have no idea why they are there. And when that combines with vain attempts to organise chaos, I sometimes ask myself the same question.

'Okay,' they are told, 'put the hurls down in front of you. Now pick up your hurls up with the hand that you write with.' One boy picks it up with his left hand. I check with him, just to be sure. 'Which hand do you write with?' And he confidently thrusts out the empty right hand.

And it seems that no matter how many times you tell a child to hold a ball, just hold it, they never fail to bounce, throw or kick it – sometimes for remarkable distances that they seem unable to achieve when that is the actual purpose of a drill.

Efforts to grapple with even the most basic of skills force me to wonder on one level how county teams come about? How do some of them get to the stage where 84,000 people will pay money to watch them in Croke Park? On another level, it begs the bigger question of how did we manage to send people to the moon, or split the atom, or merely invent the toaster if this is how we start off as a species.

The Cuala academy's year culminates in the week-long mini All-Ireland held in June. It is the highlight. And that is where we are off to in the car, the Pogues accelerating our pulses as we go to our Croke Park for the day: Hyde Road.

The weather had threatened the final day. Our fears that it would be called off are dispelled when we find we have to park miles away from the club and walk with scores of others, as though we are refugees, through the downpour. Despite the forecast, this deluge does not clear, but sits over us like the cloud over the donkey in Winnie the Pooh.

Already drenched, we stand in the open under Dalkey Hill and sing the national anthem. Then the children, in teams representing every county except Dublin (which would be deemed to give an unfair advantage to one team) parade round a field flanked with every flag. They follow not the Artane Band, but a lone piper. We all have newfound allegiances to Wicklow, Clare and Waterford.

The matches begin, and I find myself exhibiting the first signs of that horrible parent on the touchline. I catch myself, but can't help it. I shout and roar because, on the pitches, the transformation is, if not astounding, certainly significant. The matches actually have the appearance of matches. There is pattern, there is ebb and flow. Unbelievably, forwards play like forwards and backs play like backs. The boys and girls, who had struggled all year, find their feet, their athleticism, their courage. Those who looked at you blankly when given the most basic instruction are now clearing their lines, hand passing the football, striking the sliotar.

They all cheer when their team-mate scores. They have a common purpose. They fight for each other. One team has lost all their matches during the week. While it is important to learn to lose, it is also important to learn that you can win. I shout and roar. I watch Jennifer and Aaron, and am quietly grateful for the rain that still lashes into my face.

End-of-the-day trophies are given to every player. The photographer uses a flash in the murky afternoon to capture each muddy, smiling, soaking team. And everyone gets a cheer.

Some of these children will certainly go on to play at Croke Park, either at school or underage level. And who knows, maybe one or two will even tog out for the Dubs one day. Of course, most will never get to play in headquarters. But what does that matter today? Today, for one day, the field under Dalkey Hill has been their Croke Park.

(first broadcast on RTÉ Radio in 2009)

THE NIGHT BEFORE
John O'Donnell

House full of whiskey and ruby-faced men
who'd played there themselves, or nearly played once

up for the match and in need of a bed
way past my bedtime, blue plume of Silk Cut

and the airs of old songs drifting upstairs
staying on the next day, though the windows

thrown wide, not wanting to leave, a shy guest
in the corner long after the others

now gone to the ground, ghosts back here tonight
to gather me up in folds of damp tweed.

(first broadcast on RTÉ Radio in 2009)

DEEP WELLS AND ALL-IRELANDS
Leo Cullen

Here is what I remember: a bus making its way down a narrow street, but hardly able to move because of the throng of people waving flags, hitting the sides of the bus and shouting, 'Welcome home, boys!' – A bus with the widest front windscreen I've seen up to this time of my young life, tall, standing men stooped within holding hurleys and small kit bags. Seated in the front seat, looking directly ahead, a pale man with lined forehead and severe crew cut, one of his shoulders and an arm completely swathed in bandages, and nestled in the other arm a cup trophy. And despite the clamour of adulation reaching to him through the open windows, seeming a little removed from it all – a little, you might say, haunted.

Here is what I know: it is a Monday night. The year is 1962. The bus is the home-coming chariot of a victory team. The team, collected from the train at Thurles station, is heading down narrow Friar Street, will eventually squeeze through the West Gate to be feted and drowned by the blaring loudspeakers on Liberty Square. The near riot on Friar Street is because my brothers and I, and many others like us, are too impatient to wait on Liberty Square, the commands of our fearful parents unheeded. The man in crew cut and some pain is Jimmy Doyle of Thurles Sarsfields, the year's team captain. The cup nestling in his arm is the Liam

McCarthy Cup. The beaten team, beaten by a mere two points, is valiant Wexford.

Here is what I had learned: The shape of my county, how it cuts off adjoining counties, hurling counties all: it is bowl-shaped, surrounded and protected on all sides by mountains. My teacher from County Cork told me that one. He surely knew; his men of the Rebels could only peep in through the gap between the Galtees and the Knockmealdowns. The Comeraghs cut us off from the fair hurling men of the Déise. Up our eastern flank, keeping stripey Cats at bay, were Mother Slievenamon and the Hills of Slieveardagh. The hurlers of south Laois and Offaly could only stand tiptoe and look at us from the foothills of Slieve Bloom. And the Banner, the Treaty and Tribesmen could only loiter like corner boys beyond that column of Devil's Bit, Silvermines, Slieve Phelim and aptly named Keeper Hill while Rackard men of Bargy and of Forth stood firm, but from afar.

And here is what I didn't know: About Jimmy – why did he look so haunted on that humid Monday night? Was it from the pain of the injury suffered on the day before? Was it the dizziness of his achievement – captain of a Tipp team, he whose life had been given over totally to the game of hurling – Setanta of the solitary, every night training with his black and white sheepdog whose job it was to race him to each ball he pucked? Was he overpowered by the adulation? Did I only imagine his haunted look? Could it be I was protecting that little stick wizard? 'Yellow,' my father used to say of him. My country-prejudiced father – he hadn't fancied Jimmy's 'townie' crew cut, or maybe his aesthete artistry, and so had dubbed him 'yellow.' Jimmy was never yellow. Ask any Kilkenny man.

When I became an adult, a wage earner, and less affected by hero worship, I once, in the course of my worldly duties, had to make a farm inspection on a farmer near Athy – not at all hurling country. When this slow-talking, slightly withdrawn farmer from beside the canal heard I was from Tipperary, here were his exact words: 'Jimmy Doyle of Tipp, I "folleyed" him. Every Sunday my parents went to a pub in Athy and left me at home and I had a

145

great time listening to Micheál O'Hehir on the radio say: "And the ball has gone to Jimmy Doyle. He strikes it and the ball has gone over the bar." Every time he got the ball, I knew Micheál O'Hehir was going to say it "has gone over the bar." I loved Jimmy Doyle.'

So why wouldn't we of Tipperary love him? My father too softened. In time he told me of Doyle's pedigree – his father, Gerry, Tipp goalkeeper. His uncle, Tommy, half-back with Tipp, who once marked and held the dynamo Christy Ring of Cork scoreless over two drawn encounters, as well as the extra time in the second encounter: two and a half hours. And my father's farm workman of those days, Jamesy Corbett of Coolquill, told me about that second drawn game: a red hot day in Limerick, the crowd peeling from the merciless sun of mid-century Ireland. At full time, the Cork team had stayed out on the pitch, their shirts off while waiting for the extra time, while the Tipp team had been withdrawn to the dressing-room. There had Jamesy, Mick Blake and a team of masseurs from the Athletic Club of Coolquill brought a twenty gallon churn of water. They had filled it from the deepest well of Tiobrad Arann – the well of Arann – and with that cool, clear water they had rubbed down hurting muscles until the players were fit to 'lep' out of their skins like Toomevara greyhounds.

Out of such deep wells come stories.

Again today the story-seekers are marching on Dublin, from every shaded or sunlit corner of the bowl-shaped county they come. Water is rising from the deep well of the Doyles. Toomevara greyhounds are lepping out of their skins. The traps are sprung. Now! Skin the Cats!

(first broadcast on RTÉ Radio in 2009)

KILKENNY'S MARTIAL ARTS

Joe Kearney

There is a saying in Kilkenny that states: 'The men of Ireland were hurling when the Gods of Greece were young,' and indeed, there may be some truth in this claim.

The annals record a mythological battle between the Tuatha Dé Danann and the Fir Bolg in 1272 BC. The battle is claimed to have lasted four days and approximately 4,000 warriors were slaughtered in the encounter. The site of the engagement is given as Moytura, near Cong, in County Mayo. In the days preceding the battle, a great hurling match was played. The finest warriors from the opposing sides lined up, twenty-seven on each team. This was a warm-up to the main event, a little limbering up before the battle, just to get the adrenalin flowing. Records are confused regarding the outcome of the hurling match, with some accounts stating that the Fir Bolg won and immediately killed the twenty-seven of the opposing team. If this were the case, it proved a little rash, as the Tuatha were victorious in ensuing battle.

Nowadays, we import a substantial quantity of our hurleys from China and it is, perhaps, worth considering that this is the culture that gave us Kung Fu and similar martial arts. Students of these forms of combat will know that everyday items were pressed into use as martial arts weapons, examples being rice flails, fish-hooks etc. One can but speculate at the uses the camán might have been put to in those centuries of Chinese feudal history had they discovered the beauty and balance of the famous ash stick.

Hurling is known to have evolved as a form of battle training for Irish warriors. In the eighth century, under the Brehon laws, it was used as a vehicle to solve local disputes between neighboring villages. The laws went as far as setting out a scale of compensation for the families of anyone killed in these spirited, sporting encounters.

I grew up amidst echoes that may have rumbled back to these long-running tribal disputes. In the days prior to school transport schemes, we walked to and from school through the scattered hinterlands surrounding the small town of Callan in County Kilkenny. Our house was a mere sliotar puck from the Tipperary border, so we shared our school journeys with natives of that hated county. All-Ireland Finals changed conker-hunting, blackberry-stained school chums into the darkest of rivals, and all as a result of our chanced geographical locations on the scrawled map of the region. It would take us weeks after the 'final' to lose this enmity. We would be well into the season of the field mushrooms and hazelnuts before we became once again united in mischief and mutual adventure.

One teacher encouraged us to read the literature of our area. He suggested the diaries of Humphrey O'Sullivan, a nineteenth-century resident of our own town, or the novel *Knocknagow* by Charles Kickham. But, as no prophet is appreciated in his own country, we ignored the advice and returned to our comics. I'm sure if we'd persisted with our homegrown authors our understanding of this inter-county rivalry might have been better understood.

Kickham's novel is homage to hurling. He illustrates it as a sport allowing young men opportunities to display traits of strength, agility and ingenuity, qualities that might attract young women. He wrote of it as a sport capable of settling grudges that would otherwise spill over into violence.

For those of us following the black and amber, though, the novel's setting, around the village of Mullinahone in County Tipperary, soured our appreciation. It was the nearest rival village and the focus of our antagonism. Humphrey O'Sullivan, in a diary entry, records a hurling match on the Fair Green in Callan. It is understood that this was one of those grudge matches from across the county boundary.

'29 June 1827... Feast of Saint Peter and Paul, a holiday... hurling on the green... the sticks were being brandished like swords. Hurling is a warlike game. You could hear them striking from one end of field to the other.' He then goes on to write: 'I was knocked down by a young brat, but it was nothing to be ashamed of, as I brought him down as well.'

When we wielded our camáns as improvised weapons, we were unaware that our youthful rivalries were nothing new. They were mere evocations of ancient war cries whispered down the centuries and perhaps, even, the millennia that preceded our childish scampering.

Asked for his opinion on hurling, Jack Charlton once commented: 'I'm always suspicious of games where you're the only ones that play.' But how can you explain the lure of a game that predates Homer by over 500 years, and that will draw more than 80,000 followers to its home arena today?

Sometimes there are no words capable of expressing the innate love that is lodged at the very core of our hearts.

(first broadcast on RTÉ Radio in 2009)

TEAM PHOTO

John O'Donnell

One joker up on tiptoe at the back;
centre, the proud captain, holding ball. Arms
Folded in a swagger, we were ready

for anything the world could hurl at us.
Pirate beards, teen-idol hair – the glamour:
We were sure to knock 'em dead

in the bar after. Boots crusting with pitch-muck
and tradition; the jerseys that on fired-up afternoons
we'd sworn we'd die for. And (not in picture)

the all-in-this-together of it, lingering here
like the reek of Deep Heat in the changing-room
as players take the field to scattered cheers.

(first broadcast on RTÉ Radio in 2009)

ELIZABETH THE FIRST HADN'T A CLUE

Cyril Kelly

Elizabeth I hadn't a clue. Hadn't a clue about politics or human nature. Not an iota about Gaelic Football. And the proof of these wide-ranging and fairly damning assertions is The Munster Plantation. First, take Gaelic Football. Admittedly, in the late sixteenth century, that name hadn't yet been coined. In fact, three more centuries would elapse before the GAA was founded. But if Walter Raleigh or Edmund Spenser, or any other Undertaker for that matter, had stood on the desolate reaches of the Derrynasagart Mountains or the wild foothills of Mullacharadharc, and watched a game of *caid*, the inter-parish football equivalent of the time, they could have told Good Queen Bess that lumping Cork and Kerry together in a Munster Plantation would never work. If they had only witnessed Ballyvourney versus Kilgarvan say, or maybe Knocknagree against Scairtaglin, they would have seen the irreconcilable, passionate rivalry of able-bodied men, men who were prepared to spend all day Sunday running, lepping and wrestling, booting a pig's inflated bladder, endeavouring to bring it across the parish boundary, to eventually get it between a pair of pale ash stumps. Any account of such carry-on would have warned the Virgin Queen of the foolhardiness of trying not alone to subdue but conjoin such diametrically opposed, elemental forces.

As for politics, wouldn't you think that any woman who was due to revel in history's acclaim as being the conqueror of the Spanish Armada would have instinctively known that rebels and royalty would never gel; the Rebel County was, and always would remain, separate from the Kingdom. To quote Kipling, her fellow-countryman, 'never the twain shall meet.'

But possibly the most damning of all is the assertion that Good Queen Bess was a poor judge of human nature because, unlike the game of *caid* and the business of politics, where, in both cases, she was beholden to advisers, here it was her own independent action that caused so much trouble. In a sphere where female intuition regards herself as superior, if not supreme, namely the choice of a man, her judgement proved to be flawed. As Surveyor General for Ireland she chose Sir Valentine Browne, the man who would oversee the Munster Plantation. He let her down big time. After the Statutes of Kilkenny had expressly forbidden any dealings between the Ascendancy and the local peasantry and riff-raff, there was the bould Valentine becoming *Hiberniores hibernis ipsis, níos Gaelaí ná na Gaeil féin,* more Irish than the Irish themselves, to such an extent that the renowned bardic poet Aogán Ó Rathaille wrote a poem in honour of his generosity and patronage. At any rate, The Nine Years War that followed, although not a success, proved the absolute impossibility of joining the Rebels of Cork with the Royalty of The Kingdom.

And talking of Nine Years, that figure has been bandied about on the highways and byways of Derrynasagart and Mullacharadharc in recent weeks. In those mountainy, windswept frontiers on the Cork–Kerry border, in remote villages and townlands, at marts, markets and agricultural shows, among the weanlings and Charolais rams, store heifers and Freisan Shorthorns, the Droimeann Donn Dílis, the silken kine, such reminiscing stories. Amid aromas of competing porter cakes and hanging baskets, where the talk is all about pedigree, progeny and performance, those knowing nods, those sceptical sideways glances have, inevitably, as night follows day, turned the talk to football folklore. The famous draw of 1943, Fitzgerald Stadium 1945, that Cork victory in 1966, with Niall Fitzgerald's fabulous winning point, nine long years after he was on a county team that last had the measure of Kerry.

And in the fading autumn light, those darkening parish pitches; Noel O'Leary's Kilnamartra or the green and white of John Miskella's Ballincollig, where the under-twelves, fourteens, minors, whatever, have just finished another joust of backs and forwards, with excited, youthful voices scattering through twilight towards the distant streetlights, the mentors, the trainers, the go-fors, huddled on the pitch-black pitches, pose the eternal All-Ireland question: oh do not ask what is it, as T.S. Eliot said, let us go and make our visit; to that woman in Anthony Lynch's Ballyvourney, who goes daily, not to Seamus Murphy's St Gobnait in the graveyard but to her holy well, and 'tisn't praying for a cure that pious soul is; to Declan O'Sullivan's Piarsaigh na Dromada, to the majestic Chorca Dhuibhne where the Ó Sés have been leaping as high as Sliabh an Iolair, to the clubhouse of Tommy Walsh's Kerins O'Rahillys on Tralee's Strand Road, where lines of hope, history and expectation converge on the features of the giants of the past, Dan O'Keeffe, Dan Spring, John Dowling.

And the *caid* of conversation has been repeatedly thrown in during these past days, all over the Rebel Cork and the Kingdom of Kerry, mobile phone and internet, the length and breadth of the island, neighbours near, neighbours far. And the ball of talk has bounced capriciously, as on the forty. And the conversation has jinked and soloed, twisted and turned. There were know-all pundits, there were less-certain souls who practiced the Virgin Queen's motto *video et taceo*, I see but I remain silent.

And now, this fateful morning, up past the hairpin bends, with sunlight scudding on ridge and fold, dipping into glens, into gurgling gullies and water glashas, amid the blood red of rowan, the green and gold of furze, there are fleet-footed deer, fox and feral goats, all bounding across the tawny moorland, as if, in the cosmic silence of the mountains, some portent in the air has alerted them, alerted them to an impending natural phenomenon, today's titanic confrontation.

(first broadcast on RTÉ Radio in 2009)

GHOST JOURNEYS
Joe Ó Muircheartaigh

The 'Ghost Train' is as much part of Kerry football history as All-Irelands won and lost, and is woven into the tapestry of the GAA in its 125 years. It was the train immortalised by Sigerson Clifford's poem that talks about leaving Caherciveen Station in the dead of morning and steaming to Farranfore for a connection with the main-line train that would land you in Dublin in time for first Mass.

Back then, there were no executive-class carriages on Ireland's fledgling train system, like the ones many All-Ireland goers are experiencing this very Sunday morning. It was a crude case of loading up supporters like cattle, and in as large a number as possible, for what turned out to be cramped and mostly tortuous journeys to Dublin.

Therein lies a tale; one that says a lot about Kerry football.

We've heard a lot of stories these past few years about hurlers and footballers flexing their muscles off the field – threatening strikes, and even doing the deed. And, believe it or not, there are those out there in the Fourth Estate who would have you believe that disgruntled players downing hurleys and kicking their footballs to touch is a modern-day phenomenon. Alas, they know not what they say.

Indeed, striking goes back to the 'Ghost Train.'

Go back to 1910. Kerry are reigning All-Ireland champions, and fully expecting to retain their title against Louth in the final.

Maybe it's the status as the kingpins of the game that gives them the confidence to stick their heads way above the parapet and tell the GAA that they're refusing to travel to the final unless the Great Southern and Western Railway improve the conditions afforded to GAA players on its trains.

Of course, Kerry expect the GAA to support their strike. They're All-Ireland champions after all, and the final on Jones's Road simply wouldn't be the same without them.

They're fighting this fight for themselves, but also for the greater GAA. This is nationalism as well as football – nationalism because in the not yet independent Ireland of 1910, the GAA is still an emerging and unappreciated force, and in many respects looked down upon by the agents of the State.

The Great Southern and Western Railway is one of those agents – remarkably, however, support from the 'mother ship' GAA isn't forthcoming, and the association's Central Council vote by seven to six to award the title to Louth without kicking a ball.

There's revolution in Kerry – some vow to return to Jones's Road and win All-Irelands, others, like Maurice McCarthy, walk away from football altogether. Further still, he resolves never to travel on a train again. It's the way Maurice was.

Always one of the pillars of Kerry football, it was Maurice, along with Thady O'Gorman and Austin Stack, who famously called a meeting of Gaels in the National League Rooms on Tralee's Mall in 1900 to reform the local John Mitchell's club.

From that gathering, Kerry's football fires started burning. O'Gorman and Stack captained Kerry to All-Ireland winning teams in 1903 and '04 respectively. Maurice McCarthy would go on to win five All-Irelands – that was him, a great team player, but still always his own man.

For three years after the strike, he stays true to his decision to retire, despite many overtures to return, but he finally relents in 1913, when Kerry qualify for the Croke Memorial Cup final on Jones's Road. It's not just because it's a final but because it's Louth in the final, and McCarthy even agrees to travel to Dublin by train. What's more, he makes the journey twice, as the final that attracts more interest than any All-Ireland goes to two games before Kerry win the day.

Maurice McCarthy was back where he belonged while the conditions on the Kerry–Dublin train were much improved thanks to the striking stand made by his band of Kerry football brothers three years previously.

Thing is, Maurice McCarthy never did quite manage to forgive the railways. A push bike was his best friend for travel in 1913, and remained so for nearly another fifty years. One extraordinary story bears witness to this. Come the mid-1950s, Maurice has cycled his way all the way into old age.

He's in his mid-seventies when word comes through from Liscannor in north Clare that his son Dan Joe, who was the principal in the local national school there, had fallen ill and was taken to Merlin Park Hospital in Galway.

At once, Maurice resolves to make the journey to Galway – a return train ticket is bought for him, but Maurice says no and isn't for moving. Offers of lifts come in too – again, he says no. His mind is made up – he's cycling to Galway.

But there's a bit of give in him at the same time. He leaves his own bike to one side and borrows one belonging to local Tralee insurance agent John Fitzgerald. It's a newfangled model with drop handlebars and gears.

Off he goes at 4 a.m. for his non-stop journey to Galway. You could call it his ghost journey. One hundred and thirty miles later, in arrives Maurice to meet his startled son. After the visit, he gets ready for his return cycle, only to be manhandled and bundled, bike and all, into the Tralee train at Ceannt Station in Eyre Square.

Still, Maurice returns to Tralee a hero. It's as if he's just returned from Croke Park with another All-Ireland. He's a celebrity all over again, and they talk of his famous cycle to this very day.

(first broadcast on RTÉ Radio in 2009)

WE SHUDDA WON!
Larry McCluskey

'You're comin' home this afternoon captain of the All-Scholastic Championship Team of the City of New York – y'hear?'

That's what Willie Loman promised his son, Biff in the play *Death of a Salesman*, written in 1949 – ten years before we played in the Minor Final in Croke Park.

But Biff did NOT bring home the cup. And, equally sadly, neither did we!

Five of us, all members of that Minor Team of 1959, were in the hotel in Kells recently, at one of a series of meetings to arrange the Golden Anniversary of that event. There was a silence after we looked – for the fiftieth time – at the team picture of fifty years ago. One of the men, now approaching seventy, said – simply, despondently – 'Frig it, lads, we shudda won.'

There were murmurs of agreement. 'They hadn't a buckin clue,' says Frankie. 'Sure, we weren't prepared for Croke Park at all.' 'Jaysus,' says another, 'when I came out on the pitch, after runnin down from Barry's Hotel with my togs and boots in hand, I thought the stands were goin' to fall in on top of us!'

'It was worse for me,' said Des. 'Hugo and myself went to the wrong gate! The stewards wouldn't let us in… till we showed them the boots! We were late getting to the dressing-room, then the top priority seemed to be that we get out on the pitch at exactly the right time!' In that confined and frenzied space, advice about the game or tactics or anything like that went well over our bedazzled heads!

Sunday, 20 September,1959, All-Ireland Final day, fifty years ago, Galway versus Kerry in the Senior Final; Cavan versus Dublin in the Minor match. We were playing for Cavan.

Now, there may be fifty reasons why footballers remember the day they played in an All-Ireland Final in Croke Park; but for the losers, there's only one: that they didn't win!

Standing on the front steps of the college in Cavan that bright September morning, light-headed with excitement and fitness, defeat was unthinkable. Paul Fitzsimons' Volkswagen Beetle came up the avenue, two players already in the back seat. Three more of us piled in, and off we headed for Dublin. Outside Navan, we stopped along the road for one of the lads to get sick.

Into the city, to Barry's Hotel for tea and sandwiches, apple tart and custard. Then, suddenly, everything was frantic. Half walking, half running through the crowd across Mountjoy square, down Fitzgibbon St. into Jones's Road, to the Mecca itself: Croke Park, famed in song and story, then as now – my first time there!

Dressing-room a-bustle, the sacred Cavan jerseys being handed out, mine: No.13! Everyone shouting instructions and advice, all of it confused, much of it contradictory. Paddy Flood, our becalmed captain, with his bottle of 'stuff.' What was in it? I often wondered since. Probably egg-flip in those innocent, pre-wintergreen days!

Out to the pitch, a thunder of sound, a blaze of colour! 'The ball is in and the game is on!' Early in, I score a flukey goal, get a wallop that splits my eyebrow and have to go off. 'One of our best players,' I hear Mick Higgins, our trainer, say, and the pain eases a bit. At half-time, Dr Carroll stitches the cut. No anaesthetic, of course. I feel sick in my stomach as I'm ushered back into battle for the second half, of which I remember little, except my brother Declan scoring a point, and the sinking realisation that we are going to lose.

Then it's all over: 1–4 to 11 points. Coming back out on the sideline to watch the senior match, Patsy Marron from Magheracloone shouts hello through the wire, the only familiar face I see that day, though our parents – their first time, too – are also in Croke Park. Afterwards, to Clontarf Castle, where we aren't part of whatever celebration is going on!

Then, tired, dejected, silent, the long road back to Cavan. No cup, no crowds, no bonfires! Cavan's heady days of All-Ireland victories were over. But we didn't know that. We, at seventeen, were sure we'd be back in Croke Park the following year. How wrong we were! No Cavan team has been in Croke Park on All-Ireland Final day since.

And now, fifty years later, we gather to celebrate, 'renewing our deeds of past glory,' as the song says. But to celebrate what? What might have been? What could have been? What nearly was, but wasn't? 'We shudda won!'

In Kells, the talk turns to the set of jerseys we are ordering for the event. One supplier has joked that, for an extra tenner, he'll throw in a shroud as well! The sample jersey reads: 'All-Ireland Finalists, 1959.' 'I don't like "finalists",' says Hugo; 'it begs the question: did yiz win? Just say "Final".' Then Tony says: 'Ah, to hell with "Final", put "WINNERS" on them. Sure, at this stage, who will know but ourselves?! And, anyway, we shudda won.'

And so it is that, on this All-Ireland Final Day, a full Cavan team and subs, less only the three who have gone to their eternal reward, where finals are NEVER lost, will each don a Cavan football jersey bearing the legend: 'All-Ireland Winners, 1959'!

And, sure, in the twilight, isn't it often difficult to see things clearly, to tell the difference between what is and what ought? And isn't everyone, especially old footballers at this time of year, entitled to dream? And aren't All-Ireland Finals the very stuff that dreams are made of? Sure, didn't Shakespeare tell us that?

Ah, dammit, lads, we shudda won!

(first broadcast on RTÉ Radio in 2009)

LIKE A BAT OUT OF HELL
Theresa Farrell

I remember the feeling of excitement and nerves as I travelled to Dublin to watch Galway play Limerick in the All-Ireland Hurling Final. It was 1980, and I was just seventeen. That year, the McCarthy Cup was brought west of the Shannon for its first such journey since 1923. Fifty-seven years is a long time in hurling history, though the significance of that was probably lost on me at the time. I had watched the nerve-racking semi-final in a friend's house a few weeks earlier. We were thrilled with the win, and in our excitement vowed to go to Dublin for the final. We were not just going for a day-trip to see the match, we were planning a weekend in the city.

My friend and I sat our leaving cert exams that year, so of course we were now officially grown up. We were also fortunate enough to have friends living in Dublin, so accommodation was not an issue. Besides, we had saved some money from our summer jobs. We were met at Hueston station by our friends I now liken to characters from a Patricia Scanlan novel – sorry girls! They had traded country life for the city, leaving school before the Leaving Certificate, and now had jobs for life in the civil service in Dublin.

They lived in a flat in Rathmines, had their own money, a great social life, freedom, and of course records. There was very little food in the flat, but that didn't matter. They told us they had locked away some of their wages in the office at work on Friday evening, otherwise they would have spent it over the weekend, and I don't think they meant on food. We were suitably impressed. In lieu of nutrition, they seemed to exist on enjoying life.

We got to know the joy of Dublin, which at the time was living in flatland, and were introduced to music we hadn't heard before. Our friends had recently bought a record that everyone they knew owned. Perhaps this was everyone in the civil service under the age of twenty, but we were enthralled. The backdrop to our first weekend in the city wasn't 'Summer in Dublin' or 'What's Another Year.' No, the two quiet country girls who were up for the match were rocking to the new sounds of *Bat Out of Hell*. Yes, we discovered that Meatloaf was big in the civil service in 1980, and we just had to have a piece of it.

His lyrics were risqué, and made Bagatelle and Johnny Logan songs sound almost hymnal. On Sunday, after a breakfast of dry Cornflakes and black tea, we crossed the Liffey to Croke Park for the match. We donned our 50p maroon-and-white hats, and crammed ourselves onto Hill 16 to watch seventy minutes of spectacular hurling. We watched Joe Connolly mount those famous steps to collect the cup on behalf of our county, and with whatever voices we had left we cheered his every word.

I doubt there was a television or radio in Galway that wasn't tuned into the match that day, but we were there in person on that famous Croke Park grass.

After the match, the crowd spilled out onto Clonliffe Road. We met friends and neighbours celebrating our enormous win. Sunday dinner was from the chipper and it was brilliantly liberating to eat from a bag, standing on a street in Dublin.

Next day, the Patricia Scanlan girls headed back to work in the civil service, and we were heading back to Galway for the team's home-coming. Clutched in my hands as we headed to the train station was my very own copy of yes, *Bat Out of Hell*, purchased that morning in Woolworths. We were going to introduce Galway to some real music, just as it got over the excitement of winning the 1980 Hurling All-Ireland Final.

(first broadcast on RTÉ Radio in 2009)

DAISY-CHAIN
Noel Duffy

Sometimes on Sundays we'd take
the old canal bank walk
from Broom Bridge to the Ashtown Cross,
my father picking daisies as we went

between questions of *How is school?*
and *Did you score any goals this week?*
my embarrassment at his interest
saying, *Fine* or *Only one this time.*

Often he would talk about the past,
of how his grandfather passed this spot
every day for nearly twenty years
as he drove the train from Castlebar

to Connolly Station, the canal water
his sign that he was nearly home,
until his early death in a red-brick
terraced house near Great Western Square,

my father saying, *I only knew him*
by a photograph the way you know my father
through me, as an image and likeness,
as a man about whom stories gather;

and all the while his fingers working
the stems, binding them together one
by one, a chain of flowers slowly forming
in his hands until joining first to last

the circle was complete and he'd
give it to me to throw into the canal waters.
And forgetting school and football,
we'd watch it floating on the surface,

bobbing slightly in our world of lost
connections, the frail wreath pulled
slowly downstream by the current, towards
the distant, steady thunder of the lock.

(first broadcast on RTÉ Radio in 2010)

UISCE FAOI THALAMH / UNDERCURRENTS
Leo Cullen

Today I'll be roaring in Croke Park's amphitheatre: 'Up Tipp,' and be carried far away from my needs. Or is it carried with longing for all that I am – drowned in a crowd, a wiry little shouter? Am I the man that now calls 'Up Tipp, the blue and gold,' hard muscles around my jaws like the chain of a bike? Or am I my brother, writing poems beneath a whitethorn bush in the pouring rain, those few years before he died? For that's what I remember about him the most. And trembling lips on a day that Tipp – it was 1967 – lost against Kilkenny.

We were on the old Cusack, the wind clattering the roof stays, the aluminium of them flashing off his forehead; he was cold, he was fifteen, cohort after cohort of black and amber men roaring defiance, while he sucked his thumb with each surrender: blue his lovely lips, yellow his blood dry thumb.

As a child, he had sucked the thumb on his ciotóg hand. And even once when he won a rosette at a juniors' gymkhana in Boherlahan/Dualla – the belly button of Tipperary – in went the thumb. Despite mustard the elders coated up to his elbow to stop the sucking, in went the thumb; it was the big stage of it all – everything smelling of the same drama: pony droppings, ointment for horses' bruises, lady judges' hair lacquer beneath posh hairnets.

And here I am again today, my muscles tense as a hurley stick, remembering my brother in his disappointment at his first and last All-Ireland in the capital. And I had wanted to offer solace for how can it be when you are child, without insight or wisdom. But my own grief that day was enough for me, the older brother, unable to smother him with love and say 'it's okay, boy.'

Time moved on from that Sunday, walls gathered moss, road surfaces changed colour, and my brother fell sideways one night at the side of the mountain of Slievenamon and was laid out and we followed his funeral cortège, like he had become one of his own heroes: Pat Taaffe the jockey, Pat Stakelum the hurler, lithe Cúchulainn, Fionn Mac Cumhaill of the Fianna.

He told me once about the time that Fionn arranged the race for the fast women to the top of Slievenamon – starting in Kilkenny and ending in Tipp - to decide which of them would be his wife. A goddess slid open the cave to the underworld letting the women pass through, and Fionn, attemping to enter before it could slap shut, managed only to prise in his thumb. So Fionn's thumb, said my brother, glimpsed the underworld. And what would any warrior do then, but stick it in his gob, in the hope that the knowledge of the underworld might course from his thumb into his heart!

Brother, are we lost in our fathers – setting off at dawn on our old cattle-fair gatherings, to give praise over beautiful calves in creeled carts?

Brother, are we lost in our mothers, like the rapparee of Aherlow, Patrick Sheehan, hiding in the empty Galtee Mountains above the Glen he called home? Brother, beneath a whitethorn cloud you wrote that night. And the wind blew and the sunshine peeped through some corner of the earth.

Today, for Boherlahan, for you and for your eternal longings, I will swell up my chest muscles into a harp. And please suck that thumb. And ask your man, Fionn, please to suck his.

Then let the underworld undercurrents spring up, Uisce Faoi Thalamh, and wash over us all.

(first broadcast on RTÉ Radio in 2010)

TRAPPED IN AMBER
Joe Kearney

The hearthstone on which our fireplace sits is made from Kilkenny marble. This is no cultural contrivance on my part, just a chance inheritance from the previous owner. It is the place I rest my feet and indulge in dreams in evenings of reverie. When you consider the fossil shells trapped inside the black, polished stone, you can't help thinking of the sands of time, the finely grained carboniferous limestone a testament to the age of our planet.

It is this prized paving-stone that gives the city of Kilkenny its nickname of the Marble City. Transported along the Nore from the famous black quarry since the seventeenth century, it is believed that it is here, on top of this same quarry, that Oliver Cromwell positioned the cannons he aimed at the city.

Today, other sights are focused on Kilkenny. Their intentions may not be so bloody, but nonetheless are as passionately ambitious. I didn't always love hurling. Reflecting on it now, what I remember about those early All-Ireland Sundays is intense boredom. It's amazing what can change with the passage of time. When I consider those afternoons of ennui, they seem as strange to me as the fossilised sea shells trapped in Kilkenny marble. I have clear recall of one September afternoon at my Uncle Jimmy's house in Bally Keeffe, located a few miles outside of Callan, right in the shadow of another blackstone quarry. It would have been in the late 1950s. The men were gathered around the Pie set.

Uncle Jimmy manhandled the big, clumsy contraption up onto the window-ledge as far as the flex would allow, so that those gathered outside might hear the ebbing and flowing of the game in Croke Park.

The fossilised stones are testimony that once upon an ancient time the spot where the men stood was governed by its own tides. I sat inside the window, watching a spider wrestle a fly to the depths of its complex lair, little knowing that I was being slowly reeled into my own lifelong love affair with hurling. Golden light filled the window opening, reflecting the resplendence of golden stubble in the adjacent fields. The fly was trapped in the amber gleam as securely as if it were cased in precious stone.

Pliny the Elder, in his *Naturalis Historia*, recorded the presence of insects in amber. The Ancient Greeks called amber electron. Possibly its first historical mention was in the fourth century BC, when it was discussed by Theaphrastus. Certainly the light and the atmosphere was charged with electricity that afternoon in Uncle Jimmy's.

It was a serious gathering. I was not encouraged to make any distractions, hence my attentions on the misfortunate fly with whom I believed I had so much in common. The audience was still dressed as they had been for Mass. Some opened their collar studs in deference to the sunshine, but when they cocked their ears to the radio their eyes were elsewhere. They never saw the spider, or the fly, or even the amber light. All concentration was on the game played inside their heads: Kilkenny against Waterford that year.

These are statistics I know now but not then. I can recall the grunts of encouragement from the men, the roars of 'Go on, Mickey' startling my daydreams. Mickey Kelly, captain of the Kilkenny side. I imagine them holding their collective breath as I will do today.

In folk medicine, amber crystal is believed to possess healing powers. It is reputed to have a calmative effect. The healing ingredient in the stone is attributed to the presence of succinic acid, an agent used in anti-aging creams. We will need amber today. If it is rubbed against fur, perhaps a cat's fur, it produces a static electrical field that acts as a magnet for light objects. In Uncle Jimmy's that Sunday, the air was charged, hair standing on end right up to the final whistle, Kilkenny scraping through by just the whisker of one solitary point. Over time, through a form of osmosis, the love of the game leaked into my being, the black limestone quarry and the amber light fusing into something timeless and irresistible. I am as helplessly captive to the game as that fly trapped in the amber lambency of my memory or the fossilised maritime husks encased in the marble of my hearthstone.

(first broadcast on RTÉ Radio in 2010)

THE MOON BEHIND THE HILL: KILKENNY'S REAL ANTHEM

Gerry Moran

Win, lose or draw this historic hurling All-Ireland, 'The Rose of Mooncoin' will be sung the length and breadth of County Kilkenny tonight. Four-in-a-row will not be, will never be, forgotten. Should Kilkenny win the historic five-in-a-row, 'The Rose of Mooncoin' may well be sung every day and every night, in every hostelry and tavern throughout the county for the next ten years. Or more.

'The Rose of Mooncoin' is, of course, Kilkenny's hurling anthem. Or is it? There are those who would disagree. Once upon a time, and not such a long time ago, when the Artane Boys' Band strode on to Croke Park at half time to play the anthems of the competing counties, it was anyone's guess as to which song they'd play for Kilkenny. Would it be 'The Rose of Mooncoin' or would it be 'The Moon behind the Hill'?

As someone who has been at every Kilkenny All-Ireland Hurling Final since 1963, when I sat on my mother's knee, I have always been curious as to how the Artane Boys' Band chose between the two songs. I am even more curious as to how they eventually settled on 'The Rose of Mooncoin' and abandoned 'The Moon behind the Hill.'

My older brother, who is wiser and more intelligent than me, or so he says, held a theory that if the Artane Boys' Band played 'The Moon Behind the Hill' at half time, Kilkenny lost. If they played 'The Rose of Mooncoin,' Kilkenny won. He cannot, however, substantiate his theory, and I think it's the stuff of urban, or rather rural, legend.

My brother, domiciled in Dublin for almost fifty years, may, along with hurling folk from Kilkenny, be surprised to know that there is a movement afoot to reinstate 'The Moon Behind the Hill' as Kilkenny's real anthem. That movement is spearheaded by myself and a gentleman called Charley. To be honest, we are the movement, a movement we formed, some while back, over a passionate discussion in the middle of Kilkenny's High Street. Since then we have been joined by Pat, who eats, drinks and breathes hurling and sings 'The Moon Behind the Hill' at the drop of a hat. Pat was taught the song on his father's knee and, like his father before him, firmly believes that 'The Moon Behind the Hill' is Kilkenny's true anthem.

As for 'The Rose of Mooncoin,' it is after all a love song, and has little to do with Kilkenny apart from the mention of Mooncoin. It was composed by Watt Murphy, a patriotic, Catholic schoolteacher who fell madly in love with a young, Protestant girl, Elizabeth Wills, the local vicar's daughter. Watt was fifty-six, Elizabeth was barely twenty, but age difference aside, the union was doomed due to their different social and religious backgrounds.

When Vicar Wills got wind of the relationship, he swiftly packed Elizabeth off to England, and Watt Murphy died of a broken heart in the 1850s, but not before penning the love song in which Elizabeth Wills, the vicar's daughter, becomes Molly, 'The Rose of Mooncoin.'

Oh Molly, dear Molly, it breaks my fond heart
To think that we two forever must part
I'll think of you Molly where sun and moon shine
On the banks of the Suir, that flows down by Mooncoin.

As touching as the song is, it has little to do with Kilkenny. Furthermore, it's the River Suir, a Tipperary river for God's sake, that features in the chorus.

As for 'The Moon Behind the Hill,' it too was written by a patriotic schoolteacher, William Kenealy, who died, coincidentally on this very date, September 5, in 1876. William became editor of the *Kilkenny Journal* newspaper, and was twice mayor of Kilkenny City. 'The Moon Behind the Hill' is also a love song, but a love song about Kilkenny, a place Kenealy yearns for while domiciled abroad. More importantly, it's the River Nore, that flows through Kilkenny City and county, that features in the song, as does Kilkenny castle:

> *It brought me back my own sweet Nore*
> *The Castle and the mill*
> *Until my eyes could see no more*
> *The moon behind the hill*

Bring back 'The Moon Behind the Hill,' I say, as do Charley and Pat and countless others, I feel sure. But perhaps not yet. Perhaps this unique, this historic year in the annals of Kilkenny hurling is not the year to be rocking the boat, or making changes. This year maybe we should stick with 'The Rose' who has stuck with us over the last amazing decade of Kilkenny hurling. Maybe next year, with the historic, five-in-a-row securely under our belt, maybe then we'll go about reinstating the REAL Kilkenny anthem, 'The Moon behind the Hill.'

(first broadcast on RTÉ Radio in 2010)

I NEVER SAW MY DA HURL
Cathy Power

I never saw my Da, Mattie Power, hurling. Well, I never saw him hurling on a pitch with a black and amber jersey on him. He had retired from the inter-county game about eighteen years before I was born. I was still under ten when he died, but by then I was able to solo the length of the big grass area in Mountjoy Square and hit a ball out of my hand because he showed me how. He showed me how so well that, years after his death, when I was old enough to play camogie in secondary school, I kept getting sent off for playing hurling. Back in the 1960s, the distinction was greater, and the female game more subdued than it is now.

Although I remember spending lots of time with him on sidelines and in stands (they told me I went to my first All-Ireland at the age of two), I think I didn't know he was a famous hurler until his funeral. He wasn't a man to make a big deal about things to do with himself.

It was decades after his death that I learned he had the record for holding the most Leinster senior hurling titles. Between the years 1922, which was also his first All-Ireland, and 1937, he had been on the winning side in twelve provincial finals. Fair play to him, he held on to his record for seventy-three years, and that's a rare thing, especially these days in Kilkenny when records are falling like tenpins.

He was helped by the having played for Dublin in three triumphant Leinster finals. He played with the Garda Hurling

Club, and even won an All-Ireland with Dublin in 1927, when they say that not one Dubliner was on the team. It was a time when there was no county panel, and whichever team won the County Final represented the county in the All-Ireland. Gardai, even then, were culchies.

It was Michael Kavanagh from St Lachtain's of Freshford who matched Mattie's record last month.

We knew the record was close to being equalled, and we didn't mind at all that Michael Kavanagh was the man about to do it. We love him in our house. He won his first Leinster in 1998, when my son was six, going-on-seven and my daughter was only three. And here we are with my son off to college and my daughter doing her junior cert in June, and Michael Kavanagh is still winning provincial titles.

He is a quiet full back, and he is the safest of defenders. With our hearts in our mouths, for twelve years now, we have reassured each other in the stands, shouting to each other when some cheeky forward tries to make inroads: 'Kavanagh has it, go on Kavanagh, you have him.'

If Kavanagh takes to the field today, he will have equalled another of my father's records: the most appearances in All-Ireland Finals. Mattie had eleven and, as you are hearing this, Michael Kavanagh has ten. We hope that by the time the sun sets, he will have eleven. To be honest, my father's record of playing in eleven All-Irelands included the two replays in 1931, whereas Michael Kavanagh's titles came one year at a time.

After the Leinster Final this year, I was lucky enough to be in Erin's Own hurling club in Castlecomer when Michael Kavanagh came to visit, and got the chance to shake his hand and congratulate him. All over Kilkenny every July, young hurlers and camogie players go to the summer hurling camps. This year nearly 1,700 youngsters took part.

When Michael Kavanagh came to talk to the ones in Comer, about 150 of them sat down to ask questions and listen to him. It was raining, and the day was getting chilly, but the Q&A session stretched on as he showed infinite patience with each and every young one. 'Who's the hardest man you ever played on?' 'What does Brian Cody say to you at half time?' 'Who takes longest in the shower?'

He was entertaining and humble in equal measure. You could hear a pin drop when he told them that, not so long ago, he went to summer hurling camps too, and that he loved to see members of the county panel come to visit. Most importantly, he told the children, they too could strive for the highest honour: to wear the black and amber jersey and represent Kilkenny on the field of play. He had come on his lunchtime from work, taking off the suit jacket and putting on a fleece before stepping out onto the pitch in the rain and in the wrong shoes to talk to the young ones. He didn't get paid for it. The guy leading this particular camp came from his own club, and he did him the favour.

It is because there are men like him that Kilkenny wins All-Irelands and the tradition goes on. I hope that Michael Kavanagh matches my father's record today, and I have no doubt that Mattie Power does too.

(first broadcast on RTÉ Radio in 2010)

IT'S ONLY A GAME
Theresa McKenna

'It's only a game,' says my friend. Only a game, I think. The game is due to start at half-past three, and I have prepared for a feast of hurling, drinks and food to be close at hand so that I won't miss a puck of the ball. Croke Park sparkles in the August sunshine. My heart swells with pride as the Tipperary team springs onto the field. It's 'do or die' now, with a place in the All-Ireland Final at stake. My emotions seesaw from great expectation to terrible dread. The whistle blows and the game is on. In the first few minutes Tipp drive two wides and then Waterford get a point, too much for a soul to bear. It looks like a disaster. I have to leave. I just can't stand it. Out I go to the kitchen to wash a few plates. 'Calm down will you, it will be all right' I say to myself as a plate falls from my grip. Returning to the match, I am overjoyed to find that we have four points on the scoreboard. Thank God, I can settle down for the rest of the game.

Then 'goal, goal, goal!' I roar at the top of my voice as I jump around the kitchen with joy.

'Do you think they can hear you?' my friend asks bemused, as she covers her ears with her hands. Tipp are flying now, lovely hurling, dancing the age-old dance, hurls flying, passions are High. McGrath and Corbett, Mahony, Maher and Kelly mirror the great hurlers of the past. It's magic as the two teams battle it out in the second half. 'Don't throw it away now!' I cry, as victory looks like a real possibility. My heart is pounding as the match draws to a close and I prepare for the All-Ireland with hope blossoming that we might just do it this year. 'It's only a game.' I hear the words, but feel my father by my side every time I watch Tipperary play, and know it's much more than a game for me. And we're there. The big day has arrived. It's 5 September 2010. Croke Park buzzes with excitement. My heart swells with pride as the blue and gold colours flutter in the breeze. Strains of 'Alone, All Alone' waft through the stands of this historic stadium. The spirit of Doorley, Hassett, Ryan, McIntyre, McLoughney and McKenna courses through my bloodstream, explode in a frenzy of excited anticipation that results in a loud, rasping roar of 'Up Tipp.' 'Lar Corbett is on top form today, boys.' 'Shefflin will have his work cut out for him if O'Brien is at his best' I hear from supporters beside me.

It's a sunny September Sunday afternoon in the 1960s. It could be any of the the All-Irelands from 1961 to 1968. Micheál O'Hehir's sweet voice echoes through the house. Across the years we hear 'It's John McKenna, or "Mackey" as he's affectionately known in Borrisokane, McKenna to Nealon, Nealon to Doyle… and it's a goal, a goal for Doyle.' My father hurls every ball with his brother Mackey, holder of five All-Ireland medals in the 1960s. He shouted a lot over the years as no less than five members of the McKenna, or 'Kenna' family from Borrisokane won All-Ireland medals. This is the legacy enshrined in black and white photographs that the Tipperary team carry onto the the pitch today. As the scream rises from the sea of blue and gold, every Tipperary heart beats faster, as mine does today.

Memories of our hurling past, pride in our county, appreciation of the speed, skill and poetry of the game are part of who we are. Past, present and future merge as deep in our hearts we pray that this will be the day, the day that Liam Sheedy's brave warriors will bring the precious chalice to its rightful guardians. Kelly, McGrath, Corbett, O'Brien, Sheedy and O'Shea carry the hopes of all our clubs from Borrisokane to Borrisoleigh, Lorrah to Littleton, on their shoulders as they stand poised ready for battle on the sacred turf of Croke Park. I pray that Kelly, McGrath, Corbett, O'Brien, Sheedy and O'Shea will play with skill today. I sit ready for battle too, aware that the black and amber are a formidable foe, remembering my father's words: 'Killenny are never beaten, not until the final whistle blows.' Well, perhaps 'it's only a game' for my friend, but it means everything to me: pride in my heritage, fond memories of those who have gone and the hope that dreams can come true. I see Eoin Kelly and the team stand shoulder to shoulder as they cruise toward victory, and smiling in the background stands my father as his beloved Tipperary head for home with the McCarthy Cup held high.

(first broadcast on RTÉ Radio in 2010)

I CAN'T WAIT TILL NEXT YEAR
Noel Ellis

For five years it was like an annual pilgrimage. November in Scoil Mhuire meant only one thing: a trip to Croker to support our school football team in the Cumann na mBunscol Final. From 1994 to 1998 we made six visits (yes, two in one year) to the home of Gaelic Football, and we thought it would last forever. Of course, it didn't, and maybe that's what makes those years so special, especially for the boys and girls who were lucky enough to pull on the Scoil Mhuire jersey and run out onto the sun-splashed carpet in front of 82,000 screaming fans and a TV audience of mill... Ok, ok.... Our memory is playing a few tricks on us here.

It was more like a few hundred.

And the weather was pretty miserable.

And somebody somewhere probably has a video recording of the match stashed away in a dusty attic, probably focusing on his own darling child doing his best to keep warm while a goal is being scored off camera at the opposite end of the pitch!

But did we care?

We were in Dreamland.

We were in Croker.

And we had a ball.

And for every one of our six adventures, the teachers' prayers were answered, as we always got an early slot for our final instead of the dreaded 2.15 graveyard shift.

The excitement would begin with the children getting their wristbands and banners and hats and colours ready in art class in the days leading up to the match. Articles would be submitted for the match programme, and teachers would be pulling their hair out as money arrived in for the bus.

'Me da wants to go on the bus. Can me sister and her friend come?'

'Me brother is in fourth and me sister is in first and I'm payin' for the three of us. Do we have to pay the whole lot?'

'Me ma says I can't go cos last year I got sick on the bus on the way back 'cos I drank me full two-litre bottle of coke.'

But between the jigs and the reels, it'd be all sorted. Then, on the morning of the match, the shout would go up.

'They're here!'

And a fleet of double-decker buses would pull up outside the team hotel (sorry! getting carried away again). Children from first to sixth class were allowed to go, and it became customary for the infants to wave the supporters off as the buses pulled out. On one of these auspicious occasions, a senior infant was overheard commenting to his pal:

'Can't wait till next year.'

Scoil Mhuire expected!

Rumour has it that some of the poor Dublin Bus drivers who brought our supporters to Croker are still receiving counselling for the torture they endured while being subjected to 'You'll never beat Scoil Mhuire' and 'ninety-nine bottles of beer on the wall,' over and over again.

And then we'd arrive, and even though Croker at the time probably had more in common with a building site than a stadium, as it underwent a massive makeover, it was still Croker, and we were there. When we felt an odd drop of rain, or when the biting November wind started to make us shiver, we just thought to ourselves: 'This sure beats school,' and the wet and the cold didn't feel so bad after all.

As for the finals themselves: Played six; Won two; Lost four.

Bare statistics.

Not important.

But if you were one of the lucky ones captained by Raymond Doyle or Mark Gerety or Dan Gallagher or Thomas Hayes or Colin O Donnell or Michael Kirwan...

Or if your name is Niall Flynn and you played in five of those finals...

Or if you were Shauna McCarthy or Siobhán Flannery or Yvonne O'Neill mixing it with the boys and giving as good as you got...

... You have the memories.

... Those wonderful memories.

... Don't pretend that you haven't revisited Croke Park over and over and over again in your mind's eye.

And maybe in that mind's eye the sun *is* beating down;

And the stadium *is* full;

And for a few brief, shining moments you are a child again.

(first broadcast on RTÉ Radio in 2010)

THE OATH

Bairbre O'Hogan

Sometimes the answer is so obvious when you hear it that you wonder why you never asked the question. I always knew my grandparents' marriage had GAA roots. He was John J. Hogan of Tipperary, a hurler, a referee, an office holder. She was May O'Kennedy from New Ross, of the famous footballing family.

My grandfather was educated with the Christian Brothers in Nenagh. Following exams for the British Civil Service, he was employed as a postal sorter in London. There were plenty of Irish working in the London Postal Service around that time, including Sam Maguire, Liam MacCarthy's mother, and a couple of years later, Michael Collins. In 1902, John J. Hogan transferred to the Central Sorting Office in Dublin. Within a year, he was on the winning team in the Dublin Junior Hurling League. Was it in his role as player or referee or Chairman of the Leinster Council that he met up with the O'Kennedy brothers, Tom, Seán and Gus – brothers who were to be instrumental in bringing Wexford to six successive Leinster Football Championship wins and four successive All-Ireland wins. The friendship between the men somehow led to an 'introduction,' and John J. Hogan met, courted and married their sister May. His friend, fellow referee and Chairman of the County Dublin Committee of the GAA, Harry Boland, was best man. May's bridesmaid was her cousin, Nellie Cooney from Waterford; in the newspaper reports of the wedding, the bride and bridesmaid were described as being 'members of popular and rightly respected families.'

Life was busy with GAA business in the newlyweds' home – my grandfather was one of nine trustees who signed for the purchase of the Jones's Road grounds in 1913. Hospitality was regularly extended to family and friends, who travelled to watch my grandmother's brothers embark on the historic run of football successes. Seán already had a 1910 All-Ireland Hurling medal. He captained Wexford in 1915, 1916 and 1917, but was in hospital for the 1918 Final. Gus, his younger brother, was one of nine who played in all four Football Finals.

So, the GAA was central to the comings and goings of the growing Hogan household. And yet, my father, the eldest boy in a family of eight girls and six boys, played cricket and hockey as a young man, two of the games banned by the GAA as 'foreign games.' Although he passed on his love of Irish, and of Irish history and archaeology to me, there was no transfusion of the GAA blood in him, blood that he inherited from both sides.

It often seemed strange to me that there was no follow-on in his life from his parents' involvement, and no burning desire in him to rekindle the GAA spirit in his children. But on a recent visit to the museum at Croke Park, I found an answer – maybe not the definitive one, but certainly a possible one.

As a Civil Servant, working in the Postal Service, my grandfather had to take the Oath of Allegiance to the Crown, that or lose his job. The Central Council of the GAA had adopted a Resolution in December 1918 relieving any member who had taken the Oath of Membership, pending the next Convention. Sadly, his erstwhile great friend, Harry Boland, was one of those who championed the expulsion of the civil servants, which, incidentally, also included national school teachers, to the detriment of the association at the time.

My grandfather, having taken the Oath for his job, had to step down from his role as Chairman of the Leinster Council. Though nominated as Chairman again at the April 1919 Congress, he had already made his mind up not to stand. He thanked those who had nominated and supported him during his terms of office.

The GAA in turn thanked him for 'improving the discipline, punctuality and good order generally,' and for his thorough knowledge of the rules and the impartiality of his decisions.

My grandfather's traits of discipline and punctuality, of knowledge and impartiality, and of integrity, are exactly what I would also associate with my father. So even if my father wasn't imbued with a love of the GAA, the GAA and I have shared the benefits of those Hogan qualities.

(first broadcast on RTÉ Radio in 2010)

MOORE STREET MAN
Joe Ó Muircheartaigh

As Cork folk head for Dublin this Sunday, whether on planes, trains or automobiles, there will be no spot prizes handed out for guessing what the predominant topic of conversation will be.

All-Ireland Football Final day in Croke Park, and there are Rebels everywhere expecting to finally bring Sam Maguire back to his native Cork after twenty years of heartbreak.

And without a Kerryman in sight to spoil the party, the sense of expectation will be so palpable and real that they'll have the cold texture of Sam Maguire silver on their hands in mind as they travel.

With that will come the stories.

Stories about All-Ireland wins past.

Dinny Allen climbing the steps of the Hogan Stand to lift the cup in 1989; Larry Tompkins making the same journey on one leg in 1990 when Cork truly ruled the GAA land as hurling and football champs in the same year. King Billy Morgan captaining them from the goal in 1973.

'I'll tell ya boy Teddy Mac was mighteee, de greatest of dem all,' someone will venture. 'Two All-Irelands in the same yeeuur like.'

'But ye wouldn't have won without the Kildaremen Tompkins and Fahy,' a neutral in the conversation would have to say.

'True boy,' Rebels would concede, before moving swiftly on to others.

'What about de reeeal Taoiseach Jack Lynch in 1945, or Jimmy Barry's skinhead haircut in 1973? He was super like.'

So too was Tadgho Crowley, Clonakilty's finest, who was reputed to have been able to clear Chetwynd Viaduct on the Bandon Road with a one fling of a road bowl.

But another one of Cork's greatest probably won't win any mention in All-Ireland day dispatches on the way to Croke Park.

Captain Mick Tubridy, who was on the Cork team in 1945 with Tadhgo, won't register at all.

'Sure Tadhgo was captain in 1945 like, not Captain Tub... what did you say his name was again?' they'd say.

Tadhgo wasn't the only captain though. Captain Tubridy, who hailed from the west Clare capital of Kilrush, was the other – the man who got as near to a State and full military funeral as makes no difference. He died before his time, only nine years after he did more than anyone else to bring Sam Maguire to Leeside for the first time.

He was a friend of Queen Elizabeth, a confidant of the Kennedy Clan, an international star, but always still a local Moore Street, Kilrush man made good.

When he came back to Kilrush two years after winning the All-Ireland for Cork, to line out for the local Shamrocks club against Ennis Faughs in a club championship match, such was the excitement that the local urban council all but hosted a ticker tape parade in his honour.

Local wag P.J. Mack at the fish and chip shop in the town opened a book on the game. Bets could be had also at Todd O'Dea's, Mickey Carmody's, Michael Kelly's and even at Bill Hearn's shoe shop.... Just because Captain Tubridy was kicking ball with the Shams again.

By then he'd gone international, because as part of the Army Equitation School he was blazing a trail across the world. He joined the army in 1941, and while stationed in Collins Barracks in Cork won his All-Ireland.

He represented Ireland in the Aga Khan Cup, and was individual champion of the Dublin Horse Show in 1946, and again in 1953, as his horses like Bruree, Ballyneety and Kinsale became known around the world.

When he beat a world-class field in London's famed White City arena in 1948, Princess Elizabeth asked that he be presented to her at the Royal Box, while success in America brought him into the lair of Kennedys just as rookie Congressman and ex-Army man himself, Jack, was starting out on a political career that would lead all the way to the White House.

Captain Tubridy was only starting out on his own career in civvy street when tragedy struck. He left the Army in January 1954, to take over the management of a stud farm in County Meath. But by April that year he was dead, having been thrown from a horse while out jumping at Trimblestown Stud in Trim. He was only thirty years of age.

The world of showjumping and football went into mourning. When he was laid to rest in Glasnevin Cemetery, the Kennedys sent their condolences, young Princess Elizabeth, who had since become Queen Elizabeth II, probably did too, while political and sporting figures came out to pay their respects to his family from Kilrush and his wife Dorothy.

Such was his reputation abroad that the principal event at the Mexico International Horse Show was renamed the Captain Michael Tubridy Memorial Trophy in his honour.

Now Captain Tubridy is only remembered by the Kilrush Shamrocks' playing pitch on the old Vandeleur Estate outside the town that bears his name.

It was opened in 1972, when the great and the good of the GAA and showjumping came together for the official unveiling, among them two of the greatest princes of pigskin ever to grace Croke Park: Mick O'Connell and Mick O'Dwyer.

Of course, Cork footballers past were there too.

And why not? After all, he was the Shea Fahy and Larry Tompkins of his day, the adopted Corkman who scored the first half goal that propelled the Rebels to their All-Ireland win sixty-five years ago.

He might be a forgotten figure to most now, but he'll never be forgotten on Moore Street, Kilrush. After all, he's the street's only All-Ireland man.

(first broadcast on RTÉ Radio in 2010)

UP DOWN
Conor O'Callaghan

Tomorrow will be my birthday. On the weekend I was born, forty-two years ago, County Down won in the All-Ireland Football Final. My mother remembers the two of us sitting in Newry General Hospital, listening to 'Hey Jude' on the wireless and waiting for visitors who never arrived. We had only recently moved south to Dundalk, and the tailback on the old single-lane road north was so long that nobody dared to travel.

It would be twenty-three years before Down reached another final. By then, I was living in a basement flat in Drumcondra, a stone's throw from Croke Park, beneath a landlord who was a rabid Dubs fan who would countenance support for no other county. To annoy him, I took vocal pleasure in the sea of red and black that descended on our streets.

'I thought you were from Dundalk,' he said bitterly as I was handing him the week's rent.

'I only grew up there,' I replied. 'I'm originally from Newry.'

For a few seconds, I expected my marching orders. A subject of the Queen under his roof seemed too much to bear. After a long pause, he said 'I hope they're stuffed!' and managed not to speak to me again until Halloween.

I have a British birth cert and an Irish passport. I, like thousands of others, am only exercising the dual citizenship our Constitution permits me. Call me a plastic northerner, a fair-weather supporter. I am a Dundalk man 364 days of the year, and from Newry when it suits me. Today it suits me. Today, with the men from Down travelling south to claim (doubtless!) their sixth Sam, I sing the praises of the red and black once again.

Praise County Down, home of the Mountains of Mourne and discount Christmas shopping.

Praise be the derelict house on the Newry canal where my grandfather was reared.

Praise be the ten-minute crossing from Strangford to Portaferry.

Praise be the potted herrings that Van the Man stopped off in Ardglas for in his song 'Coney Island.'

Praise be the massive dam and reservoir at Spelga, that my little brother dropped his jacket into and we had to fish out with a borrowed rod.

Praise be the lighthouse of St John's Point and the black chimney-stacks of the lighthouse keeper's house at Cranfield, and the white roofs of the caravans of Greencastle that look like a mass of seagulls from the south shore of Carlingford Lough.

Praise be unmarked customs cars patrolling the border and the foreign signal your mobile picks up out of nowhere.

Praise be Pat Jennings with hands like shovels giving us his autograph in the early 1980s, and the yellow Merc we saw outside the clubhouse of Royal County Down that everyone said belonged to Hurricane Higgins.

Praise be rivers with weird names: Bapp, Clanrye, Quiole.

Praise be the corkscrew shortcut through Hilltown and the mountains.

Praise be the slieves of Donard and Binion, and the wild cat they say prowls them.

Praise be the Silent Valley and the magnetic stretch of the B57 where your car, left in neutral, rolls uphill.

Praise be little men fishing off the pier in Gyles Quay who ask 'What about you?' and speak of the Free State as if white banknotes were still in currency.

Praise be the stream near Newcastle where St Patrick banished elongate, legless, carnivorous reptiles of the suborder Serpentes from these shores for once and for all; and the Bronte Homestead; and Phil Coulter's 'Dear Little Town.'

Praise be the neopolitan sliders from the Genoa on the square in Warrenpoint.

Praise be the fish suppers in Portavogie.

Praise be Donal McCann's Ards Peninsula accent in December Bride.

Praise be the agreements of Hillsborough and the shopping centres of Sprucefield.

Praise be The 4 of Us crooning 'Mary' in accents you could slice and butter, and Ireland's oldest pub in Crawfordsburn that has served pints to Tennyson and Dick Turpin and the first President Bush.

Praise be the Cloch Mor that Finn McCool, strong man that he was, chucked from Cooley to Rostrevor.

Praise be my son Tommy, who was born fifteen years ago in Daisyhill.

Praise be that part of ourselves that is the other side of the line, but is every bit as much a part of us as everything this side of the line, if not a little more.

And praise be the south-facing slope of Wee Binion, on which is spelt out in boulders the words 'Up Down.'

(first broadcast on RTÉ Radio in 2010)

SAM MAGUIRE AND THE RUSSIAN CONNECTION

Nicky Barry

We are an isle of mists, myths and legends. The mists are real, but I have my doubts about the myths and legends. By their very nature these far-fetched yarns are open to question, but, in the very best traditions of Celtic hokery-pokery, only a curmudgeon would doubt their veracity. It's all part of the magic. The seanachies of old were candlelight dazzlers with their yarns, and so the fairy-tales of Erin were born. As a nation we exist in that twilight world of mystical make-believe when a story, whether true or not, is worth the telling. Let me tell you one here and now, on this All-Ireland football morn, about Yuri Gagarin, County Down, and the Russian connection. Is it true, or is it apocryphal? You decide, dear reader.

Last week, President Mary McAleese led a trade delegation to Russia to boost Irish business links with the former Communist State. She met Russian President Dmitry Medvedev in the Kremlin, and no doubt he asked her about Down's chances against Cork. Down and Russia go back a long way. Forty-nine years ago, on the afternoon of September 24, the men from Mourne met Offaly's finest on a shoot-out Sunday for Sam Maguire. Down were the defending champions, and were rocked in the first six minutes by two Offaly goals right out of the blue. Down were stirred, but not shaken. The father of the present Down manager, James

McCartan, scored one of the greatest goals ever seen in Croke Park, and this was followed up within minutes by another gem from sharpshooter Sean O'Neill. Annaclone's Breen Morgan hit a third, and at half-time, after a disastrous start, Down led 3–3 to 2–3. That was the end of the goal-rush, and at the end of the day Down got home by a single point to win their second All-Ireland title by 3–6 to 2–8. Before Armagh or Tyrone, Down fans were the first northern invaders to bring banners and brilliance to Croke Park.

As southern supporters were less demonstrative, the stadium that day was a sea of red and black, and the attendance of 90,556 still stands as a record. And now for the myth.

That week the Russians launched Yuri Gagarin into orbit. He was the first spaceman, and the whole world marvelled as he hurtled through the skies in a history-making flight. It was at the height of the cold war, and needless to say, the KGB and all the boyos in the Kremlin monitored his progress with intense interest. Apparently his flight was greeted with universal apathy, except for in the capital of Ireland. Atha Cliatha was packed that day with native sons and daughters, fathers and mothers from Offaly and Down, all up from the country for the big match. Such was his reception, Yuri excitedly reported back to base that without doubt Ireland was the friendliest little country in the whole wide earthly world. Now, as the KGB reckoned Ireland to be a little backwoods somewhere off the mainland of Europe, where 'Faith of Our Fathers' was sung regularly by huge Sunday afternoon crowds, they were astounded.

Yuri's report was to the point. He told of a great, wild-eyed multitude assembled in the northern end of a city called Dublin. Half of them were delirious. They were screaming, waving, singing, dancing and roaring incomprehensible phrases like, 'G'wan Paddy Mo yeh boy yeh.' At approximately 4.30 in the afternoon, the cheering reached a crescendo. Yuri distinctly heard what was to become an immortal supplication in the annals of Soviet expansion. He could not believe his ears at the welcome afforded him. 'Come on Down, come on Down,' was the cry that rose from 50,000 throats. He reported the reception back to base, and couldn't believe the translation in his earphones. As tears glistened in his eyes, Yuri's heart swelled with gladness at the goodwill emanating from the multi-coloured throng far below.

Well anyway, to make a long story short, he never did make it down to Jones's Road, but those who knew the astronaut say that, from that day on, he was quite partial to James McCartan, and that, ever after, he always liked a little dash of red with his black rum.

(first broadcast on RTÉ Radio in 2010)

THE COMMENTATOR
Joe Ó Muircheartaigh

Sheehy's house in a place called Ballintaggart near Dingle was always surrounded by sport. A few fields away and you had Casey's land, which was home to the greatest flapper meeting of them all. Still is. Half a mile in the other direction nestled Dingle's nine-hole links in the townland of Dúnsíon, while the greyhounds and football were everywhere.

The greyhounds were brought into the Moriarty household by the original Joe Ó Muircheartaigh – the clan's Cigire who coursed greyhounds, and who had a litter brother of the great Dainty Man, the dog belonging to All-Ireland footballer Con Brosnan who won the Derby in Clonmel in 1932.

The hounds coursed around Ballintaggart, for fun I suppose, but with Joe dreaming and talking of a Derby. Joe talked football too, having won a Munster junior medal with Kerry in 1926, while he also gave golf clubs to his young nephews.

It meant they were spoiled for sport on their doorstep, but what lay beyond the front door of Sheehy's house was different, something almost mythical in attraction: a radio – the only one for miles around.

Sunday afternoons became great social occasions, as people of all ages came to listen. Micheál Ó Muircheartaigh was one of them.

The Sheehys had fourteen children – so it was a busy place – and it was there Micheál got to listen to the 1938 All-Ireland Football Final between Kerry and Galway from Croke Park.

Nobody would dare go near the radio. Back then, radios were regarded as temperamental and delicate, and if you had too many people messing with it, it could let you down. The only person allowed to touch it, turn it up, down or sideways was Mickey Sheehy.

He took his job very seriously. During the week leading up to an All-Ireland, he'd carry the battery into Houlihan's in Dingle to get it charged up, then the radio would be used very sparingly in the days leading up to the match.

You had to be in Sheehy's early or else you wouldn't be able to get in. It was a great occasion for the Sheehys because they were facilitating people and showing off their product.

That All-Ireland day in Sheehy's, Micheál's introduction to Croke Park couldn't have been more dramatic. It was Micheál O'Hehir's first All-Ireland Football Final broadcast. For Micheál and his brothers, Paddy, Náis, my own father Dónal, my grandfather Thady, and everyone else listening, the game had a special dimension.

It was the Dingle connection to the team. The Brosnans, Sean and Paddy 'Bawn,' 'Gega' O'Connor, Billy Casey and Bill Dillon were all Dingle players – Paddy Kennedy was from over the road in Annascaul.

These were the players everyone visualised in the hushed kitchen of Sheehy's. The 'Bawn' being uncompromising in defence, Billy Casey and Bill Dillon the same outside him in the half-line, Kennedy and Brosnan ruling the skies at midfield and 'Gega' leading the attack.

That afternoon, Kerry thought they'd won their thirteenth All-Ireland in a dramatic few last seconds. Tony McAuliffe, who became my neighbour in Ennis over sixty years later, passed to John Joe 'Purty' Landers, and the Rock Street man kicked the lead point, but as the ball was sailing over, referee Tommy Culhane from Glin blew his final whistle.

For Micheál, it was back to Sheehy's for the replay and more drama – this time, with Galway leading by four points with three minutes to go, a whistle from referee Peter Waters was mistaken for the final one and Galway supporters rushed the field. Kerry left, with some of the players gone from the ground and on their way home before order was restored to finish the game.

Micheál listened intently, not to know that eleven years later the same Micheál O'Hehir would hand him the microphone for his maiden voyage in Croke Park – the Railway Cup Football Final between Munster and Leinster – his own voice coming out of Sheehy's radio, or from the one his Auntie Mai brought back from America and sat proudly in the middle of the Moriarty kitchen in Dúnsíon.

And so it began. Our family's radio man, who's touched our hearts and others with his words – the way he says 'em, the bilingual journey through the GAA ages, but always rooted in the present day.

Everyone has their favourite Micheál moments from Croke Park.

The Donegal man will speak of 1992, when he talked the Annals of the Four Masters from 1616 – An Bráthair Bocht Micheál Ó Cléirigh, his brother Conaire Ó Cléirigh, Cuchoccríche Ó Cléirigh and Flaithaire Ó Maolchonaire. 'Wish they were here,' said Micheál.

The Meathman will pick the blitzkrieg move for that goal in Game Four in 1991 that broke Dublin hearts; the Downman will think of DJ Kane – or 'Lawrence of Arabia' as Micheál called him – returning to battle with headgear like Peter O'Toole's famous character; the Kerryman doesn't know what to pick because he has so many big days.

The list goes on and on, but I'll aways go for Clare. My adopted place, my home, my family's home. The Clare shouts around Michéal in 1995 when they came in from a desert of eighty-one years and won an All-Ireland. The way he rattled off the names of the 1914 Clare team when Jamesie O'Connor scored the final point.

Fowler McInerney, John Shaloo, The 'Dodger' Considine, John Fox who went straight from Croke Park to the Western Front but who lived to tell the tale, James Guerin who got three goals in the final but was a victim of the Great Flu epidemic a few years later, captain Amby Power and Sham Spellissy and more.

And there's more, because other Clare folk go back to the famous Oireachtas final of 1954 in Croke Park, when Clare beat Wexford.

The commentary was as Gaeilge, and Big Dan McInerney became Dónal Mór Mac Airchinnaigh; Nicky Rackard became Nioclás Mór; Jimmy Smyth was Séamus MacGabhann and so on… and Wexford was Loch Garman.

And therein lay a tale.

Clare won, and believed there'd never be another bad day, with local Ennis wag, Peter 'Slavery' Guilfoyle going down in history when he said: 'My God, that fella Gorman must be a great player, he's all over the field, he's brilliant.'

That was Micheál. You didn't have to be able to understand him to love him. We'll miss him on big match days from Croke Park and everywhere.

But, I'll tell you what. The radio was on in Sheehy's of Ballintaggart on Saturday evening for his final match commentary from Croke Park after sixty-two years, and in Auntie Mai's old kitchen too.

And all around Ireland, and beyond.

And it was emotional.

(first broadcast on RTÉ Radio in 2010)

CAT FIGHT IN CROKER
Gerry Moran

The 'clash of the ash' in Croke Park, this All-Ireland Sunday, is virtually a clash between fifteen 'stone-throwers' and fifteen 'Cats.' Logic would imply that the 'stone throwers' are in with a much better chance. Feline fur against solid rock is a no-brainer really – except for the fact that cats are clever, and tenacious, and cats have nine lives.

The 'Cats' in question this Hurling All-Ireland Sunday, are the 'Kilkenny Cats,' who may, or may not, have nine lives, but what is inarguable is that they have thirty-two Hurling All-Ireland titles to their credit while the Tipperary 'stone-throwers,' lagging behind with twenty-six, are more than anxious to close that gap.

As it happens, there is no gap between the counties of Kilkenny and Tipperary – a thin line on the map is all that divides these neighbouring counties, a thin line that accentuates loyalty and allegiance and rivalry, as only bordering counties can appreciate and understand.

And it is that thin line between Kilkenny and Tipp that gave rise to Tipperary's nickname of 'stone-throwers.' The story goes that faction fights occasionally broke out after major hurling matches between Tipp and Kilkenny, particularly along the border around Urlingford, which resulted in, among other things, stone-throwing.

Why the good people of Tipperary were left 'holding the stones,' so to speak, and became known as the 'stone-throwers' I have no idea. The activity, I feel sure, must have been mutual, as I can't imagine the people of Kilkenny standing idly by while being pelted with rocks. So perhaps the true origin of the nickname 'stone-throwers' goes back to the Land War of the 1870s, 1880s and 1890s when Tipperary agitators, so the story goes, were particularly militant and adept at throwing stones.

Kilkenny's nickname also originates with aggression. The people of Kilkenny are known as 'The Cats' because of the constant squabbling that arose between the town's two corporations, one Irish and one English or Anglo–Norman, who viewed each other suspiciously across a border also.

That border was the River Breagagh, which flows through Kilkenny and separated Irishtown, the old Gaelic quarter around Canice's Cathedral, from English or High town, where the Anglo–Normans had settled and built their castle. That cat-like squabbling went on until the two corporations were amalgamated in 1843.

A more colourful explanation of the nickname 'Kilkenny Cats' comes from Cromwell's occupation of the city in 1650. The story goes that Cromwell's soldiers, for their amusement, were wont to tie two cats together by their tails, throw them across a line and let them tear each other asunder, a practice frowned upon by their officers.

One evening some soldiers were involved in the practice when they heard an officer coming. The soldier responsible for the cat-fight slashed the cats down with his sword, leaving only their tails, still tied to the line. 'Have they eaten each other down to that?' the commanding officer inquired. That episode quite possibly gave rise to the rhyme:

> *There once were two cats from Kilkenny,*
> *Each thought there was one cat too many,*
> *So they fought and they fit,*
> *They scratched and they bit*
> *Till excepting their nails,*
> *And the tips of their tails,*
> *Instead of two cats there weren't any.*

Whether today's All Ireland Hurling Final will be a cat-fight, or a dog-fight, I have no idea, but one thing is certain: it will be a fight, perhaps even a battle royale. Tipperary will leave no stone unturned to retain the McCarthy Cup, while the wily Kilkenny 'Cats' will fight tooth and nail to regain the 'holy grail of hurling' for a thirty-third time.

Meanwhile, in my local hostelry in Kilkenny, a 'watering-hole' favoured by several Tipperary men domiciled in our city, not even a thin line separates the 'stone-throwers' from the local 'Cats.'

Jowl by jowl we sit sipping our pints, and tonight, as the inevitable post-match analysis takes place, words undoubtedly will be exchanged, tempers may flare and insults may well fly, but no stones will be thrown. Instead, an uneasy truce will prevail until such time as the victors calm down and the vanquished cheer up – sometime NEXT September, I reckon.

(first broadcast on RTÉ Radio in 2011)

LORY MEAGHAR'S SWALLOW
Joe Kearney

Paddy Dowling was as strong as the proverbial ox. There was a great demand for his services whenever it came to haymaking. The joke was: how many pitchfork handles would he break in the season? Even when the barn was almost filled to the galvanised roof, he never slackened – and that was when he usually broke the fork handle!

You'd hear a shout from him that was part groan and part victory roar.

'Over the bar says Lory Meagher.'

Ah, yes, those were the days when we still believed in legends.

As a boy, up there on the ascending bench of sweet, new hay, Paddy was as much my hero as Lory Meagher, that legendary Kilkenny hurler, was his.

On the dizzy heights of the rising haystack, I was eye level with the swallows as they inscribed arcs and aerial wizardry between the uprights of the barn. Small fledglings, with heads sleek as dolphins, would peep out from mud-ball, adobe dwellings and duck back as yet another swarth of Paddy's hay sailed up and momentarily blotted out the sun.

As well as forking hay, it was a marvel to watch him eat and swallow potatoes. Nothing less than sliotar-sized tubers would satisfy his hunger.

In the afterglow of mealtime, he liked nothing better than to eulogise about his favourite hurling legend: 'Over the Bar' Lory Meagher.

I know that famous All-Ireland Final of 1931 as if I'd been there myself, Kilkenny against Cork. Two drawn games and the final not hurled until November. Before that last encounter, Lory had broken ribs and was unable to line out for the Cats. Kilkenny lost... badly.

'Sox'd relate about the time Lory hit a ball from midfield in a Leinster Final against Dublin. The umpires lost sight of the sliotar. The only thing that fell to earth was a dead swallow.' He'd lean back in his chair, full to bursting with flowery spuds, and explain the secret of Lory's greatness.

'Swallows – he learned to knock swallows out of the air, in the fields behind his father's house.'

My hope was that he was wrong, and hope is the blessing of childhood. It is a thing we must never lose. In the words of Shakespeare, 'True hope is swift, and flies with swallow's wings....'

The birds are lining up on the wires again, and it saddens me to see them prepare for departure, huddled side by side, as if posing for one last team photograph.

A swallow tattoo is popular amongst nautical men as a symbol of safe return; the tradition is that a mariner has this tattoo, of the wandering bird, inscribed after sailing 5,000 nautical miles, and a second swallow could be added after 10,000 nautical miles.

If hours of training were nautical miles, then the hurlers of Kilkenny are entitled to decorate their bodies with an entire flock of the birds. But my hope is that Brian Coady has not indulged in any Lory Meagher training techniques on the practice field.

(first broadcast on RTÉ Radio in 2011)

OLLIE WALSH: HURLING HERO
Cathy Power

August is the time for the poc fada, and on a Saturday last month I found myself watching a competition on the lawns of Stormont as part of Belfast's Féile an Phobail. The hurlers were competing for the Edward Carson Trophy as, it seems, Carson played hurling while he was at Trinity College Dublin.

They pucked the ball down one side of that mile-long avenue and up the other, then down and up again. It was a surreal experience to watch the progress of the contest sitting at the base of the statue to Carson, the father of unionism, in the middle of Prince of Wales Avenue, which runs from the Upper Newtownards Road to right up to the building where the assembly sits.

I had never seen a poc fada up close before, and had not realised just how strenuous it is to continuously puck the ball for such a distance. I found myself remembering my childhood poc fada hero: Ollie Walsh, regarded by many as the best hurling goalkeeper of all time. He won a just a few poc fada titles in the early 1960s, and his achievements have been long surpassed, but in our house, when I was a small child, news of his victories was greeted as if he were a close family member.

He was from Thomastown, and played with the Kilkenny senior hurlers from 1956 until 1972, going on to manage that team in the 1990s.

It is hard to believe now that Ollie Walsh was so famous back in the late 1950s, a time before even Teilifís Éireann existed, not to mention dedicated sports stations, the internet, Twitter and Facebook. In those times when mass media was the newspapers and Raidió Éireann, to become a household name meant you were really something special.

In the late 1950s, a fancy-dress competition was an annual event in the premises now known as the SFX. It was St Frances Xavier Hall then, and was attached to the Jesuit community on Gardiner Street, Dublin.

There was no question about how I, as a pre-school child, would be togged out for the competition. My black and amber hurling gear was made by sewing strips of black crêpe paper onto an orange jumper knitted by my mother. Add white shorts, a hurley with the name Ollie Walsh written on it and a number one pinned to my back.

I have only the vaguest recollection of it, but there is a photo somewhere of me, smiling shyly having won a prize. It was no surprise that a child of our house would be sent out dressed up as Ollie Walsh, but the fact that a panel of Dublin inner city judges would award me a prize says something about his fame.

Ollie Walsh's name was known the length and breadth of the country. He was handsome and blond, which helped, but above all he was a brilliant goalie.

He played senior hurling for sixteen years, and won five All-Irelands, ten Leinster titles, two National Hurling Leagues and three Railway Cups, among other titles. In 1967, he was the Texaco Hurler of the Year, the first goalkeeper to win that honour.

He inspired the famous headline on the now defunct Gaelic Sport magazine after the 1967 hurling final: 'A stitch in time saves nine.' That day Ollie had played a brilliant game, denying John Doyle of Tipperary his ninth All-Ireland medal. The Kilkenny goalie had played with several stitches in his wrist, having injured himself on the train to the match that morning.

He was at the helm, as manager, of the Kilkenny senior hurlers when they won back-to-back All-Irelands in 1992 and

1993. Having failed, however, to get out of Leinster in 1995, he resigned as manager that year.

The following year, I was a volunteer-working in El Salvador. It was at a St Patrick's Day gathering of Irish people in Central America that a Kilkenny man working in Nicaragua told me the sad news of Ollie Walsh's sudden death a week earlier at the age of only fifty-eight.

Just five years later, the people of Thomastown gathered on Mill Street, where Ollie had lived as a young lad, to unveil a statue to him, just across from the gate where they say he honed his goalkeeping skills by practising night and day with hurl in hand.

The monument immediately became the place where teams travelling to away matches gather to get lifts or board buses, where people stop to chat about hurling and from where buses are leaving for Croke Park this very morning carrying supporters to the All-Ireland Final. At this time of year, a flag is put in the hands of the bronze statue and never, ever has anyone removed that flag or done anything to disrespect Ollie's statue.

Carved on the plaque behind him it says:

They called him lynx-eyed and fearless.
They spoke of his brilliant catching,
His long striking,
His devastating sidestep.
He loved hurling, his native parish,
The black and amber.
To us he was Ollie, Prince of Goalkeepers,
The greatest of them all.
Ní bheidh a leithéid arís ann.
Beannacht Dé ort, Ollie.

Indeed, Ollie, and if you are looking down on us today, send us luck and send the goalie some of your skill, so that when the buses empty in front of you this evening, it will be a happy occasion for the black and amber.

(first broadcast on RTÉ Radio in 2011)

THE FIRST SUB
Leo Cullen

You take them for granted, the characters of All-Ireland Day: the small man with the big banner, John 3:7 who sits behind the goal; the balladeers on the canal with banjo, guitar cigarettes and Rocky Road to Dublin; the women selling apples, oranges, pears, ripe bananas and the last Mars Bars; the fellow peddling senior and minor colours, flags wrapped around his neck and arms like the vision of Medjugoria. The man I talk about is none of these: a man with rolled up raincoat and newspaper who hangs around outside pubs, except not for match tickets but match songs.

He's the man you won't know, who travels up every year for one purpose – to find a pub, two pubs – in which he can sing the songs of the competing teams. After that he has done his bit, he has given his all for both sides. Drinker of three pints, singer of two songs, he doesn't go to the game; he's already waiting at the station by the time the final whistle blows.

A lean man with a long nose, a back-of-the-church man, he lives on oranges and ballad songs. Oranges because at club matches back home he loved to watch the players suck orange peel during half time; ballad songs because his father sang them before him. He lives in a county that is generally neutral, not having contested a Hurling All-Ireland since 1949. If you ask where he comes from he'll give you a clue: 'Which is the only county in Ireland that doesn't touch a county that touches the sea?' Hurry up with your answer. It's County Laois. His house is within sight of Ballybrophy; railway junction of furze bushes and small cattle from where once he got the train to Dublin; now he gets it at Port Laoise, or as he calls it, because his father before him called it, Maryborough. Yes, he's old-fashioned; old names of towns, old songs, old fleadh cheols are his Hymn and Holiness and Hosanna.

He travels with his two songs. He alights at Heuston Station among the hordes of jersey-wearing followers; this year the black and amber, the blue and gold. He holds on to his white neutrality. He heads for the first pub; makes certain it's packed exclusively with the followers of one county. He awaits his moment, a lull in the storm of talk and pints and dazed children. Then he launches into song, the song of the county; he pounces like a hurler pounces on a loose ball. And when he's got attention and the followers join him, when he's lifted their hearts to endeavour, when they are transported, so is he. And then quietly he leaves, on to the other pub – and assessing no bodies are there from the first crowd, he sings the song of the second crowd. Again he shows fervor – fanaticism – that's important: loyalty, or as he says himself, 'loyality.' For both teams, he is the first sub.

Last year, for Kilkenny, instead of 'The Rose of Mooncoin' he'd sung so many times before, he sang the 'Louse House of Kilkenny'; and nearly brought the house down, such was the laughter. Another year, for the men of Tipp, instead of 'Alone all alone by the wave washed shore,' he sang 'She lived beside the Anner at the foot of Slievenamon.' And how oft in his thoughts has he sung 'The Banks' for the followers by the Lee? He loves it when a new county makes an appearance – a first coltish breakthrough, or the re-emergence of an old giant: Offaly: 'The Offaly Rover,' Limerick: 'You're A Lady,' Wexford: 'At Boolavogue as the sun was setting,' Waterford: 'Dungarvan My Home Town,' Galway: 'and see the sun go down on Galway Bay' and 'My Lovely Rose of Clare.' He has high hopes one day soon of singing 'Molly Malone' for the Metropolitans. And how he gloried in the timbre of his own voice the September Sunday of 1989 when Antrim appeared, the saffron men. And awaiting his moment among a crowd of men whose accents were strange to him, he got up and hushed the sea of faces with: 'Far across yonder blue lies a true fairy land.' For at that moment he knew he was in those Green Glens, and the Antrim men knew they were in an All-Ireland.

One thing he'd love is for his own county to get there. Laois, that doesn't touch a county that touches the sea, the blue and white. 'Lovely, lovely Laois,' he'd sing. But it's the song that is the saga, not the contestants, not the winning or losing… This year he'll crack out something new for the Marble men in a pub near the station, then he'll crack out his hard-boiled egg and sandwich and then he'll dart up to Barry's hotel where he'll crack out something old for a phalanx of Tipperary stone-throwers. He'll give that extra bounce to the day like a banjo gives to a session. Watch out for him, but if you catch him in one pub singing one song, and then in the other, singing the other, say nothing, just join in, just clap to his ambidextrous spirit.

Let him go with the remains of his day, and while the sliotar flashes like lightning around Croke Park, let him savour his slow walk back up the quiet quays; let him read the names of the pubs, the old Dublin drinking-houses, let him visit, one, two, three. His vocal chords at rest. Job done. Session over.

(first broadcast on RTÉ Radio in 2011)

HURLING FINAL GIRL
Mary Ledwidge

'Miaow, Miaow,' said the stray cat on the ledge outside my kitchen window. 'Miaow, Miaow,' I replied, for I too am a cat, a Kilkenny cat from Hurling Country. It was 6 September 2010, the day after the All-Ireland Hurling Final – a final in which Tipperary, the old arch rival, had put an end to Kilkenny's hopes of five in a row. Was the stray cat there to comfort me? Or was that a look of triumph on his face? Before I could say another word, he disappeared into the hedge in my back garden, leaving me to reminisce about past Hurling Finals and growing up in Kilkenny, where hurling is in the blood. I can remember playing hurling from a very early age. We lived on a farm, and when our chores were done, out over the yard wall we'd go into the field, where we'd hurl for hours.

Every September, on All-Ireland Hurling Final Day, we'd gather round the wireless in the kitchen to hear Micheál O'Hehir's commentary from Croke Park. The pageantry, the atmosphere, the passion were brought to life by that wonderful broadcaster. He could paint pictures with his words. Of course, the day was even more special whenever Kilkenny were playing, and if they won, oh the joy of it! But if they lost, my Auntie Jo would say 'No need for disappointment now. Remember, in an All-Ireland Final, both teams share the glory.'

In my lifetime, Kilkenny reached the All-Ireland Final on thirty occasions, and brought home the Liam McCarthy Cup seventeen times. For me, the most memorable final of all was in 1971 – Kilkenny versus Tipperary. Since that day, the Hurling Final took on a whole new meaning.

Early that Sunday morning, my husband Tom and I set off for Dublin and joined the heavy traffic bound for Croke Park – cars bumper to bumper, fans cheering and waving flags – black and amber for Kilkenny, blue and gold for Tipperary. Oh, the excitement!

The colourful cavalcade made its way to the outskirts of the city, and headed for Croke Park, but we took a right turn down the Longmile Road. We had a very different destination in mind that day – not Croke Park, but the Coombe Maternity Hospital. You see, my daughter Catherine had decided, three weeks ahead of schedule, that she wanted to be born on All-Ireland Hurling Final Day! After I had checked in at the hospital, I panicked. There was no television. How was I going to see the match? I pleaded with the nurse (who happened to be from Tipperary). 'Please, please, can I watch the Hurling Final somewhere? I'm from Kilkenny and I've never missed a Hurling Final in my life.' She smiled at me in a conspiratorial way and said she'd check. A few minutes later she returned, and wheeled me, lock, stock and hospital bed into a small room where a television had been set up for staff. The game had just begun. Oh, the excitement, the anticipation. Contractions were relegated to second place! The Tipperary nurse dashed in and out regularly to check on my progress (and on the progress of the match). It was such a closely contested final, ending in victory for Tipperary: 5–17 to 5–14. Ah yes, Tipp certainly had the measure of the Cats that day.

Later in the evening, my daughter Catherine was born, three weeks early and weighing only five and a half pounds. When the Tipperary nurse handed her to me, she said 'Here she is, your own Hurling Final Girl.'

As Catherine was growing up, every September we'd sit and watch the Hurling Final together and she'd say 'Tell me again about the day I was born,' and I'd retell the story of that special Sunday in September 1971, when Tipperary beat the Cats, and she arrived in time to share the glory. To capture the magic of the day, I wrote this short poem for her.

HURLING FINAL GIRL

You made your entrance in the wake of Hurling Final rapture,
Clash of the ash, roar of the crowd,
Banners waving, whistles blowing, dream teams
Breathing life into your first cry.
Serene against my heart, we made our lifelong pact
And shared the glory of McCarthy's silver cup.
My lovely one, my Hurling Final Girl.

(first broadcast on RTÉ Radio in 2011)

THE BUS JOURNEY
John Allen

For those lucky enough to be involved at this level, All-Ireland Hurling Final Sunday is a special day, ending a unique journey that began years before in the backyards and local GAA fields of many of the exponents of this sacred, ancient game. To be involved in an official capacity is an enormous privilege indeed. I had that honour on numerous occasions and in various roles, the last few as team coach and manager.

For the followers who travel to the capital the previous evening, there's the added bonus of a night out in Dublin. For the team there's another night in. The players are well used to nights in though. The life of Ireland's professional amateur hurlers is indeed a Spartan one. It's a life of matches, training, recovery sessions, stretching, core work, fields, gymnasiums, swimming-pools, personal eating plans and many, many nights indoors.

For most of these elite athletes, who dream of being part of a McCarthy Cup-winning team, the year ends in failure. Only for one squad of players does the season have a happy ending. The journey up the steps of the Hogan Stand is the nirvana of the fortunate few.

But there's another journey that both teams get to experience on All-Ireland Final day in which there aren't any losers. It's a journey that never failed to raise the hairs on the back of my neck. The power one felt on that particular journey gave one a sense of what it must be like to be the President of Ireland, or a visiting dignitary.

That special voyage begins about two hours before throw-in from the team hotel. Given that the players have spent the previous night and the morning of the game in a bit of a bubble, away from the madding crowd, it's only when the time arrives to head to the stadium that the seriousness of the occasion really kicks in. The arrival of the Garda motorcycle outriders means there's no turning back now.

The players are, at this time, in the team room. Many are semi-togged. Some are on the masseur's table having a final rub down. The team medics are buzzing around like pollinating bees. The water and hurley carriers are busy ensuring that all the necessary equipment makes their way onto the team bus. High-decibel battle-music invades the tension-filled air. Most players have their own iPods with their personal choice of inspirational words and music. Conversation is scarce.

Soon it's departure time. The physios' tables are hurriedly folded. The room is silent.

Everybody is on board the coach at this juncture. The doors whoosh to a close.

There's no turning back now.

The outriders' lights begin to flash. The sirens' high-pitched wail announces the beginning of the journey to the coliseum that is Croke Park. The bus is silent until the battle-music decibels invade the air.

It's not unusual to have a group of loyal fans waving off their heroes as the bus pulls out onto the Dublin streets.

On the last September Sunday afternoon that I sat on that bus, the Southside streets were quiet. Traffic-light colours were ignored, as they always are by these elite motorcyclists who lead the charge. Traffic began to build as we crossed Samuel Beckett Bridge onto the city's Northside. That power sensation returns again, as cars pulled off right and left to allow these heroes through.

Soon, as on every All-Ireland Final Sunday, the hats, flags and colours begin to illuminate the footpaths. Attracted by the sirens, many heads turn. The stadium is in sight. There's no turning back now.

The crowds are milling outside various pubs as the bus whizzes past. The applause is heart-warming. The area is now a sea of colour, excitement, activity and heightened expressions as we approach the back of the Cusack Stand.

We slow to a stop. A Croke Park official boards, and as team manager I greet him. The final leg of the journey begins, deep into the bowels of the stadium.

Soon, the dressing-room door is visible. The name 'Corcaigh' jumps out to meet the eye.

The select welcoming media party, for many years now, always included RTÉ's ever-friendly Micheál Ó Muircheartaigh and Ger Canning. 'Hello, lads. Everybody's fit and ready?'

'Any changes?'

There's no turning back now.

This unique journey is over, but blood, sweat and tears will be shed before it's time for the next unique journey up the steps of the Hogan Stand.

Tá an-áthas orm an corn seo a ghlacadh….

(first broadcast on RTÉ Radio in 2011)

ALL-IRELAND SUNDAY

Josephine McArdle

It's All-Ireland Sunday, and the fans are converging on the capital. The faithful have been to Mass and got the blessing.

The sandwiches are made.

Phone credit bought.

Flags are flying, and the anticipation is mounting.

O'Connell Street is buzzing. Mobiles are ringing. Shreds of conversation rise and fall. Eyes scan the crowd. Waiting and watching. Watching and waiting. Fathers and sons. Brothers and sisters. Mothers and daughters. Tall hats and baseball caps, rolled-up flags and bugles.

The networks are connecting mobiles and blackberrys, iPhones and smartphones. Everyone's talking. It's good to talk on an All-Ireland Sunday morning.

The boys from Ballincollig and Banbridge have arrived. Girls from Gneuieguilla and Glanmire, Mammies from Mallow, Dads from Downpatrick, uncles from Dunmanway, aunties from Ardglass, grannies from Castlewellan and grandads from Drimoleague.

Emails are coming in from Beijing and Shanghai too, where daughters and sons are waiting for the starting whistle. In Melbourne and Sydney, Perth and Darwin, our scattered diaspora are Skyping their good-luck messages. Separated friends are Twittering. Girlfriends are capturing and uploading images. Texts are flying back and forth.

Brothers are remembering.

Meanwhile, the players are loosening up, managers are mentoring and physios are massaging.

The referees are ready.

At the hallowed ground, the stewards have arrived and are receiving their instructions. Programmes were delivered and sellers are at their stations. Catering staff are *in situ*. Counter assistants are preparing for business, hot dogs are standing by; milk is poured. Around the country, the ticketless Kerry and Dublin supporters in Athlone and Athlumney, Kenagh and Crinkill are readying up too for the afternoon's GAA fest, the most prestigious inter-county gaelic football competition, and culmination of another year.

For its hundreds of thousands of members and fans, the GAA is a way of life.

In every parish in Ireland, from Ballyheigue to Ballyfermot, there's a club.

Today, O'Sullivan is representing Glenbeigh while Fennell is flagging St Vincent's Marino.

The O'Sheas fan the pride of An Ghealtacht, and the Brogans line out from St Oliver Plunkett's on the Navan Road.

The flag is flying too for Finuge, for Ballymun Kickhams and for Whitehall Columcilles. For Duagh, Ballyboden, Scartaglin and Cromane because there's surely a GAA pitch every ten miles in Ireland.

In every club, a cohort of volunteers has given their services on a weekly basis to train and manage teams of boys and girls as young as ten. Parents ferried carloads of hurlers and footballers to matches around the county. Local lottery draws raised funds for club maintenance. Mothers laundered the team kit and tied the bootlaces. Fathers taught their sons and daughters that attitude is more important than ability, and courage is more important than cleverness.

The public house was a forum for meetings and would-be selectors. Everyone was on board: auctioneers and teachers, hoteliers and carpenters, grocers and butchers, poets and publicans. One size fits all.

Because the GAA is not about personal glory, about medals, silverware or trophies.

It is about the bonds of friendship that are created.

It is where a little boy learns how to solo a ball and hold his tongue when censored.

Where we find our sense of place and community and learn where we belong.

Today, the spirit of a nation is united.

The teams may change, managers may retire, board members may be replaced, but that spirit endures.

So we take our places in the stands and wait for you, our champions, to emerge.

And your young boy's dream of running out onto Páirc an Chrócaigh and representing your parish, your county; that ember of hope that you've always managed to preserve is bursting into flame now.

Your day has come, and now with chest inflated and eyes filling up, you blink back the tears and hear the Croke Park roar.

A shiver surges through you. Shake your arms loose, hop from foot to foot, left, right, left, right. Head up. Walk, skip, jog.

Down the tunnel. In the slipstream of the greats. Of men like Jack O'Shea and Barney Rock, Paddy Cullen and Maurice

219

Fitzgerald, Brian Mullins and Seamus Moynihan. You're filling
the space they left behind.

A wash of light welcomes you.
Thunderous roars of county pride.
Applause.
Take up your position.
You're home.

(first broadcast on RTÉ Radio in 2011)

MICK CAROLAN
John MacKenna

T his afternoon the players from Donegal and Mayo will take
to the field in Croke Park, men in search of the greatest
prize Gaelic football has to offer: an All-Ireland medal.

By teatime, barring a draw, the players from one side will have
the precious metal in their hands, they'll have walked back across
the hallowed turf, as the autumn evening falls, feeling thirty feet
tall; they'll have been part of the mayhem that is the winners'
dressing-room. Some of them will have sat quietly, savouring the
hour; some will be overflowing with energy, whooping it up like
there's no tomorrow. Backs will be slapped, hands shaken, tears
will fall, laughter will echo along the corridors and out onto the
deserted field and the empty stands.

And, for others, the dream will, at best, have been postponed.

For me, All-Ireland Final mornings bring thoughts of those
monumental footballers who never won that ultimate prize, and
each of us will have our own list of men whose ability and skill
we admired, even in defeat. My list includes the great Dermot
Earley of Roscommon; Mickey Kearns of Sligo; Kevin O'Brien
of Wicklow; Willie Quinlan of Carlow; Glen Ryan and Anthony
Rainbow of Kildare – men whose playing days were days of
wonder, whose ability wove spells, who truly were the magicians
in my life.

I still live in hope of seeing Johnny Doyle and Dermot
Earley Junior lift the Sam Maguire for Kildare, but of the men

who deserved to but never did there's one man who stands above all others in my mind.

He was a colossus – a half-back on the Kildare teams between 1957 and 1975; a winner of Railway Cup medals with Leinster; an All Star in 1966; a man who played and lost in four Leinster Finals and two National League Finals. He was the epitome of a brilliant, committed, talented and sublime footballer; he never won a provincial or an All-Ireland medal, yet he was a man who never stopped believing.

And my particular memories of him come from opposite ends of his career.

The first is of a summer Sunday, sometime in the early 1960s. Kildare were playing in a championship match in Athy, and the ground was crammed with supporters. The huxters were flaunting the hats, colours and ribbons – crêpe paper hats that ran in the rain; the Luckie Luckies – Lucan ice-creams – were on sale outside the gate. Inside, we were urged to get the last of the choc-ices before the ball had even been thrown in, and the same cry was still going up as the final whistle approached.

There were no fences or security gates back then, children sat on their fathers' shoulders or squatted on the sideline, as close as could be to the action. And that's where I found myself, cross-legged, close to the halfway line, my flag – a rip of old sheet stuck with drawing-pins to a piece of stick – in my hand. At that level, every kick was heard and every tackle was felt and every shoulder made the ground shudder. And, above all others, one player dominated the sky and the ground that afternoon; one man rose to field every high ball and to launch attack after attack from the half-back line. That man was Mick Carolan. To me, he was everything I wanted to be: tall, handsome, athletic, fearless and talented. He was Kildare.

When the heavy-laced football thudded out of play beside me and he came to take a sideline kick, I was as close to him as I'd ever been, so close that I must have been in his line of fire but, instead of asking me to move, he reached down and ruffled my hair before steadying himself and putting the ball over the bar. Had the hand of God reached from the clouds and anointed me, I wouldn't have felt any more deeply or wonderfully blessed. I had been anointed by the touch of greatness.

Years later, in 1998, when Kildare reached the All-Ireland Final, I wrote about that incident and, a couple of days later, I got a phone call asking if I could meet Mick Carolan. Can a bird fly? Can an elephant remember? Of course I could meet him, and I did. And he brought me a gift: the jersey he'd worn in the 1958 League Final – he might as well have given me the Shroud of Turin.

So, when the teams launch themselves onto the pitch in Croke Park this afternoon, I'll be sparing a thought for the gifted players who have never won the Sam Maguire: Earley, Quinlan, Kearns, O'Brien and – above all others – the great, great, great Mick Carolan.

(first broadcast on RTÉ Radio in 2011)

IN THE BEGINNING THERE WERE RUMOURS

Cyril Kelly

In the beginning there were rumours. Hearsay… hints… ráflaí. I gCorca Dhuibhne, in Castleisland or Castleknock, in Dromod or Drumcondra. But then there are always rumours. 'The garsún is barely able to walk and already he can boot a ball thirty yards. His left is as good as his right.' And rumours of rumours. 'He's as sure of foot as a puck goat; he has the gimp of a gamey greyhound. I heard it from a man who's a second cousin once removed of the mother.'

Every street, district and circle, every town, parish and riding throughout the land has, over the years, endured sporadic rumours about the latest legendary incarnation. And if you want to check out any of these ráflaí, an old footballing stalwart is your only man. You're bound to meet him in one of his usual haunts, watching the evening's retreat towards the Equinox, ensconced, maybe, on a hummock of heather high above some Kingdom shore. Or perched, perhaps, on Binn's Bridge, memories floating on the Royal Canal, disappearing round the bend at Croker. But regardless of location, when the talk turns, as inevitably it will, to the solemnity of football, and you broach the subject of the latest prodigy, you will have to be prepared for the long pause that will ensue. You will have to be prepared for the askance glance, the tightening purse of the toothless mouth. Eventually, deciding that soft talk and discretion have no place when football worth is being weighed up, your companion will want to know the pedigree of the latest putative prodigy. 'Is this kid going to take after the uncle, Billy-the-braggart? That cúirliún would solo up and down the wing all day if the team was on top, throwing all kinds of hair-oil shapes, togs and geansaí starched and spotless, but the same lad'd run like a rabbit if the going got tough? Or is the kid, maybe, going to have the gumption of his great gran'aunt, the Spinster Sweeny, who ran the Tans that stormy night they came pounding rifle butts on her door?' And with the sudden thought of another year – in a long line of years – losing ground, our stalwart might give Sigerson Clifford an airing, recalling the invincibility of proven football legends:

Plough and spade and seine boat shaped them for the deeds they were to do,
Street and school and mountain heard their victory cry.

And this afternoon, thirty likely lads will come bounding from the ancient shadows, into the catharsis of Croke Park. Likely lads who are the rumours made flesh, rumours of rumours personi-fied, stamina and strength and prodigious skill. Likely lads whose mettle has been tempered in combat over the years; street leagues, Cuman na mBunscoil, under age, minor.

And there will be those of us there of a certain vintage who have borne witness to it all before. Ah yes, the famous final of fifty-five, the mythical rivalry of the 1970s. Images will come swerving once more past Neanderthal backs who'd gladly use an elusive forward's guts for garters; elemental John Egan, Hanahoe lording it like a magistrate, mercurial Mickey Ned. And still we'll struggle anew with that old black magic we know so well, that same old voodoo in the veins every time we watch Dublin and Kerry teams march in tandem to the countdown for another All-Ireland Football Final. During those interminable minutes before the ball is thrown in, there will be aficionados in the stands and on Hill 16; in watering-holes from intergalactic time zones there will be wayfarers transfixed by television and radio sets, wanderers clinging to any god-forsaken intersection of longitude and latitude scattered across this hurtling sphere, all voluntarily submitting to the same rush of helium to the head at precisely 3.30 p.m. today, CMT, Croker Mean Time. And then, with a sorcerer's sleight of hand, the referee will throw the pale ball high in the air. The ivory orb will hang on high for a nanosecond; four midfielders will leap like stags; four stretching pairs of antler arms; eight soaring hands; limbs caught in a tableau of levitation, spreadeagled against the sky.

(first broadcast on RTÉ Radio in 2011)

SKY BLUE
Colbert Kearney

It took me a long time to appreciate the beauty of Kerry football, to take pleasure in the languidly elegant play of the likes of Mick O'Connell and Maurice Fitzgerald, to concede that they caught and kicked with a sweetness few outside the Kingdom ever emulated.

My resistance began *fadó fadó* when my father lifted me over the turnstile at Jones's Road, steered me through the masses of supporters, past hawkers – 'Wear your team's colours' – and dealers – 'Get yizzer ripe William pears' – and up the steps behind Hill 16, so steep and endless that all I could see was the vast blue sky, as if God and his angels and saints were wearing our colours. I was absolutely confident of victory, my mind unable to imagine we could be beaten by a team of countrymen; but some instinct suggested that all precautions should be taken – just in case – and so with this in mind I addressed myself to God up there in his upper upper stand. I was respectful – 'O God, I realise your constant concern to guard all Mankind against the wiles and schemes of the Devil won't leave you much time for the game this afternoon...' – but that didn't stop me from making myself perfectly clear: '... On the other hand, God, this game means an awful lot to me and my Daddy and we'd both be eternally grateful if you could keep an eye on Croke Park and make sure Dublin win.'

Time has kindly erased much of what followed; only nightmare flashes remain.

Compared to Dublin in their stylish blue, the Kerry players looked a bit *hicky* in their green and gold but, from my perch on the wall at the bottom of Hill 16, I couldn't fail to notice that they were bursting out of those jerseys and socks, that their eyes were the eyes of men possessed, that they were superhumanly fit and fast and strong, their midfielders soaring like birds, their forwards not bothering to work the ball in close to the goal but belting over points from unlikely distances.

Shocked and heartbroken at our loss, I followed Daddy down the silent steps, my faith in a just God convulsed, my faith in my fellow human beings shattered by the traders' cries. 'Wear your winning team's colours! Get yizzer ripe Kerry pears!'

Eventually we did it, in 1958, 1963 and 1974, but not against Kerry. Every All-Ireland is cause for celebration, but Kerry are the benchmark; and only when you have beaten them can you really consider yourself the best. That's what made 1976 special.

In 1974, Kevin Heffernan had taken over and began putting a team together that could beat Kerry, coaxing Jimmy Keaveney out of retirement, one of the few whose ability to kick the ball was up to the highest Kerry standards. Expectations were great in 1975, but yet again Kerry were there to dash them. The two teams met again the following September in a game that no Dublin supporter will ever forget. Dublin beat Kerry in an All-Ireland Final for the first time since 1923. No wonder, when asked how he felt, a happily exhausted Jimmy Keaveney replied: 'I don't care if I never won another bloody match; I'm happy now.'

To beat Kerry, Dublin need all the game's physical strengths – and something else besides. Few Dublin players have the traditional Gaelic talents their counterparts have inherited over the winning generations. The Dublin style is less pure, more influenced by the soccer most of them played while growing up in housing estates. Hence the instinct for close-range goals where others might settle for high-sailing points.

Nor can you undo the Kerry players' pride in their footballing achievements; you have to match it and beat it; to do this the

Dublin players must draw on the sense of proud superiority and good fortune conferred by birth in the capital city and, when the going gets rough, find strength in the knowledge that when they take the field they will be – as ever – one against thirty-one.

The player who best epitomised Dublin's hybrid athleticism was Kevin Moran. Fearless, utterly indomitable and always with a hint of buccaneering swagger, his driving runs were so untraditionally direct that it took highly skilled and experienced Kerry backs a while to come to terms with them, and by then, in the final of 1976 and the classic semi-final of 1977, it was too late: he'd blown away their aura of invincibility. In 1978, he signed for Manchester United, with whom he won two cup medals, and went on to play more than seventy times for Ireland, becoming a driving force in Jack's Army, as he had been in Heffo's.

Many see the 1977 semi-final between two teams at the top of their form as the greatest display of modern Gaelic football. Kerry people might disagree with the legendary status this game has acquired, and point out that in the count that matters – Sam Maguires – they came out on top over the series. What is undeniable is that between them Kerry and Dublin created a rivalry that has become a classic, bringing Gaelic football to new heights and making today's game the All-Ireland all true neutrals would want to see.

Let's see again the hell-for-leather daring and breathtaking skills of those great encounters in the past. And let's hope that God gets it right this time.

(first broadcast on RTÉ Radio in 2011)

BEST OF TIMES, WORST OF TIMES
Joe Ó Muircheartaigh

It's the best of times yet the worst of times, because it's a tug of love that would put 'Tadhg an Dá Thaobh' in the ha'penny place. Kerry versus Dublin in high September in Croke Park.

Sam at stake in the ultimate of all city-versus-country clashes. The Jacks against Culchie Kerry – the ultimate bonfire of the vanities in Gaelicville. Which way to turn, which geansaí to wear?

Didn't know as a seven-year-old in short trousers in 1975, when hopping over the turnstile and sitting on my father's knee in the Hogan Stand.

Don't know as a forty-three-year-old, who wouldn't be let out in short trousers.

Every Dublin house of Kerry parents is probably the same, but growing up the crisis of conscious that was Dublin versus Kerry always seemed more magnified in our Blackrock home. Yes, it was a bad day in Blackrock when Kerry and Dublin got ready to rumble.

Everything about the house was green and gold. My schoolteacher father giving us a history lesson on how big Ned Roche put the shackles on Kevin Heffernan in 1955, and how Jerome O'Shea, Micksie Palmer, Dr Jim Brosnan, Tadhgie Lyne et al put the Dubs in their place. He just about stopped short of singing Bryan MacMahon's ballad about the game, but we got the message, again and again.

My mother chipping in with her tale of being in the swell that gathered outside the Canal End entrance that same year and burst through the gates for free, how she marvelled at her fellow teacher and fellow-parishioner and pin-up of the Kerry team that was Sean Murphy from Camp.

I never did get to know if mother and father met after the game in the Shakespeare Bar on Parnell Street that's always the west Kerry haunt on All-Ireland day, fell in love over football and got married, but what I do know is that they were newly-weds in September 1959, and back from their honeymoon in time to see Kerry win their next All-Ireland.

You see why this Kerry thing runs deep, deeper still when my granduncle started coming home from America for the All-Ireland every year. Mickey Moriarty was larger than life itself, billeting himself in the Carney Arms Hotel in Dún Laoghaire, where he'd entertain all comers at all hours of the night with his tales about playing host to Kerry touring teams of the 1920s in his Manhattan 'Speakeasy,' and with his yarn about coming home on holidays in the early 1930s with two members of those teams, Phil O'Sullivan and Jerry 'Pluggy' Moriarty.

He always told that story because it was no ordinary holiday. Mickey brought his big-bumpered Buick with him for show and for company, and it became the talk of Dingle, and of Cobh too, after the first leg of the journey back west was interrupted when they smashed into a water fountain seconds after hitting dry land.

My granduncle Mickey was my hero, and if all that wasn't enough, my indoctrination in all things Kerry was completed by being ritually ferried up UCD to watch Mickey's nephew and my uncle Mícheál train the members of the Kerry team based in Dublin.

There we'd play fetch-ball for Jack O'Shea, Mick Spillane, Charlie Nelligan, John O'Keeffe, Ger Power, Barry Walsh and more. It was a privilege being a ball boy to some of the greatest players of all time, but I was still a Dub with 'Blue' blood.

Schooldays in Scoil Colmcille on Marlborough Street and Coláiste Mhuire on Parnell Square were always about Sam

Maguire being brought on show by past pupils Brian Mullins and Robbie Kelleher.

We mimicked Mullins and Kelleher in the Scoil Colmcille clós and then out in the Mhuire's home at Longmeadows in Islandbridge. While there it was always Dublin for Sam and Kerry for the holidays.

It was why myself and my younger brother Dónal played fetch-ball with Dublin jerseys on our backs.. My nylon geansaí had Tony Hanahoe's number eleven darned, or maybe it was ironed, onto the back of it. Dónal's had Jimmy Keaveny's number fourteen.

We were Dubs, but how committed were we? That was always the question when Kerry loomed on the horizon over Croke Park. Hand on heart we could never really answer it. The worst of times, but the best of times, because the 1970s and 1980s are remembered by Dublin versus Kerry in Croke Park and the roller-coaster it all entailed.

In the 1977 All-Ireland Semi-Final, I was ribbed by a Kerry cousin when bursting into tears mid-way through the second half as the Kingdom looked to have the game by the throat. He didn't know it, but the tears were because of a very bad nosebleed that had dried up by the time David Hickey and Bernard Brogan blasted the Dubs to their most famous victory of all.

Suddenly it was my cousin's turn for tears.

In 1978, I didn't know whether to hand-pump the air with joy when Mikey Sheehy put the ball in Paddy Cullen's net, or head for Strasbourg and demand a hearing for Cullen and Robbie Kelleher in the European Court of Human Rights.

It was tough being torn between two teams and two cultures in those years. I screamed for the Dubs in 1975, but they lost, was in Kerry's camp in 1976, but they lost, yet was still was at the head of the queue in Scoil Colmcille a few days later with my autograph book when Mullins and Kelleher came calling.

A Dub, but behind it all a closet 'Ciarraíoch Mallaithe.' It will be the same this All-Ireland Sunday. It couldn't be any other way.

(first broadcast on RTÉ Radio in 2011)

GAILLIMH ABÚ
Mary O'Malley

It is a winter evening, bitter and cold. The silence is broken by the cries of children at play. My makeshift hurley, the rough edges hurting my hand, shudders against the finger bones when it strikes another stick, hurting all the way up the arm. There is a hoking underfoot for the ball, a push, the stick snakes between my feet and the ball is gone. It is pucked way down the pitch, which is short and full of rocks.

I am seven years old.

Or a summer's evening, towards nightfall. Children at play. A real hurley, the ash smooth and beautifully hefted, an effortless extension of the hand. Not as sore when the sticks clashed, more a ringing up the arm, the life of the tree life still evident in the timber, like Ulysses' oar. The connection between the ash and the game is ancient and sacred. The small ball, not a real sliotar, is curving towards my goal. I lift the hurl, intercept the ball, pick it up on the stick, hop it and give a long puck, out of danger.

The sky is clear and darkening so that the deep blue line that will be visible up to midnight is gaining definition over the ruined coastguard station. The Slyne Head lighthouse scans the village like radar, picks up the blip of the ball as it speeds towards me. I raise the cuman, nervous of missing. There is a lightening in the air, a slowing down of the ball's trajectory.

Between me and it, there is another dimension. In this endless moment, I discovered magic. And physics. The dimension of the present moment, which, the distinguished Czech immunologist and poet Miroslav Holub tells us, in his essay of that name, lasts three seconds. I was taken aback to read this, as I have always considered the present moment to be infinitely elastic. Battalions of angels could be flying within its boundaries, or radio waves from outer space. More likely the latter. I was never much visited by pretty angels. 'Now I lay me down to sleep, I pray the lord my soul to keep.' At that age you expect whiteness, and gold. The ones I saw roosting at the end of my bed had the look of fourteenth-century Venetian corner boys. Distinctly fallen.

With a bit of discipline, they'd have made lovely hurlers.

Until we got our first television, when I was about thirteen or fourteen, I had never seen a proper hurling match. Before that we used to listen, gathered around the radio on Sunday afternoons, entranced by the dramatic skill of the virtuoso commentator, Micheál O'Hehir. We listened, to 'Amhrán na bhFhiann,' the ball was thrown in, a roar from the crowd and O'Hehir's voice calmed us again for the first long puck, the pass, the gathering speed of an early attack. He, almost uniquely, had perfect pitch and measure, his delivery a miracle of timing.

Since radio is creative listening, and since each had to rely on his own knowledge of the rules, it is certain that five people in the same room were watching five different games. Some of them may have resembled rounders as much as hurling. Television changed that. The Gods had faces, and very visible bodies. They didn't always move as gracefully as on radio. Many a young girl would have cause to remember Kavanagh's words: 'That I had wooed not as I should a creature made of clay.'

Only with radio would all five of us in that room be playing our own variation on what was happening in Croke Park.

Beautiful motion. Perhaps much of our love of the game really is connected to a love of freedom, not in the narrow, nationalistic sense of the 1940s, but its opposite: a freedom from restraint, from that straightjacket of shame and repression that has informed the body language of Irish people over generations, through colonisation, Victorian values, a joyless Church, a rigid nationalism and, above all, the loss of the Irish language.

Because hurling at its best, regardless of the spoken language of the players, is a game that throws a couple of hundred years of surface English off, and does it lightly. Its roots, its 'dúchas' as Breandán Ó hEithir might have said, are deep in the linguistic structure that underpin what has become known as Hiberno-English. There is a synchronisation between the action of an All-Ireland Final and the accent and expression of the commentator that is undeniable, which could be why today, as always, I'll switch down the TV sound and listen to the match on Radió na Gaeltachta.

I am a dilettante, unworthy of even a passing glance from a proper fan. Yet I harbour a dream that one day I will get tickets for a final in Croke Park.

I want to go, as much for the chance to see Irish men impassioned and liberated by physical grace, when the parallelogram of the pitch is transformed into a universe of near perfect symmetry, one that moves not towards the ever possible chaos, but is governed by laws of mass and motion and held in almost perfect order.

Today, if the old gods are guiding play and Macha is on duty, she will have conspired to bring onto the pitch only those young men whose Latin souls trapped in Northern bodies lend the game a grace and speed that makes it legendary, and of those heroes, the bravest and best will be decked out in maroon jerseys and the prize will come West.

Flann O'Brien would approve, I think. A little hyperbole never killed anyone.

At any rate, a good game provides what Frost demanded of the true poem: '... not necessarily a great clarification... but a momentary stay against confusion.' Taoiseach take note.

And so we watch, season after season, year after year, and never tire of the endless permutations of two teams of fifteen men giving us yet another staging of an old play, hopeful each time that this will be an inspiring, even a unique performance. A bit like Shakespeare. Agus Gaillimh Abú.

(first broadcast on RTÉ Radio in 2012)

HURLING CHOSE ME

Eamon O'Shea

I never chose hurling. It chose me, and many others like me. And it has never let go. Back in the 1960s, when growing up in Cloughjordan, County Tipperary, I played hurling – not sometimes, not often, but continuously. Alone against the gable-end, one against one in the garden, two versus two on the road, at lunch break in the schoolyard playing full-blooded matches on small-scale pitches without a helmet or a health and safety officer in sight. Townies versus country lads – it was hard to know the difference – just throw in the ball – every day. Back then, though the world may have been opening up to revolution, where I lived we were more concerned with exploring the hurling hands we had been given.

In my parish, all young hurlers came with question marks. Is he any good? Is he strong enough? Brave enough? Skilful enough? Made of the right stuff? As good as his father? Would he even make the club team? The answers ultimately determined your position in the local hurling pantheon.

What about me? The genetics were promising. My older brother Liam was so good that he set scoring records for the juvenile team – even at age ten I knew that must mean something for siblings coming behind. But would I ever be a hurler? A real hurler? Somebody once said that I did look like a young Jimmy Kennedy, who played for Tipperary in the late 1940s and early 1950s. I took that comparison as possibly relevant, albeit noting only decades later that nobody ever said that I played like the great Jimmy Kennedy!

As irregular relationships became more permissible in 1960s Ireland, so hurling gradually became me and I became hurling, and a love affair had begun; one that was readily sanctioned by family and community. The excitement of waiting for my father Ned to come home from working the land so that we could travel to see my older brother play in County Finals in the nearby faraway fields of Thurles, Holycross or Cashel. My mother had his dinner ready, good clothes laid out and shoes at the door, so that there would be no delays, even if time was always more of a friend to all in those days. The procession of cars to and from these matches – hope on the outward journey, sometimes disappointment on the return, but never so much as to extinguish hope for the next time. Endless talk of chances taken and chances missed, of heroes and villians, of maybes and maybe nots.

On then I went to vocational school in Borrisokane, and the curiosity of the early morning assembly. Every morning we marched into class listening to Mocky Dunne, the school principal, preparing us for the day that some of us might walk behind the Artane Boys' Band in Croke Park on All-Ireland Final day. He called out the names: Hogan, Ryan, Burke, O'Neill, surely one of you will play in Croke Park – the straining of the ears for the sound of O'Shea on that list – the sound of silence still felt four decades on. Pilgrimages to the Munster championship now allowed, I always watched the parade behind the band as carefully as the match itself, just in case.

The game impacted on everyone in the parish, directly or indirectly. As hurlers, we played our scripted roles on different teams at different times and waited for chance to make its mark. For others, the game provided the narrative for everyday life, the canvas where connections could be made in the shops, post office, creamery, and of course the public house. My Uncle Willie preferred the sanctuary of the latter whenever we played, hearing the reports of the match later from and an endless list of confidants and always letting me know 'Ye were good today' or 'Ye will have to improve.' He didn't really need to see the game, the second-hand accounts were almost always better than the real thing; third-hand, and after a few pints, they became even better.

Today, anchored and marooned in later-age in Galway city and long-time separated from these early fields of gold, I watch my own urban children try to create their own futures in an uncertain world. Will hurling be for them the constant that it is for me? So many games played and watched, but each remembered for mattering most, until the next one – and 'Dad, we have heard this story before you know' – oh sorry.

All enduring love affairs must ultimately capture the heart, the soul and the imagination. For me, hurling does that better than any other sport, mainly through the ties that bind us to people, places and local communities. Looking back now at a life lived under its spell, the game seems so interwoven into the fabric of that life that they are but one and the same. Does any other game bind and set you free at the same time, allow you to look forward and back in equal measure. Surely not!

(first broadcast on RTÉ Radio in 2012)

THE HUNGER GAMES
Gerry Moran

'Lads,' he said, 'How can you possibly eat at a time like this?' It was half-time in the All-Ireland Hurling Final between Kilkenny and Galway in Croke Park, and Jimmy and myself were tucking into our home-made beef sandwiches. 'We eat at a time like this,' I told our fellow-Kilkenny man, 'because we're going to need all the sustenance we can get to roar on our team in the second half of this All-Ireland Final. And besides, we're hungry.'

And boy did we need those sandwiches. Because for sure things were looking glum – glummer than glum at half time in Croke Park that second Sunday in September, and I didn't blame our man for losing his appetite. Indeed, as Jimmy and myself demolished our sambos and sated our appetite we wondered, as did a lot of Kilkenny people, where the Kilkenny team's appetite for hurling had gone. What had become of last year's savage hunger against Tipperary, because for sure Galway looked hungrier and meaner and leaner? In fact, they looked ravenous, and capable of devouring our 'boys' whole and entire, which they did in certain parts of the field of play.

That first half of the Hurling All-Ireland was a tame affair, from a Kilkenny point of view, and about as tasty as a ten-day-old trifle; whereas we were anticipating a mouth-watering soufflé of hurling skill and style, the only soufflé dished up in the first thirty-five minutes of that encounter with the Tribesmen was as flat as the proverbial pancake. Flatter even. If anything it was Galway who were dishing up the mouth-watering and jaw-dropping hurling, giving us, and Kilkenny's management team, lashings of food for thought.

There were a lot of puzzled and confused Kilkenny faces in Croke Park at half-time that All-Ireland Sunday. A lot of folks, including myself, were thinking: one roasting from Galway was a misfortune, but two would be downright careless (to paraphrase one Oscar Fingal O'Flaherty Wills Wilde).

And when our sandwiches were gone, Jimmy and myself tucked into the sweets, tasty butterscotch ones, the more of which you eat, the more you want to eat. To a neutral observer (if there was such a species in Croke Park that Sunday – and there wasn't), it looked as if Jimmy and myself were having ourselves a merry little picnic. Not so. We needed every crumb of bread, every scrap of meat, every sweet to fortify us, to keep our sugar levels up and sustain us against succumbing to the high-octane suspense and, of course, to stave off cardiac-arrest.

Oh, and to shield us from that thunderous and deafening roar of 'GAL-WAY, GAL-WAY' that resounded around Croke Park every ten minutes. And there was no use in the Kilkenny crowd responding with 'GO-AWAY, GO-AWAY,' as it just sounded like 'GAL-WAY, GAL-WAY,' and simply added to the decibel level of the Galway support.

Thankfully, our boys eventually rediscovered their appetite for the game (whetted, no doubt, by some serious grilling at half-time), and dished up the kind of hurling we have come to expect on an All-Ireland Hurling Final menu. Had he goaled, Henry's penalty would have been the icing on the cake for Kilkenny, as would Joe's two frees, had he not missed them, for Galway. So, in the end both teams, I reckon, got their just desserts.

Henry's hunger for a historic ninth All-Ireland Hurling medal was not to be sated that second Sunday in September, nor was Joe's hunger for a first All-Ireland Hurling medal. Both players would have to wait for another day, today, as it happens, when hopefully these two mighty hurlers and their equally mighty teams, Kilkenny and Galway, will serve up another feast of hurling, and Jimmy and myself will get to enjoy our batch of beef sandwiches.

(first broadcast on RTÉ Radio in 2012)

DREAMS OF A RAGGEDY BUSH
Joe Kearney

I am a sceptic, an irreligionist, someone who finds it hard to admit that I might be superstitious, so I rarely confess to counting magpies. Its hard to reconcile my freethinking notions while intoning 'One for sorrow, two for joy…' in the silence of my mind whenever I catch sight of the bird whose call resembles the rattling of old bones. But I do this for the ingrained, innate paganism that is part of my make-up. I don't walk under ladders. I am careful not to spill salt and I never, ever break a mirror.

In this I am not alone. Drive along the twist of road between Kilkenny and Kells, and on a bad bend you will come across St Patrick's Raggedy Bush. The first time I witnessed this apparition was on a misty autumnal evening when the light was failing. It loomed out at me, pale as a spectre from the hedgerow. For those who have never seen it, the raggedy bush is a three-metre-high hawthorn, almost entirely covered in torn rags and assorted scraps of clothing. It resembles some notion of a Tibetan offering of prayer flags in a place where you might never expect to find them; located, as it is, on a dangerous bend, where unsuspecting motorists have been know to swerve on first sight of the Raggedy Bush.

This particular tree is a nice example of the melding of the Pagan with the Christian. It is symbolic of confused sceptics, like myself, who don't like the notion of darkness, or getting out of bed on a Friday the thirteenth, yet who are brave enough to berate the notion of *piseóga* in the bright light of day.

Legend has it that Fionn MacCumhaill and St Patrick were breakfasting together on the heights of Slievenaman, when Patrick accidentally ate Fionn's portion of porridge.

The giant was renowned for his short temper, so Patrick took to his heels. He ran all the way through Mullinahone and Callan, with Fionn in pursuit. When the giant ran out of steam somewhere near Windgap, he borrowed a hurley from a sporting youth and pucked a sliotar after the escaping saint. Now, as most Kilkenny people will contend, Fionn was a Tipperary man, so the ball missed its mark, and landed up in a hawthorn tree on the Kells road. Patrick was so grateful for his safe delivery that he promptly dropped to his knees beneath the bush and offered thanks. The stone on which he knelt still carries the imprint of his knees. He wiped the sweat from his brow on a piece of cloth that he then tied to the tree. Thus are legends forged?

Over time, a tradition emerged where a scrap of clothing from an ill person was tied to the bush, as the colour faded and the rag rotted it was believed the illness would depart from its victim and enter the spirit of the tree.

Multiple dreams and hopes are hung upon the branches.

This is evidenced by the multiplicity of strange and wondrous items suspended from the tree. When examined, it is clear that many of the attachments are placed with other than religious motives. Delicate strips of underwear flutter alongside the domesticity of tea towels, hair bands and babies' bibs. Some are fading from their former glory, but the more recent additions retain the vitality of magenta, coral, saffron, even some maroon and white! A tatter of black, gauzy lace flutters and spirals around the leg of a thick, athletic sports sock in perpetual tango that some might regard as heathen in this sacred place.

The hawthorn tree that became the Raggedy Bush most likely started life as a seed in a pile of bird droppings. It flourished in the face of adversity, survived ruminant livestock and was never harvested for firewood.

It may have become lopsided under the weight of hopes and dreams, yet it lives on to grant wishes and listen to the prayers of the hopeful who genuflect in the moulded grooves of St Patrick's knees and sprinkle themselves with pooled rainwater.

In its branches today, there are ribbons and streamers in black and amber. These have not faded. They are fresh and strong and vibrant. Time has yet to dull their glorious banner.

Down the road is the ruin of the twelfth century Kells Priory. Nearby flows the King's River – the one in which King Niall Caille drowned, attempting to save one of his servants in 844. A lot of history collides at the bend where the Raggedy Bush grows.

And on this day of days in the hurling calendar, some may pray for glory, but I will tie my black and amber dreams to the thorns of the Raggedy Bush, keep my fingers crossed and… hope!

(first broadcast on RTÉ Radio in 2012)

MICHAEL WALSH: A HURLING LIFE

Patrick E. Walsh

Hurling bubbles in our family's blood, so for the life of me I couldn't fathom how I had never seen this book before. Staring out at me from the pages of *Kilkenny Senior Hurling Champions 1887–2003* was a picture of my father, Michael Walsh. The picture identified him as the winning captain of the Rower-Inistioge team of 1968. The book would make a wonderful Christmas gift for what we knew would probably be his last.

From the middle of November it was obvious that he would never leave the house again. One of our last big days out was to the funeral of former Kilkenny All-Ireland winning captain, Micky Kelly, who was married to Josie, my Dad's sister. Afterwards he shared pints and stories over a long afternoon with men he hurled against long ago.

The great bundle of energy that is Sam Carroll said to him, 'It will be your turn next year,' referring to the County Board's policy of honouring the champions of the past.

Without missing a beat, he smiled and said that he was looking forward to it, but both of us knew his illness would have taken him from us long before then.

These days his limited eyesight was saved for the donation to the bookmakers' benevolent fund that was his daily trawl through the racing form. I offered to read to him the pages covering the 1968 final from the book.

He would never have asked.

That was his way.

A few days after Christmas, I sat at his bedside as he asked me to write to the author of the book, Dermot Kavanagh, who had also played on the team. He wished to thank him for the honour of the separate picture identifying him as captain.

That evening I heard for the first time his recollections of the 1968 championship. He became frustrated as a torrent of memories flooded his head, and their delivery was slowed by the damming effect of his shortness of breath.

He recalled being picked out of position at centre back against Éire Óg in the first round to curb the threat posed by Tommy O'Connell, the Kilkenny forward.

The quarter-final versus Thomastown was postponed until the Spring of 1969 to allow Ollie Walsh to return from a suspension, following a Kilkenny–Tipperary brawl in the National Hurling League. Again he was picked to do a job. Cha Whelan had to be marked, so he started full forward.

Freshford were the opposition for the semi-final, and he was positioned to stop Pa Dillon, the great but fearsome Kilkenny full back of the 1960s. From his bed he told me, in slightly less than parliamentary language, that he feared for his life, and that if Pa were to walk into the bedroom there and then, he'd still be afraid. Pa Dillon today is one of the most softly spoken, obliging Kilkenny heroes of the past.

Two days later I read to him Dermot Kavanagh's touching reply. 'Believe me it was no problem giving your Dad due acknowledgement. He was a brilliant hurler and sincere servant of the club….' He '… was always picked to play on other such greats as Paddy Moran, Martin Coogan and Sean Buckley when the occasion demanded… I can safely say that all the senior statesmen of that team were great men, none more so than him… probably his greatest outing for the club was last September when, at very short notice, and clearly unwell, he led the guard of honour for Pudsey Murphy's funeral.'

When I finished, he smiled and his eyes filled up as he reached out to grip the back of my hand.

Nothing was said, because nothing needed to be said.

That was his way.

His funeral six days later conveyed to us the sense of brotherhood that embraces not only the Rower-Inistioge team of 1968, but the hurling community in general.

Lining both sides of the street in the rain opposite the Ollie Walsh Memorial in Thomastown were the teammates whom he had led into battle to claim his parish's one and only county title. Over their shoulders were slung the club jersey that was their battledress on that memorable day.

I still think the lid of the coffin lifted as his chest swelled with pride at the sight of these great men providing a guard of honour along the streets where he had made his home for over forty years.

The rain relented as the sporting gods smiled on the amount of hurling men that had gathered to bid farewell. The 'Men of 68' led the cortège to the church, and his three sons and three grandsons carried him to the altar, where waiting for him was the Tom Walsh Cup, which he had received nearly forty-three years previously.

We have no picture of him being presented with the cup on County Final day, so it's a sight that will be branded on our memories forever.

At the graveside, a face we all knew approached my mother.

Before he could offer his condolences, she smiled and said, 'They tell me he hurled the socks off you.'

Seamus Cleere, the prince of Kilkenny centre backs, laughed and hugged her.

He had been picked centre forward in the County Final against Bennettsbridge to stop the peerless Seamus Cleere.

In the *Irish Independent* report of the match, neither of them got a mention.

Job done. He never said anything to us about it.

That was his way.

(first broadcast on RTÉ Radio in 2012)

A JOURNEY NOT A ROUTE
Cathy Power

When I was a child in Dublin, a trip to Kilkenny was a big deal. Depending on how you were travelling, of course, but whatever the vehicle, it was still the kind of trip where you'd wish someone the best of luck when they were setting out on it.

There were people in digs in our house who used to hitch, and people, as a rule, would give you a lift, with neither hitcher nor driver particularly worried about any risk.

There were student nurses who used to cadge Saturday morning lifts in vehicles from Fit Remoulds, the Kilkenny tyre company, whose drivers stayed in our house from Monday to Friday.

The roots of my claustrophobia came when as a child I stood on the footpath on Gardiner Place watching young women, seated on a throne of tyres, disappear from view behind the sliding door of a Volkswagen van for a journey to Kilkenny, alone, in the windowless back of the dark, rubber-smelling vehicle.

The train was always great, and even better if, because of a whisper from CIE, we knew in advance that the following Sunday's Mystery Train was going to Kilkenny. While other Dubliners speculated on the destination, we had our day planned in the Marble City. Not only was it a cheap and comfortable way to travel, but we could do it with an air of superiority since we were the ones in the know.

The best of all, though, was when, with my father and mother, I travelled in the Ford Prefect. My mother drove, and my father navigated our way from hotel to pub to the next pub, and at every stop he was sure to know someone. I drank Club Orange until I was sick, and my mother drank tea and coffee, at least until we got near enough that one would do no harm.

Naas, Kilcullen, Athy, Ballylinan, Castlecomer, Kilkenny or to be more precise: Lawlors, The Hideout, The Leinster, The Pedigree, the Avalon and Langton's.

The journey took all day, but that was the point: the journey was part of the experience to be planned, savoured, enjoyed, shared on return and remembered in the future.

'Do ya remember the day we met the man with the dog in Kilcullen?'

'Who was the man who sang the song for us at the Pedigree Corner?'

'Wait til I tell you who we met in Comer.'

At least the first half day of any visit following a journey like that would be taken up in conversation about the trip itself.

Last year I got a job in Dublin, and from May to December drove up and down from Thomastown to the city centre every working day. My parents would have thought it an unnatural and impossible way to live, and they would have been right.

It used to take me about twenty minutes to get from home to the motorway, and maybe another forty-five minutes from Newlands Cross to the city centre.

I nearly died doing it. It was about two hours door-to-door. Mornings weren't so bad, but evenings I hated it. The motorway might be quicker, but it is a hell of a lot more boring.

Some evenings, when my daughter phoned for a progress report, I couldn't even tell her where I was, because one stretch of it looks much the same as another. There was no time, there was no fun, there was speed, stress and fatigue as I tried to live on a diet of caffeine and petrol.

The M9 is a road, the quickest way from one point to another. It is a far cry from the old way: a journey involving people, towns, stops, drink and food, landmarks and the creation of memory. I look back on it as a priceless luxury and joy. Motorway or not, however, when as late as last year, on the morning of an All-Ireland, my children and I would decorate the car, and wearing my black and amber waistcoat we would head for Croke Park on the M9, it was still magic.

We loved that journey, the big breakfast, the excitement, forgetting the tickets and having to go back for them, the examination of other cars' colours, speculation about the match, the traffic, the bulls' looks at opposition vehicles and the hope of seeing the team bus *en route*.

But now that commute is a thing of the past too, and this morning, for the first time in my daughter's memory, we will make our All-Ireland journey not from Thomastown, but from Drumcondra.

My identity crisis continues: a Dublin woman, with Kilkenny parents, who went to live in Kilkenny and now is back home in Dublin, walking to Croke Park in a black and amber waistcoat.

Tomorrow night I will be in Kilkenny to welcome home the team, as I have always done, wherever I was living at the time, but now that I am back living where I was born and bred, the question remains: where is home?

It is a question I may ponder until the day I die, but today there is no doubt about my allegiances in Croke Park. Mon the Cats!

(first broadcast on RTÉ Radio in 2012)

MY MOTHER'S COUNTY
Leo Cullen

Sean worked on the farm in my mother's county where I went on summer holidays. He was my hero. He had wistful green eyes that dreamed all day of football men. He put the halter on the horse and mended the bridles and talked football.

Henry Dixon lives up the road in Claremorris, he said. Sean Flanagan comes from Ballyhaunis.

Hay and oats for the Galway goats, he said, eggs and rashers for the Mayo slashers.

Tom Langan comes from Ballycastle by the sea, he said. Now where are they?

The great Mayo All-Ireland wins came in 1950 and 1951, Flanagan, Langan and cohorts had the medals. Though only ten or so years had passed since those Olympian wins and winners, my hero Sean's adulation for them was fading. It seemed like a lifetime; what does it seem like sixty years on? Sean, are you still here?

'Do ya think?' he used to ask in his accent that each year I carried home in the car with me at holiday's end to my hurling county in the South. 'Do you think?' he'd look into the far heavens, or into the wires of the radio through which he'd heard those names jump like sparks of lightning. And then he'd name the Down team that were currently all the rage – he'd recite the awesome litany of names from one to fifteen. And he'd ask, whatever happened to Mayo, 'Do ya think will they be back any year again? Do ya think would they ever beat these boys from the North?'

After Sunday Mass, Sean bought ice-cream wafers as wide as steps for me and my cousin, and laughed when we couldn' get our mouths around them. Following a pint or two then, he travelled off to club games; those to which I didn't go with him I imagined I had. Club games were held in a variety of terrains. In the parishes of Ahgamore and Bunnyconellan locked in by rushes and snipe grass, the sod squelching under the feet of the footballers. In sandy pitches on the coastal wilds of Achill Island. In parks on the edges of towns – Ballina, Claremorris and Ballinrobe. Followers drove long distances, sometimes even taking the boat out to Clare Island, fortress home of the O'Malleys, football boots and jerseys hanging out over the boat instead of sword and shield. Wherever the game was played, the players attempted to uphold the standard and style of Mayo football: leap highest, catch the ball cleanest, kick it on! Cheers of appreciation would ring out. Sean would scratch the bristles of hope and imagination on his chin. And along with my Mayo accent I would carry home in the car with me to the South my memory of men rising high, grasping the ball in careful hands, turning in the air clean as the twist of a corkscrew.

Back home I went, to my Mayo mother, and when she asked me what I was doing, and I said 'Going to football matches and talking to Sean,' she said, 'Oh, silly laddie, keep away from that rough old game and from that Sean fellow for he'll fill your head with rubbish.' And I thought, could anyone so disown their legacy as my mother?

She died while still a young woman, and after that there wouldn't have been much talk between my father and me about her. The way I understood it was that he wanted to protect me, my brothers and sisters from memories, and in return I didn't want to disturb him. So I don't know when or how it was that one day I asked him if she had taken an interest in those great wins of 1951 and 1952. 'Taken an interest?!' he responded. 'Those games nearly stopped her heart!' He laughed thinking back on it. 'She hid under the bed,' he said, 'Micheál O'Hehir blaring the match commentary out of the radio, and she hiding beneath the bed, her hands stuffed in her ears, and every now and then calling out: "Who's winning? Is it finished yet? I can't bear it!" And then, when it was all over, she crept out from under the bed and filled herself with gassy lemonade and sang all her songs: "Patsy Fagan," "If I were a Blackbird," "Moonlight in Mayo." She was a child at heart.' My father shook his head then until he too became like Sean, lost in his reminiscences.

And I wonder was I beginning then to understand that here was one thing my mother shared with Sean, and it was generosity of spirit. And another was passion; passion for her county. They were both children at heart, both children of Mayo.

But a tenacious phalanx too of men and women, you Mayo children are! I can see you early this morning rise up out of every corner, gather by shadowy clubhouses of Garrymore, Ballintubber and the Mullet – by coast where currachs beach on sandy dunes, or on Moytura's Plain where black cattle graze alongside limestone walls. I can see you travel from the land where fuschia is blood red and grass is vivid green and the ball drops down from the sky and young men ascend on wings to claim it. For Mayo are magic!

(first broadcast on RTÉ Radio in 2012)

HOUSE OF PAIN
Tom Rowley

A few years ago, a book came out entitled *House of Pain*. Casual passers-by catching a glimpse of the title in a shop window must have conjured up all sorts of disturbing images of sadistic goings on and, generally, a lot of misery, anguish and suffering. And they would not have been too far off the mark. The book, by sports journalist Keith Duggan, is about Mayo football and that seemingly endless, grinding quest, stretching back over sixty-one years, to clasp the Holy Grail: the Sam Maguire Cup, and bring it back to the county.

House of Pain is subtitled 'Through the Rooms of Mayo Football.' And like hundreds of thousands of others, I have been in and out of those rooms, one minute bright with expectations, the next warming in the glow of anticipated victory and then, so often, shivering in the clawing chill of damp defeat.

I think my mother must have sensed all of this ages ago, back when we would be striking out with red and green banners to support Mayo in a Connacht final. She would ambush us at the front door and fling splashes of Holy Water over the colours. If we trudged back in the evening, banners lying low, we would be greeted with her same, consoling refrain: 'Ah sure, maybe it's for the best, at least now your miseries are over for another year.'

Agony and ecstasy, twinned and entwined, year after year, through the rooms of Mayo football. And the decades rolled on, as triumphs, to a point, and disappointments, all sloshed about and mingled. Great names, heroic games, and still no Sam Maguire. Mayo endured, sensing deep down that football is about more than winning and losing. It's about a sense of identity, a certain dignity and the layers of history that have shaped the county and its people.

The night before Mayo do battle in an All-Ireland Final in Croke Park I am reminded of this when I put on singer and fiddler Dessie O'Halloran's version of 'The Boys from the County Mayo.' For years I treated this song as overly sentimental, the line 'Treat each like a brother and love one another' grated. Then Dessie, drawing on his own times on the building sites in England, simply changed the word 'love' to 'sub,' extracting a sentimental vein and replacing it with a back-straightening dose of reality.

To 'sub' someone was to dig deep and help out a fellow county man, or another Irishman, usually with a few pounds, until the next pay day. So when Dessie gravelly lilts 'Act each as a brother and sub one another' I am seeing the motorway construction sites across England my own father worked on.

And Mayo has no monopoly on tales of the emigrant's daily struggles. Mayo men have subbed skint fellows from Donegal, and many a Donegal man came to the rescue of a hard up Mayo labourer. And now, as emigration again weakens these counties, I've no doubt they are again subbing one another.

As the drama unfurls this afternoon in the cauldron of Croke Park, I will be remembering way back to when, as a boy, I played out my Mayo football fantasies in our Acre field, after the hay was tossed and piled into cocks. Tearing down the field, soloing the ball, bending and weaving as imagined defenders, in reality static cocks of hay, loomed close. The scenario was always the same. It's All-Ireland Final day. Croke Park. Micheál O'Hehir's voice swirling in my head: '… the seconds tick away, the sides are level, Mayo launch one final attack.' Morley combs the shy, brings down the ball and passes it to Joe Corcoran. Now I was Corcoran, cutting in field, jinking past defenders, steadying myself, taking aim, shooting, the ball swirling high like a thing possessed and dropping between the posts. In my case, just inside the ESB pole in the middle of the hayfield and the imagined other upright.

And so today the many Mayo legions, banners on high, will merge into the red and green army and converge on Croke Park. And maybe, this time the door of the House of Pain will creak open, a red and green tinted light will creep in and, bit by bit, light the rooms. And maybe, just maybe, a young boy's football fantasies, played out years ago in the Acre field, will finally become a reality. The final seconds ticking away, the sides level, a player in red and green cuts inside, steadies himself, aims, shoots, the ball soaring, swirling and dropping... dropping... into history.

(first broadcast on RTÉ Radio in 2012)

CON HOULIHAN
Cyril Kelly

So there we are, in the photograph as if lined up for mugshots. There are four of us, sitting side by side a couple of years ago on Christmas Day in the morning. Four representatives of the Kerry Mafia domiciled in the metropolis. The location: a Dublin Garda station – our backs to the wall. Two of the four were stout members of the constabulary, the third was the late Con Houlihan, plus, I'm afraid, myself. Before us, on a round Formica table, a few condemned high-rise towers of empty glasses, brimming pints gathered together like a cosy little thatched village, a cluster of Castle Island mediums. I have to admit that this could be seen as a snap of four 'found-ons,' as in found on a premises for the purpose of consuming alcoholic liquor on a date and at a time prohibited by law.

Con Houlihan wrote about the 'found-on' phenomenon many times. In the photo I am sitting next to him. He has one great lapa of a left lámh on my elbow, another great lapa on the right, restraining the elbow of one of the Detective Sergeants, and he is looking intently into the camera lens. Wearing a chunky, green geansaí, green anorak, he has the noble head of a Native American chieftain. His high forehead is embossed with primal wisdom fished from the depths of the Gleannsharoon River, whose waters course down from the foothills of Sléibhte Gleann an Ridire.

And Con's hands, a pair of lock forward's paws; as deft of touch as a thatcher, they could wield the pen as a fly fisherman wields his sally rod, whipping whistling music overhead, unfurling the line onto the skin of the river, plucking parochial images from deep in the past and tossing them up, renewed, glittering and twirling like white trout, landing them into the startled light of current time. Who could forget his account of the Football Final of 1978, particularly his depiction of Paddy Cullen's frantic attempt to foil Mikey Sheehy's mercurial free kick. Con described the Dublin goalkeeper 'dashing back towards his goal like a woman who smells her cake burning.' And on that same day, as Con himself often wrote: 'Now read on... after the second Kerry goal the Hill was as silent as Scairtaglin on a Good Friday afternoon.'

Samuel Johnson, when denouncing the Metaphysical Poets, accused them of 'yoking the most heterogeneous of ideas by violence together.' I fear that Con Houlihan's breadth of reference may have invited the opprobrium of the good doctor. In his Tributaries column for the *Evening Press*, Con could yoke together such unlikely companions as Lester Piggott and Vincent Van Gogh. He wrote: 'It may seem ridiculous to compare Lester Piggott to Vincent Van Gogh; each, however, was consumed by a passion that led to sacrifices so enormous that "normal" people can hardly comprehend.'

Con could catch the fetch of Willie Joe, his prose could dizzy with the shimmy of Martin McHugh, could banish the mist from the dip in Ballybrit to illuminate the final two furlongs, to give us a binocular close-up of those two last fences hunched in the hollow. And from time to time we got a glimpse of that other Dylan Thomas, the one in the shadow of Fern Hill where time is flying with the high fields and the farm is forever fled from the childless land.

Unlike Thomas, however, Con Houlihan's childhood fields never fled. 'My heartwater is in the Gleannsharoon River,' he wrote. 'It's almost 25 years since I fished that river and I can still remember all the runs and the pools and the shallows and the depths and the places where the trout love to run and the places where they shun.'

Con will be missed and reminisced in many an urban and rural watering-hole, no more fógras from the dogs and the racetracks, from rugby grounds and soccer terraces at home and abroad. His ghost will hover over a certain Garda Station, a couple of cic fadas from his shy residence in Portobello. And today, at the All-Ireland Football Final, there will be an abiding absence, down at the Canal End, beneath the big screen, in the miniscule high-definition screen of the mind, an absence in an anorak, leaning against one of the old crowd barriers, that inimitable Croke Park chronicler, all the action and atmosphere, the colour and valour of Mayo and Donegal, teams and tribes alike, reflected in the twinkle of his all-seeing eye.

(first broadcast on RTÉ Radio in 2012)

JIMMY'S WINNING MATCHES
Denise Blake

We are sitting in Croke Park in the Lower Hogan Stand near the halfway line for this year's semi-final football game. Donegal against Cork. All around us is green and gold. At lunchtime in the hotel, Jimmy Magee passed our table, stopped and said 'Is there anyone left in Donegal?' Those who are at still at home must hear the sound of us all in the stadium.

Donegal, pride of all. They reckon a year ending in two is lucky for Donegal: in 1972 they won their first Ulster title, 1982 first All-Ireland U21, 1992 the first All-Ireland Senior title and now in 2012 we are storming Croke Park again. As the song that is an earworm says 'Jimmy's bringing Sam back to Donegal again.'

It is not often that the past, the present and the future come together for so many people at one time. There are men sitting in this crowd who played on that famous 1992 team. Their team pictures hung in homes, hotels, pubs and restaurants throughout the county for years.

The wonder then was how young men we had known growing up had become heroes. Crowds turned up in towns throughout the county as the team stood on the back of lorries made into makeshift stages and held the cup aloft.

Now, 1992 hovers over us. Those who managed back then to get tickets, like winning Willy Wonka's prize, know where they sat in the old stadium, how they celebrated afterwards. Those of us who remained at home know exactly what we were doing.

I was in my living-room with a small baby, watching the TV with the sound turned down and listening to Charlie Collins commentating on the radio. Laurence had managed to get three tickets unexpectedly on the Friday night, and was at the game with our young sons. When Manus Boyle scored nine points and became man of the match, it suddenly became important to them that their granny was Manus's father's cousin.

We all know how our lives have evolved since, those who are with us, those who have passed on, those who weren't even born at the time.

In the spectators' stands around us there is the whole spectrum of ages from elderly, slow-walking men to newborn babies in mothers' arms. There are so many children dressed in green and gold. Generations of families are leaping to their feet in unison every time a shot is sent towards our goalpost. The experts sitting behind me are roaring conflicting advice. Laurence keeps shouting, 'Who's looking for it?' I believe this is Donegal's year, but my every last nerve is so taut it thrums.

Durcan, McGrath, McGee, McGlynn, Lacey, Thompson, Gallagher, Bradley, Kavanagh, McLoone, McHugh, McBrearty, Murphy, McFadden, Walsh, McElhinney, McLaughlin and Toye. Jim McGuinness' warriors.

Who knew in 1992 that the young player with Spanish Armada darkness would be the manager to carry the challenge? He stands in a black tracksuit – arms crossed, his long, straggly locks now short and greying. His image has become iconic as he replaces Che Guevara and Obama in posters around the county. So much fanatical energy is flowing towards him, but he remains focused. This team have signed contracts, watched their diets, worked with weights and trained with the intensity of professional footballers. Each man works to keep his place on the team. This is the new Donegal.

With time running out and Donegal two points ahead, the press photographers circle around McGuinness. The whistle blows. He leaps in the air. The green and gold go crazy. I hug Laurence, and then anyone I know. I hug a man I don't know. People are cheering, laughing, texting, taking pictures, a girl behind me is sobbing, as down on the pitch the team rejoices. I get a text from Philadelphia and an email from a friend in Toronto. My father says to me, 'Your arms must be sore, every time I looked over at you they were raised in the air!'

The PA system plays 'Jimmy's winning matches, Jimmy's winning games' as we begin to leave the stadium. All around us is elation. This has been a perfect day.

And with that, our thoughts turn to the final and tickets. Tickets! Anyone buying or selling tickets?

(first broadcast on RTÉ Radio in 2012)

MY FIRST ALL-IRELAND
Pat Coleman

As you approach Dublin city from the west, you will surely see a striking landmark soaring into the sky at the town end of the Phoenix Park. It is the Wellington Monument, an obelisk, 205 feet high, which was completed in 1861 to honour the memory of Dublin-born Arthur Wellesley, better known as the Duke of Wellington.

Now when I first saw the Wellington Monument I was completely oblivious to its illustrious history. I was eleven years old, it was 1966 and something much more important was the focus of my attention! I was on my way to my very first All-Ireland Final, my first visit to Croke Park. My father turned our little red Volkswagen off Conyngham Road up into the Phoenix Park, pulling up just a few yards from the monument. The monument itself was not the reason we stopped – it was the fact that there was a park bench there that would serve as our picnic table. My brother, my three sisters and I wasted no time in tucking into the beautiful picnic that my mother had lovingly prepared hours earlier. Ham and cheese sandwiches followed by sweet cake and a flask of tea made a beautiful meal. Then there was time for a quick game of football in the shadow of the monument. No doubt the game was a subconscious effort on our part to emulate the heroics we would witness later in Croke Park.

On to Croke Park then, and we parked our car in Fitzroy Avenue, quite close to the stadium. My father produced his ticket, and the four of us children were lifted over the stile – Health and Safety regulations, which now demand that the tiniest baby must have a ticket, were still a long way in the future. Inside the ground we were treated to a short history lesson. My father showed us the plaque displaying the names of fourteen people who were shot dead in Croke Park by British Soldiers on Bloody Sunday, 21 November, 1920. The dead included the Tipperary footballer Michael Hogan, after whom the Hogan Stand is named.

Up the steps, and we got our first glimpse of the actual pitch. Looking down on it, that pitch seemed like no football pitch we had ever seen! It was greener, larger and perfect in shape and orientation. There were no hills or hollows and, most importantly, the goals had real nets, perfectly hung of course. We sat with our father in 'our' seats until halfway through the minor game, when the official ticket holders arrived. We were then escorted down towards the sideline, where we sat with our backs to a low wall and we were, literally, just yards from the action. As big match time approached, the excitement reached fever pitch. The colour, the atmosphere and the anticipation all combined to create a very special occasion indeed. And when the famous Artane Boys' Band struck up the strains of 'Amhrán na bhFiann,' 60,000 spectators and the thirty athletes on the field stood to attention and faced the tricolour. I remember that as a spine-tingling moment, one of the highlights of the day.

The game itself seemed to pass by in an instant. Our team, Galway, defeated Meath to claim their third All-Ireland in a row.

Further intensifying the sense of pleasure was the fact that our club, Dunmore MacHales, was well represented on the team, with 1960s household names Keenan, Donnellan and Leydon in top form.

As I look back on it now in black and white footage from *Reeling in the Years*, I see the grey ordinariness of a bleak, undeveloped stadium, and the pedestrian nature of the football, but back then it was pure magic! 'Ice-creams here. Tubs of ice-cream, get your ices here!' cried the hawkers as they moved through the spectators. Spectators with unsophisticated flags and crude hats made from crêpe paper showing their county colours all added to our sense of wonder on the day.

I have returned on at least thirty-five occasions to Croke Park, that theatre of dreams, for the All-Ireland Football Final. I always enjoy the occasion, and fondly remember my first time there. And sometimes, to the absolute horror of my now adult children, I even bring the flask and sandwiches and have a little picnic in the shadow of the Wellington Monument!

(first broadcast on RTÉ Radio in 2012)

BANQUET OF DREAMS
Joe Ó Muircheartaigh

It was Bob Dylan who said that Muhammad Ali 'served the world a banquet of dreams.'

This much is very true, but narrowing it down to the local, and it doesn't get much more local than the GAA, it's true to say that Kevin Heffernan also 'served the world a banquet of dreams.'

The GAA world; the world for those of us whose life danced to the beat of the GAA drum.

The treks to Croke Park on winter and summer Sundays. Haggling with the 'lock-hards' looking for the price of a pint for minding our Hillman Hunter.

Climbing in over the stiles for free and soaking it all up.

Croker was a grey old place then, but it had history and it had stories, and it was home to the Dubs.

We loved the place and called it home.

Yes, we also had split personalities in our house. Kerry one day, Dublin the next, Kerry the day after again, and on it went as we grappled with our peculiar predicament.

Dublin-born, yet Kerry-ified from the cradle. Intravenously from a Kerry mother, who had fallen for Seán Murphy the 1955 day when she was in the throng that broke down the gates of the Canal End and saw Kerry beat Dublin in the mother and father of all All-Ireland Finals.

Don't worry, Mam, all the girls fell for Seán Murphy because he was the man, the man for the big day and the big crowd – the Duncan Edwards of the day.

Us Dubs were fed Kerry by my father too, who religiously brought us up to Belfield, week after week, to see Jack O'Shea, John O'Keeffe, Charlie Nelligan and the rest of the Dublin-based Kerry lads train.

We loved it, but we loved the Dubs too, because the Dubs came to our primary school, Scoil Colmcille on Marlborough Street, with the Sam Maguire.

Past pupils Mullins and Kelleher let us hold Sam after the win in 1974, lift it in the air and made us dream of Croke Park.

These were Heffo's heroes. The Jacks were back and we, without or with Kerry blood, saw ourselves as being the newest recruits to Heffo's Army.

The Hill and the way it heaved – it became our Kop, way better than the one Bill Shankly built across the water in Liverpool.

It was all because of Heffo. The team he built from nothing, the team that were an extension of himself.

Tough and uncompromising, yet with a swagger that seduced a city over a few years and provided the GAA with a transfusion that has sustained it to the present day.

With the Dubs under Heffo it was rock'n'roll. It was theatre. It was sulphur. Dublin versus Kerry. Jackeen versus Culchie.

They didn't like each other, yet they only really existed because of one another.

And it was Heffo who started it all, taking a team of misfits and transforming them into the biggest things to ever hit the GAA.

As a journalist, I always wanted to interview him, but he didn't do many interviews, yet he was one of the most easily accessible county managers, whether past or present. His phone number was in the book.

I'd met him a few times down the years – nearly thirty years ago at Shelbourne Park dog track when my uncle Mícheál introduced him an to American cousin of ours as 'the greatest manager in the world.'

Another time was in the ESB, where he worked alongside my other uncle Paddy for many years.

Through them, I got the interview.

The Berkeley Court Hotel was the meeting place. We were about to sit down and talk when Heffo said, 'have you a car?'

'Yes,' I said.

'Then let's go. Follow me.'

Off we went, down towards Lansdowne Road and on to Grand Canal Street, Pearse Street and across Butt Bridge to the north side.

I thought we were heading for Croker, but I was mistaken – it as out to Fairview and up the old Malahide Road to St Vincent's.

There he sat on the high stool drinking coffee for an hour, and talked football. The Dubs. St Vincent's. As a player being beaten by Kerry in 1955, what it was like to finally beat them as a manager in 1976.

But it was his hurling story that showed the greatness of the man – and showed away from the glamour of All-Ireland Final day what the GAA was really about.

The Club. The grass roots.

A few years earlier, himself and another legend, Des Foley, put their hands up at a Vincent's AGM and enlisted for duty – it wasn't the glamour senior team, but the Junior Four team, then the lowest rung of the hurling ladder in the county leagues.

'We got them,' said Heffo, 'and we started working on them, and at the end of the year we won the championship.'

He said the satisfaction both himself and Foley got out of seeing the team progress was as good as any All-Ireland.

That was pure class, Heffo was pure class.

He served those junior hurlers a banquet of dreams.

(first broadcast on RTÉ Radio January 2013)

YERRA
Maurice Cashell

Terry Dolan's *A Dictionary of Hiberno-English* is a fabulous cornucopia of words, phrases, proverbs and sayings in English as it is spoken and written in Ireland. Some are rarely heard, others are alive and evolving. One such is the word 'yerra' that, according to Professor Dolan, expresses mild disbelief or surprise or indifference. Maybe. Much depends on how you say it.

My father, from Tralee, resented his exile to the Midlands, the only place where he could get a teaching job in the mid-1930s. For him, there was only the Kingdom.

Anois teacht an Earraigh beidh 'n lá 'dul chun síneadh,
'S taréis na Féil Bríde, ardóidh mé mo sheol.

He'd say at Christmas, quoting Raftery the Poet, 'We'll go home for Easter.'

A 300-mile round trip for a family of six in a 1950 Ford Anglia was no picnic, but for us it was the stuff of adventure. Ten miles from home, just before Athlone, we'd head south at Cornamaddy School, and from that point on we were on the Road to Kerry, our own personal Yellow Brick Road, proverbial path to hopes and dreams. It was a road rich in images: the transmission pylons of Radió Éireann. The tuning dial of a radio of that time had a multitude of broadcasting stations from around Northern Europe. Athlone was up there with Beromunster, Hilversum, Luxembourg, Droitwich, Warsaw and Moscow. Passing the pylons linked us to far-away places. We picnicked at the Silvermine

Mountains, forever trying to bring about a detour so that we could try our luck at finding some silver. The last ritual halt was a pub on the Limerick–Kerry border, where my father would stop for his first pint. Raftery provided poetic licence:

I gClár Chlainne Mhuiris bhéas mé an chéad oíche,
'S i mBalla taobh thíos de thosós mé ag ól.

We'd roll into Tralee about teatime. When everybody was seated, Granny would launch into the annual update: who was dead; who was sick; who had emigrated; who had bought and sold land. Once our ears were attuned to the accent we began to discern words and phrases unusual in our house: 'wisha,' 'wirrasthru,' 'whisht,' 'avic,' 'moryah,' 'bad cess to them,' 'her and her figaries.' There was a liberal sprinkling of 'Yerra's. Grandfather, who spent his entire working life as a gardener in the Bon Secours Convent, was quiet and withdrawn. But before bedtime he'd bring me out to the front gate to reassure me that the mountains were still at the end of the street, and that when I was a bit bigger we'd climb to the very top.

It never happened. When I was about nine, we were told he was dying. We went to Kerry to say goodbye. I don't remember it as particularly traumatic. What I do recall is being told that he had a special present for me. I had visions of a new football. Or money. He produced five or six tennis balls and pushed them into my hands.

'I kept them for you,' he said.

They were old, moth-eaten, bald and empty of bounce. My mother caught my disappointed eye, tossed her head and whispered 'yerra.'

On one of those trips we visited a hotel somewhere in West Kerry. While my father and his brother visited the bar, I sat in the dining-room with my lemonade and biscuits. There were photographs around the walls. Kerry football teams. My father had played with Kerry in 1933 and 1934. What if his photo was on the wall and he didn't know about it? I searched enthusiastically, but couldn't find his teams. I asked the waiter about the missing photos.

'Yer Da, I suppose,' said he.

'Yeah,' I said, 'he played with Kerry.'

'Win an All-Ireland, then?'

'No.'

'Yerra.'

And off he went with his tray, collecting salt cellars and bottles of brown sauce. Never was a word so full of meaning. This was Kerry. No medal, no fame. No fame, no photo.

The last time we travelled together to Kerry I was in my early teens. Daytime I accompanied my father to his favourite beaches or walked with him the mountains of my forebears. Most evenings I kicked football with the lads on the local green. One evening, as we passed the Bons Secours Convent, one of them pointed it out and said:

'There was a gardener there once who kept every ball that went over that fence. A right bosthoon. Never threw them back. Can't remember his name.'

I know what you're thinking. Did I volunteer the information that the gardener was my grandfather? That their lost balls were my inheritance?

Yerra!

(first broadcast on RTÉ Radio in 2013)

DUBLIN'S LAST SENIOR HURLING ALL-IRELAND IN 1938

William Nolan

By 1938, Dublin had won the All-Ireland Senior Hurling Championship on five occasions: 1889, 1917, 1920, 1924 and 1927. In the same period, the county had won fourteen All-Ireland Senior Football Championships, suggesting that football was a more popular and successful sport than hurling. Dublin was represented by its champion clubs: Kickhams, Collegians and Faughs, in its first three All-Ireland victories, but the focus changed thereafter from the county champions to players drawn from all clubs. In 1936, Dublin City, in which the hurling clubs were concentrated, had a population of 367,364, of whom 119,693 were born outside the county. Hurling drew its recruits mainly from the hurling counties of Leinster and Munster, with Galway providing the western contingent. Hurlers worked as civil servants, teachers, garda, what Seán O'Casey referred to as 'cushy jobs.' They could also be in the army or students in UCD.

In the 1920s, hurling in Dublin had been dominated by Eoin O'Duffy's Garda team, which was so successful that it was voluntarily disbanded for fear of discouraging less successful clubs. Kilkenny please take note in 2013. By 1938, the county team had players from seven clubs: Army Metro, Faughs, Young Ireland, Eoghan Ruadh, New Ireland, UCD and the revived Garda. Dublin advanced to the Leinster Final against Kilkenny, its perennial rivals and constant conquerors at a time when there was only one door in the championship house.

The first match was drawn. Kilkenny, perhaps for tactical rather than spiritual reasons, attempted to have the replay delayed, claiming that the date fixed coincided with the annual pilgrimage of the diocese of Ossory, in which the county was located, to Blessed Oliver Plunkett's shrine at Drogheda. The match went ahead, and Dublin won on the score of 4–9 to 3–5. Pat O,' pen-name of Patrick D. Mehigan – greatest of all GAA commentators – reported: 'Dublin were far the better trained team: they outstripped Kilkenny in every race to the ball, and their brilliant early opening was never seriously challenged.'

Dublin were through to the All-Ireland Final, in which its surprise opponents were Waterford. Tipperary, All-Ireland champions in 1937, had been installed as favourites, but had been suspended after the Central Council upheld an objection by Clare, who Tipperary had beaten, that the Tipperary team played Jimmy Cooney, who was under suspension for breaching Rule Twenty-Seven: the Ban – after having been spotted by a vigilante attending an international rugby match on 12 February.

The All-Ireland Final was played in a revamped Croke Park. Hill 16 had been terraced, and the double-decker Cusack Stand had been officially opened on 21 August 1938. The purists, accustomed to watching Kilkenny, Tipperary, Cork and Limerick, were unimpressed with the standard of hurling. The *Irish Press* report observed:

> … stylish play on the Kilkenny or Limerick model was absent. The ball scarcely left the ground at times, and the play was cramped and somewhat dull, stoppages were frequent, and the St John's Ambulance men were called with monotonous regularity.

Pat O' s verdict was:

> Jim Byrne of Eoghan Ruadh, a native of Dublin and a product of the city school's hurling was the best of the lot.

Forde kept a good goal, Gill and Farrell with Byrne completed a half-line on which Dublin's victory hinged, they had Waterford's attack in a vice.

Indeed, a photograph in the *Irish Press* showed Charlie MacMahon of Young Irelands and Dublin with Sean Feeney, his Waterford opponent, in such a vice grip. MacMahon, a dual player, had a steel plate in his head because of a wound received during the attack on the Custom House in 1921.

Dublin won its sixth, and sadly its last, All-Ireland Senior Hurling Championship on the score of 2–5 to 1–6. Dublin's goals were scored by Mark Flynn, the garda, and Bill Loughnane, the medical student at UCD. Bill, subsequently a Fianna Fáil TD for Clare, had a son, Tony, who played for UCD and Dublin in the 1960s, and Ger Loughnane, their kinsman, was to manage the Clare teams of 1995 and 1997 to All-Ireland victories.

Major Tom McGrath, Dublin team mentor and former county chairman, had played for Clare in the 1914 All-Ireland, and had been a member of the East Clare Brigade of the IRA. He also served as chairman of the Dublin County Board. The trainers were Mick Mockler and Barney Crosby, a fitness expert. Harry Gray, the blacksmith from Rathdowney and greatest Laois hurler of all time, played at centre field for Dublin. He was to play with Faughs from 1937 to 1954, and was centre forward for Laois in the All-Ireland of 1949. Both captains, Mick Daniels of Dublin and Mick Hickey of Waterford, were natives of Carrick-on-Suir, but Hickey was on the Waterford side of the river. Daniels played with such intensity that he physically collapsed and had to be substituted in the second half. There is a wonderful photograph of him with the Liam McCarthy Cup, and his four young sons around him shyly glancing at their father-hero.

Jim Byrne remains the only Dublin-born hurler who played on an All-Ireland Senior Hurling winning team. There were others who lost out. Mick Leahy, also of Eoghan Ruadh, was injured for the final. Tommy Treacy of Young Irelands had played for Dublin in 1934–5, but then declared Tipperary his native county, as did Ned Wade of Faughs. Both were sidelined when Dublin, with whom they would have been automatic selections, won through. Such were the vagaries of the infamous 'declaration rule' that caused so much disruption to Dublin hurling. Dublin contested All-Ireland Finals in 1941, 1942, 1944, 1948, 1952 and 1961, but 1938 remains the last time the county lifted the Liam McCarthy Cup.

(first broadcast on RTÉ Radio in 2013)

FATHER, SON AND SLIEVENAMON
William J. Smyth

I learned to play hurling with my four brothers in the fields around our farmhouse in North Tipperary. We played for hours, imagining ourselves as the heroes of that era: Joe Salmon of Galway, Pat Stakelum and Tommy Doyle of Tipperary or Nicky Rackard of Wexford. My mother knew that a match was over when one of us came in crying from the well-field; a match would end more quickly when the ball crashed through the parlour window. Which reminds me of the mother of the three famous Rackard brothers admonishing her sons 'not to hurl by the dairy door.' We put together scrapbooks of hurling heroes, and competed again at night to name correctly the famous Tipperary teams that won three All-Irelands from 1949 to 1951, or the teams of their opponents. We listened avidly to Micheál O'Hehir's radio broadcasts. My mother said that I always kept careful note of the scores when Tipperary were winning, but that my pen dropped when Cork or Wexford surged ahead.

I got my first taste of Croke Park in September 1962, when we played the Minor Hurling Final against Kilkenny. It was a brilliant feeling to run onto that famous pitch and enter that special arena of sound and sporting combat. A year and a half later, in March 1964, we – UCD, that is – won a great Fitzgibbon Final, defeating the holders, UCC, in Croke Park. The body memory of that event is still intact. Croke Park was flooded with sunshine, and the sod was perfect as I took up my right corner back position under the Cusack Stand. That September I was back in Croke Park, this time on the sidelines as a far-out sub on the Tipperary senior team that defeated Kilkenny in the 1964 All-Ireland. Twenty years later, the Gaelic Athletic Association decided that the centenary All-Ireland should be played in Thurles, where the GAA was founded in 1884.

All of Tipperary wanted their countymen to get to and win this special All-Ireland. Cork stood in the way. My son Cormac – then nine years of age – accompanied me to Thurles for that 1984 Munster Final. He was decked out in the red and white of Cork, while in blue shirt and yellow tie, I – if a little less overtly – supported my home county. We went to live in Cork in 1977, and Cormac and his brother Neil grew up in that sporting city. I always encouraged them to support their own county, and that they did with a vengeance. Their sister Peigín – not so passionate about hurling perhaps or more strategic perhaps– kept closer to her father in matters of county loyalty. (Until she married a Corkman, that is!) It was as usual a great and fiercely contested game. With a few minutes to go, I was so confident of a Tipp win that I tried to speak sympathetically to Cormac, noting how crestfallen he was. Then the Tipp goalie, reaching high to bring down a certain point, saw the inrushing Seánie O'Leary flash the ball into the net, and Cork were back in the match. As Tipperary's midfield faltered, Cork surged ahead to victory. It was my turn to be crestfallen. As we left Semple Stadium, this young nine-year-old Cork supporter told me: 'Ye weren't good enough anyway.' Not a word of sympathy from my son. Yet it was a good moment as father and son diverged. A young boy was carving out his own separate identity.

A Tipp victory came three years later in the famous replay in Killarney. Nicholas English, under enormous pressure and with a possible goal in the offing, wisely handpassed the ball over the bar to earn a draw for Tipp at the end of normal time. In extra time, a youthful Tipperary team outplayed a Cork team that had dominated Munster hurling for some years. It took ages, it seems, for the Tipperary players to reach the victor's rostrum as their blue and gold supporters swarmed around them.

Cormac and I joined the carnival occasion on the streets of Killarney as the Tipp contingent celebrated and the Cork supporters – gallant as always – joined in to tell their stories and sing their songs. Tales of Munster Final battles were recalled; of the rivalry between Cork's ageless Christy Ring and the peerless Tipp. goalie Tony Reddan; how Ring flashed the sliotar past Reddan into the net only for Reddan to double on the ball as it rebounded off the back staunchon and send it flying up the field. The umpires never noticed. Only Ring and Reddan knew, and Ring's protests went in vain. Or the story of the newly elected TD for Cork, Jack Lynch, thundering into Reddan's territory and giving the goalkeeper a heavy shoulder before disappearing swiftly. Reddan could not follow him, but with an angry stutter instructed the nearby Ring to warn Lynch that if he, Lynch, ever invaded Reddan's territory again, there would be an 'effin by-election in Cork.' The stories and banter helped Cormac to recover. On the way home, we stopped for a meal on the Cork–Kerry border, and I asked Cormac when did he know that Cork were beaten. 'When they sang "Slievenamon",' he said. And that was a full ten minutes after the final whistle.

(first broadcast on RTÉ Radio in 2013)

Clíodhna Ní Anluain

282

HOW TO SCORE IN HOTPANTS
Martina Devlin

'That's what you're wearing to the Ulster Final?' My father stared at my mother in disbelief.

She had just walked downstairs in a new pair of hot pants, looking modern and cool – in both senses of the word – on a scorching July day.

Except it was 1973 in small-town Ireland, and hot pants were considered risqué – this pair were sent to her by a fashionable sister-in-law in London.

A toss of my glamorous mother's head. 'What's wrong with them?'

My father took a step back to study the hot pants. They were chocolate brown, with a bib at the front and crossover braces at the back, teamed with a long-sleeved blouse in a psychedelic pattern. Although not particularly clinging, they showed a generous expanse of leg. Shapely leg, it should be noted, despite their orange covering of American Tan tights, which were all the rage.

'There's nothing wrong with them, as such. You look very nice. But we're going to the Ulster Final.'

'And?'

'And you're dressed for the beach, not a football stand. You'll be a distraction from the game,' he said.

'Don't be silly. Not even the Last Trumpet could distract any of you GAA men once the teams line out.'

'It's just not right,' he wailed.

'I know it's not right. The sun's splitting the stones – we should be going to Bundoran, not Clones. The children ought to be building sandcastles, not stuck in the middle of a crowd at a GAA game.'

'But how can we go to Bundoran when Tyrone are in the Ulster Final?'

'Fine, let's go to the final. The children are ready. I'm ready. The picnic's ready. You're the one keeping everybody waiting.' And she lifted her cream and brown leather shoulder-bag – even for a GAA fixture, colour co-ordination was never compromised – and shepherded all seven of her goggling offspring outside.

My father knew when he was beaten. He gathered up the flask of tea, bottle of Robertson's barley water, egg sandwiches and packet of custard creams, which always featured on our picnic menu, and followed her out to the car.

I brooded in the back seat. Mortification was waiting in Cavan. It happened every time my mother wore one of her London outfits. Men would be looking at her – men who weren't my father.

He might be resigned to it. Perhaps secretly proud of it. But I certainly wasn't. Mothers ought to wear floral sun dresses and cardigans. Mine was adjusting her Jackie O sunglasses, and adding *another* layer of red lipstick.

We reached the stadium in Clones, and eight people emerged from the tank-like Austin 1300. I stayed put.

My father did an inventory, and realised one of his children was missing. His head poked back into the car. 'Hurry up, there's a queue at the gate.'

'Don't want to go,' I said.

'But Tyrone are playing.'

Mutinous, I bunkered down. I couldn't help having a mother who looked sensational in racy (by Omagh standards) London fashions, but I wasn't obliged to sit beside her in public. 'I want to stay in the car with my library book.' As corroboration, *Little House on the Prairie* was brandished.

My father shuffled his straw trilby round his forehead. 'I suppose there's no harm in someone keeping an eye on the car.' He was always convinced it was a target for vandals and carjackers.

'It'll be hot in there – she could get heatstroke,' my mother objected.

'Open your window – not too much – and keep all the doors locked,' my father instructed.

And so it was that I experienced my first and last Ulster Final, without seeing it, from the inside of a car outside St Tiernach's Park. There was drama, tension and excitement – but I had to guess at their sources.

The loudspeaker conveyed a string of words that couldn't be separated out to indicate sense. And while the roars and groans from the crowd signified a score made or missed, it was impossible to tell whether Down or Tyrone had been lucky or unlucky. Occasionally I caught sight of the ball kicked high above the goalposts for a point – but on which side?

At half-time, an older brother delivered a sandwich and a drink. 'Daddy says do you want to come in for the second half?'

I did. There was scant satisfaction in staging a lone protest against hot pants – and not just them, but against her entire wardrobe of unmotherly clothes – when I lacked the language, never mind the courage, to explain why I objected.

Headstrong, however, I wasn't for turning. I stayed where I was.

Afterwards, the family surged back to the car park in high humour, with Tyrone lifting the Anglo-Celt Cup for the first time in sixteen years. The Red Hand men were through to the All-Ireland Semi-Finals.

To celebrate, we stopped off for sliders before crossing the border, raspberry ripple ice-cream melting over fingers, clothes and upholstery.

A blob fell on my mother's knee, and my father mopped it up with his handkerchief. '3–11 to 1–11 to Tyrone.' Contentment radiated from him. 'Now, wasn't that better than the beach?'

'It wasn't bad,' she allowed. 'But we'll go to Bundoran next weekend.'

'Anything you say, honey bunch.'

I fumed nearby, mystified at how easily he was beguiled by a pair of hot pants. I'd never grow up to wear clothes that disgraced children or manipulated men, I vowed. Although, after a few years passed, that's exactly what I longed to do.

(first broadcast on RTÉ Radio in 2013)

SEPTEMBER 1982
Paul Rouse

The very last part of the ball is about to turn under the cross-bar down at the Railway End goals. The raindrops will soon be shaking from the net. Charlie Nelligan will be on the ground in a heap, and the umpire will reach for the green flag. Seamus Darby will launch into a joyous jig, and the man in the yellow oilskin jacket in the old sideline seats in front of the Hogan Stand will join him.

The man in the yellow oilskin jacket is my father. Beside him is my younger brother David. The two of them are already standing as the ball enters the goal. Others are climbing out of their seats all around. This is the goal that will win the 1982 All-Ireland Football Final for Offaly: the most famous one-in-a-row in GAA history.

Colman Doyle caught the moment in a photograph taken from in front of Hill 16. I've brought that photograph to every place I've lived in. It is that most rare of things: a moment caught in time when you see your dreams about to be made real.

A few minutes later, the final whistle has blown and Offaly fans have breached the wire in front of the Hogan Stand. There's a glorious wildness to the crowd. The man in the yellow oilskins is running around in a manic state, drawing the TV cameras after him: who knows what he's trying to do, but it's great fun watching him do it. It's also great fun looking for my brother and not seeing him: my father has lost him (or forgotten him) in the madness. No harm: that should have been me in the sideline seat beside my father!

Away from the cameras, I'm out on the field also. I see my mother and I head towards her. Before I get there, Seamus Darby picks her up and throws her in the air. And then he does it again. He's from Rhode and she's from Rhode, and no further explanation is needed. Seamus Darby has just scored the greatest goal of all time to win the greatest match of all time to beat the greatest team of all time.

And then it ends. I don't remember the presentation of the cup, or the speeches, or talking to anyone. All I remember after that is my mother throwing myself and my brothers into our car, and driving us out to Finglas. My grandfather lived there. Dick Conroy was known in his home village of Rhode, and in certain parts of London, as 'The Boiler.' He was a huge man, great fun and recklessly devoted to the GAA, especially to Offaly football. He had played on the first minor team fielded by Offaly in 1928, and had been a selector on the Offaly team defeated by Kerry in the 1969 All-Ireland Final. He was my hero, and I was definitely his favourite, and he spoiled me magnificently.

When we arrived to the house, he was overcome by emotion; great tears streamed down his face, one after the next. He hugged my mother and hugged all of us. I was twelve, and I couldn't understand why he was crying; I understand now and I think of him whenever I see people crying after winning a match. It's about the match, and about much more than the match.

He died two summers later of a broken heart. My nana had died eight weeks previously, and he just didn't have any interest in living without her. He was brought home to Rhode to be buried. Generations of footballers came up to pay their respects in a long, snaking line. In that line were men he had played football with and brought to football matches and given jobs to – and men from the Offaly 1982 team.

When the coffin left the back door of the church to be brought to the graveyard, a small group of men – amongst them Dermot O'Brien and Billy Cashin – draped the coffin in the flag of Round Towers, the club my granddad had been so involved in when he lived in London. They had come over from London for the funeral in the middle of the week when it wasn't cheap or easy to do so; the more I remember that act, the more wonderful I think it is. The Round Towers flag lay beside the Offaly and the Rhode jerseys on that last journey.

That evening, after the funeral, the pubs of Rhode overflowed with drink. All the while, myself and my brothers and my cousins played football on a lawn in the village beside the Murphys' house. It was a warm summer's night, and we played for hours. We weren't dreaming of September Sundays or thinking about The Boiler, just playing football.

(first broadcast on RTÉ Radio in 2013)

WEARING THE BLUE OF DUBLIN
Tim Carey

It was thirty-two years before I was finally able to bring myself to put on a Dublin jersey, to publicly express my allegiance to my county, to nail those blue colours to that proverbial mast. It's not that I was ashamed to do so; far from it. It was that I did not feel, well, qualified.

If you met me, there would be little to tell you that I was not born in Dublin, that I was not a Dub through and through. I am both well disguised and comprehensively assimilated. But I do know that part of me is different.

The reason for this is that I came to Ireland in 1979 at the age of twelve from Milwaukee, Wisconsin, USA. In America, my family was not part of any Irish community, and I had virtually no exposure to Gaelic games. When we upped sticks and came across the Atlantic, my games of choice were basketball, American football and baseball. Teams called the Bucks, the Packers and the Brewers, rather than the Dubs, were the subjects of my devotion.

But I soon developed an early affinity with the city in which I lived, and also its great Gaelic football team. Living in Blackrock in south Dublin and going to Newpark Comprehensive, where Gaelic games were not played, it was only in 1983 that I made my first visit to Croke Park to see the infamous bad-tempered final between Dublin and Galway, which Dublin won.

In my later years in school, I became friends with Stephen Ladd, whose sister married John O'Leary, the then Dublin goalkeeper and captain. Through Stephen, I became a regular attendee of Dublin games. Croke Park and the Dubs became part of my summers – I even played five-a-side matches with members of the Dublin team. Although I woke on big match days as nervous and excited as anyone else, there was no question of me putting on a Dublin jersey. In my head, I remained an outsider to this world.

When Dublin reached their next final in 1995, and played against Tyrone, my girlfriend Sinéad and I, unable to secure tickets, watched it in Meagher's pub in Fairview. After the match, the place heaved with celebrating Dublin supporters, almost all dressed in blue, matching the canopy of the early evening sky. Then, out of the blue, as it were, the Dublin team appeared on the roof of Meagher's holding the Sam Maguire trophy aloft in triumph – knights bringing back a holy relic. As that evening wound down, John O'Leary, captain, gave Sinéad and I a lift across the city. I sat in front talking with the winning All-Ireland Captain just hours after the victory, while Sinéad sat in the back with, believe it or not, the Sam Maguire cup beside her.

Even after this experience, I still did not feel qualified to wear a Dublin top.

My 'Americanness' receded with each passing year. I was in the immigrant's limbo, no longer American, but not yet, and perhaps never would be, Irish. Symptomatic of that confusion was that I would sometimes wear the blue shirt of my old Milwaukee baseball team to show my allegiance to Dublin.

In 2000, after I had been working at various heritage sites – including Kilmainham Gaol – for a number of years, I had the good fortune to be put in charge of the GAA Museum in Croke Park. A strong interest in the games, their history, cultural significance and Irish heritage in general saw me overcome what might have been perceived as potential shortcomings: I'd never played the games, went to a Protestant school and did not speak Irish. When I got the job, I was reminded of the 1980s ad in which young members of a band met with a music promoter who tells them, 'You can't sing. You can't dance. You look awful. You'll go a long way.'

After being in charge of the most important artefacts of the GAA's history, and helping to interpret that history to the Museum's visitors, you'd think I wouldn't have had a problem wearing that top, but still I couldn't. In fact, I never even tried one on. My friend Stephen could not understand my reluctance. I knew as much about the game as many, was as vociferous as any and more disappointed than most when Dublin lost. But that was not the point. Those people around me were Dubs, and I was not.

Then I wrote a book on the history of Croke Park. While I felt honoured that people thought I was qualified to put down the history of what is an icon of Irish cultural life, I remained, in my own mind, underqualified to wear that jersey.

I eventually married Sinéad who had travelled in the car with the Sam Maguire in 1995. We have had two children. Before children, I, like most people, had no idea of the impact they could have on one's life. But from the moment I looked into my daughter's eyes in the very minute she was born, and felt that connection only a parent can feel, I knew my life had changed.

My children Jennifer and Aaron have 'settled me' in a way I find hard to describe. Having them has resolved many internal conflicts caused by the circumstances of my life. They have helped to define me, but also helped me to define myself. And that even came down to wearing the jersey of a sports team.

Both of them play for Cuala GAA club, and when Sinéad and I started bringing them to Dublin matches, they, of course, wore the jersey. As they got a little older, they wanted to know why their Dad did not do the same. They did not comprehend the reason for my reticence. When I tried to explain, my reasoning sounded, even to myself, as hollow hubris. Whenever we headed into Croker they wanted me to be fully part of their world, and were disappointed that I refused.

So, when Dublin played Donegal in the 2011 All-Ireland Semi-Final, I, at last, put on the top. When I met Stephen he smiled at the sight of me. Walking into the stadium and taking our seats in the Cusack Stand, I have rarely felt more self-conscious. I believed people were looking at me, saying to themselves: 'He can't wear that. He's not allowed. How dare he?' But no one said anything. I wondered why I had resisted, but knew that these things sometimes just take time.

The next match was that final against Kerry. It was a match in which years of pain for the Dublin supporter melted away as Stephen Cluxton's free floated over the bar. And at that moment I was part of the mass of blue that shook the stadium to its very core.

(first broadcast on RTÉ Radio in 2013)

REBELS AT THE DOUBLE
Bert Wright

The writer Andrew O'Hagan has said that 'a novelist is someone who might respond professionally to the sound of a
piano in another room.' The remark was aimed at his creative
writing students, encouraging them to seek inspiration in everyday sensory experience, but surely this can happen to any one of
us. A scent, a sound, a conversation overheard, a snatch of music,
can make an impression on the memory much deeper than the
weight of its fleeting occurrence.

For me, the sound of a piano in another room instantly
conjures up the memory of a house in Cork City in 1990. I had
been invited to the home of Éamonn Young, a Cork footballing
legend and retired Army officer with whom I was collaborating
on a book to celebrate the Rebel County's historic double-
winning season. We were taking a break, and Éamonn's wife
Monica had just brought in tea before leaving us to discuss the
work-in-progress.

Moments later, I was stopped in mid-sentence by the achingly
sweet sound of voice and piano echoing through the old house.
That the piano accompaniment was halting and arthritic only
added to the melancholy of the moment as Monica's tremulous
soprano hovered over that loveliest of Moore's melodies, 'The
Last Rose of Summer.' Éamonn set down his tea and raised a
forefinger, urging me to listen. I was listening already. Would she,
I wondered, risk the high note in the last line, 'Oh! Who would

inhabit this bleak world alone!' She did, and nailed it effortlessly. Éamonn beamed with pride. Monica soon joined us, and spoke fondly of the musical career her talent might have promised, a talent recognised by no less a figure than Count John McCormack, whom she had met as a young woman.

Meeting Éamonn, or Youman Young, as he was sometimes known, was equally fortunate for me. The journalist who had agreed to write the book withdrew at the last minute, and, ever-willing, Éamonn had stepped into the breach. No man was better qualified for the job; not alone had he won an All-Ireland football medal with Cork in 1945, he had also trained the team and served as a county selector. Under the *nom de plume* 'Rambler,' he had been writing a GAA column for the *Echo* and the *Cork Examiner* for many years. 'Youman's yer only man' was the advice I was given, and never had I cause to regret acting upon it.

In the early stages, the book progressed at a funereal pace; unsurprising really, since Éamonn had to hammer out his copy on the most antiquated typewriter in all of Munster. Several letters were bockety, or missing altogether, so the manuscript often took on the appearance of a failed text message. I came to dread the phone calls from the poor confused editor in Edinburgh. 'What does he mean here? Is he speaking Irish?' 'Leave it with me, I'll ask him.' Éamonn would laugh, apologise and blame the wretched typewriter, but the no-nonsense declarative prose and the love of Ireland's native games invariably shone through.

As the weeks passed, the manuscript pages kept coming. Every Friday, Éamonn would march into Waterstone's, where I worked, with the latest sheaf of pages in a crisp manila envelope. He would refuse to leave them at the cash register, insisting that he would hand them over to nobody but *Mr Wright*. This infuriated the staff, who resented being treated like mere underlings, but, being a military man, Éamonn would only deal with the officer class. Then, having offered his customary violent handshake, he'd be off up to Collins Barracks for a game of squash or along to Jury's for his swim. Thirty years his junior, I often felt as if the opposite were true.

In the scale of holy miracles, producing the book in time for the Christmas market must rank alongside the ultimate Christmas miracle. But whether by divine intervention or the industry of the Scottish publisher, the first finished copies finally arrived and *Rebels at the Double* was soon flying out of every bookshop in Cork City, primarily out of Waterstone's, who were permitted to display the Sam Maguire and Liam McCarthy Cups in the shop window.

The launch party, hosted by Waterstone's, was attended by the High Kings of Cork football and hurling, including the captains Tomás Mulcahy and Larry Tompkins, and a formidable priest, who seemed to command such deference he might have been the Holy Father himself. Tall and solid with a leonine head and a thick mane of grey hair on him, Fr O'Brien, I later discovered, was the coach of the senior hurlers and the doyen of Cork hurling. Youman was duly honoured by his peers, and the whiskey consumed that night would have flooded the banks of their own Lovely Lee.

Rebels at the Double went on to become a bestseller and, by 24 December, every home in Cork City and County must have owned a copy, the very last copies being fought over with the grim determination known only to the last-minute Christmas shopper.

By the summer of 1991, I had left Cork for America, but not before bidding my old friend Éamonn Young farewell. He was full of praise for the virtues of travel, and wished me well, declaring that together we had done the Republic of Cork some service by commemorating their double-winning season in prose. When I returned to Dublin, I often felt inclined to pay Éamonn a visit, but the exigencies of raising a young family intervened, and I regret to say I never did. His beloved Monica predeceased him, which must have been a bitter blow, but Youman, one of the noblest Corkmen of them all, lived to the ripe old age of eighty-six, and his long innings was richly deserved.

Recently, I heard Nina Simone sing her wonderful version of the 'Last Rose of Summer,' and immediately I was transported back to that house in Cork where, warmed by the glow of good conversation and John Jameson's finest, I had whiled away the hours in the company of two fine oldsters. I slept the sleep of the righteous, and awoke woozily in a strange bed in the Young's spare room, but I've never forgotten Éamonn, Monica, and the sound of a piano in another room.

(first broadcast on RTÉ Radio in 2013)

YE'LL MAKE IT TO CROKER YET
Joe Ó Muircheartaigh

There have been a few occasions over the past three decades and more that I've woken up worried from a nightmare that happened on Jones's Road way back in the fall of 1978.

And in those few seconds after it's over, the events seem as real, current and important as they were way back then – somehow your senses are on high alert, you see the things in the minutiae by being transported back to being that ten-year-old when everything has just gone wrong.

What you worked for, what the team worked for, what the school worked for, what the school saw as its vocation, birthright and real purpose in life. What all the trips to Fairview Park, the Phoenix Park's Fifteen Acres and the Whitehall pitches on the old airport road were for.

Football. And getting to play in Croke Park – and winning there.

It was deep in the second half, and Scoil Colmcille on Marlborough Street were finally footballing the dream. Playing in a Cumann na mBunscol final in Croker, the same field and over the same blades of grass that Mikey Sheehy and Brian Mullins and company had played ball on a few months earlier.

Given the chance, we'd have have got down on our knees and eaten the grass.

It was cold, it was wet, but this was as close to nirvana as made no difference. We were attacking the Cnoc 1916 end, and as we did, we imagined the phalanx of blue rockin 'n' rollin' to our every move, thrust, catch and kick.

The Cnoc would guide us home to the Cumann na mBunscol Division Four title, and we'd be climbing the steps of the Ard Comhairle to lift the cup and fill it afterwards with lemonde and feast on legs and wings of Pat Grace's finest chicken, which we were told came all the way from Kentucky, even though it was probably more like Kinnegad.

It was there for us, it really was, as we chased down what was history and immortality in our own eyes. But more than that, winning would make real what Brian Mullins and Robbie Kelleher had first told us would happen a few years earlier.

Mullins and Kelleher were our heroes because they belonged to us – we pinned posters of them to our wall instead of the Bay City Rollers, Liverpool or Leeds United.

They were iar-scoláirí who'd first learned to kick ball in the clós that separated Scoil Colmcille from the Model Schools that were also ensconced in the Department of Education Grounds on Marlborough Street.

They were there in the 1960s, but in 1974 came back to their Scoil Colmcille roots with some very special cargo in hand.

Sam Maguire.

Our principal and teacher Aodh Ó Ruairc got them to call by – Aodh was a famous man in his own right, as for decades his was the voice of authority that came over the Croke Park tannoys on All-Ireland Final day heralding the teams onto the field.

He did the same in September 1974, announcing Mullins and Kelleher's arrival as every pupil in the school packed into the one pre-fab.

I can still see Mullins and Kelleher now – two Gods and giants of men, both of whom seemed to belong more to Rome's Coliseum or a hippodrome in Olympia than a small pre-fab in inner-city Dublin.

And with their long locks and flairs they were rock stars, who by their words, their mere presence in the same pre-fab, giving us attention, made us dream. Of All-Irelands. Of Croke Park.

'Ye'll make Croke Park yet,' they said. At once we never doubted ourselves. These were the same words Mullins and Kelleher imparted once more in 1976 and 1977 after Sam Maguire came home to the Hill in those years too. Still we believed.

Then finally it happened on that December day in 1978.

This was our All-Ireland. Togging out in the same dressing-room as the Dubs under the old Cusack Stand with its wooden-panelled walls. Walking down the tunnel, then taking a deep breath, holding it and sprinting out onto the field with a determination that marked us down as having been born for this day.

This is what we believed, until it all went wrong that is, in the second half.

A few seconds was all it took. We had our opponents on the rack, and a goal would have tipped the balance in our favour, but when the chance finally came into the Cnoc 1916 goal, Scoil Colmcille's great misfortune was that it fell to me.

And what a chance it was! One on one with the keeper. What to do? Jimmy Keaveny would side-foot it home with Georgie Best-like nonchalance; David Hickey would go for power; Kevin Moran would drop-kick it, while Tony Hanahoe would palm to the net and than wheel away in triumph.

Sadly, I managed none of the above, instead I bottled it, by trying to punch a point. That was bad enough, but when it went wide and the ball dribbled to a stop against the fencing on Cnoc 1916, our chance was lost. Forever.

In the middle of the nightmare, that's the most vivid image of all – the goal that never was, the climbing of the Ard Comhairle steps that never was, the lifting of the cup that never was, the lemonade we never got to drink and Pat Grace's fried chicken we never got to eat.

But hey, that's not really what it's about.

It's about those trips to Fairview, the Fifteen Acres and Whitehall; it's about the schoolyard leagues and welcoming Mullins and Kelleher back to their old alma mater in frenzied excitement and awe.

And we did what Mullins and Kelleher said we'd do – we made it to Croke Park .

(first broadcast on RTÉ Radio in 2013)

ONLY A GAME
Maurice Cashell

I didn't keep a diary recording the joy and the anguish, the plaudits and the humiliations of my journey to Croke Park. But I do have one photograph, taken from the end line, where the umpires stand. In the foreground, the goalkeeper has caught the ball and is moving to the left to belt it outfield. Towering above him is the old Cusack Stand. Advancing towards him is Jock Haughey, stocky veteran player for St Vincents and Dublin. Frank Fleming of Civil Service and Mayo is moving towards Haughey with menace. In the background are half a dozen players who were household names in the early 1960s. I don't need a diary to remind me of what happened next.

For my first fifteen years I showed little promise as a footballer. Enthusiasm? Yes. Self-confidence to a fault. But skill? I couldn't kick snow off a rope. There are footballers who, when sides are picked, are always left for the last two places. A regular rejection in my case. And, very often, to complete that rejection, you're told to play in goals. But I got to like the position and, by the time I was sixteen, was good enough to play for the Longford Juveniles and, later, the Minors. There were no national trophies in that period, but I enjoyed the game, especially the camaraderie, the pleasure of doing something well, the occasional press coverage or photograph and, above all, satisfying one's insatiable desire to play for the county.

Two years later, now the regular goalkeeper on the Civil Service football team in Islandbridge, I graduated to the Longford Senior Team, first as a sub during the National League. After a few matches I found that sitting on damp wooden benches with the other subs began to dilute the camaraderie. I saw that my loyalty to the team depended on the extent of my active involvement in it. While I never wanted Longford to lose, I was destined to stay forever on the bench if the goalkeeper consistently played well. I hinted to the mentors that they should give me a crack at the job, maybe in a challenge match. But all through that winter I was handed a sub's jersey. I can't recall if I prayed for divine assistance. Possibly, because one Sunday, after Mass, fate intervened in the form of a burly full-forward from Baileboro. There was an altercation in our goalmouth. The forward was sent off. The goalkeeper was carried off. My moment had arrived.

There was much travel. For team members who were Dublin-based, every match was an away game.

On Thursday mornings, a postcard arrived telling me when to meet with Mick Keegan, our driver, critic and fan outside McBirneys on Aston Quay. The *Longford Leader* on Friday night carried the full team. For a period I was the regular choice. Larry Gillen was my full-back in Islandbridge, as well as for the county, and it worked well. I was happiest in the spring and summer. The ball was dry and easier to handle. We prepared and trained more thoroughly. We developed a better understanding. Autumn and Winter were different. Longer trips, often as far as Mayo and Sligo, in the National League. A leather ball when wet was slippery and twice as heavy, exposing a goalkeeper's frailities. I had good days and I had bad days.

Then came that Dublin Senior League match in Croke Park. And the photographs. Not the one of the goalkeeper bravely clearing his lines, but the four in the back page of the *Evening Press*, with the captions: 'Goal No 1'; 'Goal No 2'; 'Goal No 3' and 'Goal No 4.'

The following Thursday there was no postcard. On Friday night, there was a new goalkeeper in the *Longford Leader*. I talked to the Chairman of the County Board. Jimmy Flynn's advice was wise and gently, but firmly, delivered. It was only a game; I was young; it was time for me to move on, to get a life. For the next few years Jimmy presided over the most successful period for football in the county. The Senior Team won the O'Byrne Cup in 1965, the National Football League in 1966 and the Leinster Championship in 1968.

I was at Croke Park for all the matches. I came through the turnstiles.

It hurt not to be playing, not to be in the middle of it all. But you have to move on.

(first broadcast on RTÉ Radio in 2013)

LINING OUT
Pat Boran

They were the big lads, the strong lads, the fit lads,
with their gum-shields and groin-guards, their county colour kit-bags;
we were the bozos in the hand-me-down sad rags,
alone in our windswept goalposts, looking on.

They were the boys with the thick-knit socks
and long-lace boots, the calf muscles like rocks;
we were the castaways in cast-off togs,
marooned in our windswept goalposts, just about clinging on.

They were the ones who made every squad,
up front in the bus, all fired up like Greek gods,
they were the named, the famed, the proclaimed and the cherished;

we were the slow ones, the 'Christ sake, would you go on's,
the frozen half-dozen last to be chosen,
the nameless, the shameless interchangeable no ones,
we were the AN Others at the end of the list.

Teenaged he-men descended from bears,
blood on their knees, mud in their hair,
they were the boys with the ice in their hearts and their veins;
we were the wasters, the dodgers, the slackers,

the double vest-wearers, the chocolate snack-packers,
the most likely to get the ball smack in the kisser, and faint.

And then something happened, some fate struck a spark,
the wind changed direction, the bright sky went dark,
and the ball like a comet came down in our hands
and we held it;

And suddenly as one they rushed to our sides
in a flood of approval, a surge of pure pride,
to lift us up into the air on a tide of forgiveness;

and that sodden rectangle of tread-beaten grass
to the rear of the school, now the danger had passed,
was O'Moore Park or Croker itself, and *en masse*
the 'they' and the 'we' had been transformed at last into 'us.'

(first broadcast on RTÉ Radio in 2013)

OVER THE BAR

Mary O'Malley

R e-reading *Over The Bar* ahead of the centenary of Croke Park is a little like visiting the Ireland I grew up in, one that seems to have existed unnoticed in the public perception of Ireland Inc., having been written about mainly in another language, Irish, a world translated into English mainly through sports commentaries and dispatches from abroad, even when that world conducted much or all of its business in English.

It was the Ireland of Caitlín Maude and Cearta Sibhialta na Gaeltachta, of an aging Máirtín Ó Cadhain speaking passionately from the back of a lorry in Cois Fharraige 1969, in failing health, to young people who would not accept their fate of immigration and unemployment as submissively as it sometimes suits us to imagine their ancestors did.

As a youngster, I knew nothing about the GAA except that it led to endless arguments, but was as much a part of Ireland as the Government. Neither had much of a presence where we lived, but, like everyone else, I listened to the radio. I listened to Micheál O'Hehir. I listened to Micheál Ó Muircheartaigh. I heard Breandán Ó hEithir. I longed for Paris and Rome, New York and Valparaiso.

Breandán Ó hEithir was admired by many, trusted in some implicit way to give out a version of the world that was visceral, witty and rich in anecdote. His dislike of the cant of the Patriarchy within and without the GAA and other Gaelic organisations never robbed him of compassion. He came, after all, from a place with a deep distrust of daily communicants, without a single available flat space for a team to play any sport in, what fields there were being far too valuable to risk. The game they played with sticks wasn't quite hurley, and it certainly wasn't cricket, which I learn was played by none other than Michael Cusack, after whom the Cusack Stand is named.

Ó hEithir was young in an Ireland where men were men and girls were nurses, games were a way for young men to let off excess steam before being shipped away to England or America, and were entertainments on a slightly more serious level than fights and dancing. Dances were divided into céilís, where nobody went into a decline at the sight of a scrap, and those where teachers met nurses with a view to marriage, where the women did. But then, teachers didn't often scrap.

Breandán went to St Enda's College in Galway, but because of the Second World War, he spent the first year in Drumcondra, where he got to know Dublin and Croke Park. Writing forty years later, the sense of that early excitement and delight still shines through. He knew something all great Gaelic sports writers know: that the sport and the folklore are intermingled, that this was our picturehouse and our theatre, where history was remembered, exaggerated and misread more accurately than in the many books lining the shelves of libraries and universities and schools. A history of struggle and madness and spite, of games abandoned by team and referee, of a postcard from the wives and girlfriends of one team to a local paper declaring their fears that the neighbouring 'Gaels' would murder their husbands. Where else could you possibly have such fun?

After St Enda's, he attended UCG with mixed results. The same university that awarded President Ronald Reagan an honorary doctorate in 1986, causing secret-service men from America to peer down manholes and up chimneys (prompting one exasperated wit to ask: 'I wonder would it be any use giving that fella a brush?') banned Máirtín Ó Cadhain from speaking at the annual Irish Week in the 1950s. His story *Cré na Cille* was being serialised in the *Irish Press* at the time when he was banned from speaking 'because he was not a suitable person to address us.' Breandán withdrew from the Cumann Éigse agus Seanchas as a result.

Lest we think the university above such things, the decision to ban Ó Cadhain was, it seems, personal, and made by reason of politics, or spite, or both.

I saw Ó hEithir only once. He was opening an exhibition by a talented young sculptor from Inis Mór. Shy of someone about whom I had heard so much, I hung back. I knew he lived in Paris, was against Section 31 of the Broadcasting Act, as was I, and was old enough to realise he was someone out of the ordinary.

He was a cosmopolitan Aran man, who did not go into weaknesses at a discussion of Republicanism, loved hurling and rugby, read the great American sports writers, wrote hilariously about those extremes of heroic language penned by 'The Gael' or 'The Celt' and parodied by Flann O'Brien and Joyce, while retaining his passion for the GAA, despite the ban on involvement by players in foreign games. Yet through it all he retained a deep and exasperated love for the Gaelic Athletic Assosiation, taking the best of it and recognising that its best is in many ways the best of ourselves, making well-earned fun of its zanier moments, meetings and downright madnesses, which are, after all, our own.

Like most people from the West, he disliked orthodoxy and distrusted puritans. He came from a culture where such simple-mindedness would never do – there was too much mockery and too keen a sense of loss. Bishops were remote, and more than one had found, when forcing some Maynooth-spawned orthodoxy, that the better part of valour was discretion.

Like all good writers, Ó hEithir leaves you with questions long after the book has been laid down.

Who was the young airman who fell from the sky near Inis Mór, and, caught in his parachute harness, drowned and was fished from the sea later that day? He was buried in the graveyard at Cnocán na mBan, and when his parents came to see it after the war, they decided to leave him there, overlooking Kilmurvey Bay, because his grave was so well tended and they liked the place well.

And who was the humble GAA everyman who cycled thirteen miles in the rain and dried out in front of the oven before cycling the thirteen miles back, week in, week out, the anonymous delegate to whom *Over the Bar* is dedicated?

I know the answer to the second question: he's in Moycullen and Oughterard and Rahoon, tireless as ever and not always a he. And maybe he's training the goalie of a future Galway team to utter the words: 'Is mór an onóir dom an corn seo a ghlacadh ar son fhoireann na Gaillimhe....'

A moment, forever connected in my mind to the man I never knew. A year or two after his death, I was noticing the emerald ring worn by a striking looking woman standing in the corner of Kenny's Gallery in Galway. She smiled, recognising envy but not at all put out. Caught, I said 'That's a beautiful ring.' We talked. She was Ó hEithir's wife, Catherine. Hearing how I admired him, she said 'Breandán gave this to me,' and smiled enigmatically. Whenever I hear his name now, it is the ring I see on her finger, the colour the sea has in a certain light, off Dún Aengus.

(first broadcast on RTÉ Radio in 2013)

THE MATCH

in memoriam J.F.
for Paddy

John O'Donnell

The doors and boot banged shut, the engine not
yet started and you'd be switching on. '*He hits it*
long again'; how many Sundays did we hear
a high ball arcing through a summer sky before

being plucked out and belted back into the maw
of our car, among chocolate stains and crisps, more
toothsome fizz-filled drinks than we could finish?
'*A right shemozzle here,*' O'Hehir in the Yiddish

screeching with excitement, my young brother and I
trading pinch for pinch in the back seat as we
headed for the shore, hoping the rain would finally get bored
with us, drift off to ruin someone else's day. You'd

always drive, though you were nowhere near
the spattered windscreen. Eyes fixed in a beatific stare
beyond Strand Road, the seagulls hanging round like knives;
all you could see were goals and points and wides,

Micheál's frenzied commentary yammering non-stop
from the speaker. Even when you'd park you'd keep
the spell, carrying a transistor over still-damp sand,
a tabernacle tuned in to Athlone, the same one I'd

collected after from the hospital, with the rest of your things.
I'm turning the dial now, following the wavebands
in case I'd find you. But the only sound I hear is the soft hiss
of the sea. In the end you bowed your head, the way you'd always

done at Mass, but on those Sunday afternoons gave thanks and
praise for hurling and football; me a sherpa stumbling behind,
lugging bathtowels and a deckchair as you strode ahead to join
the congregation, stretched out beside battered radios along

the beach or in the dunes until 'The final whistle,' tinny cheers
of far-off crowds rising above us like hosannas in the air.

(first broadcast on RTÉ Radio in 2006)

Author Biographical Notes

John Allen is a former Cork hurler and footballer who also managed the county's senior hurling team to All-Ireland success in 2005.

Nicky Barry lives in Killarney, County Kerry, and is a retired PE teacher and former County Down Minor, Junior and Senior footballer, winning an Ulster Senior Championship medal in 1963. He is a noted musician, poet, songwriter and golf writer who has performed on Radio Kerry, UTV and RTÉ radio and television.

Denise Blake had her second collection, *How to Spin Without Getting Dizzy*, published by Summer Palace Press in 2010. Denise is listed in *Poetry Ireland*'s 'Writers in the School' directory, and has wide experience of facilitating workshops for children and adults.

Pat Boran was born in Portlaoise in 1963, and lives in Dublin. He has received the Patrick Kavanagh and the O'Shaughnessy awards for poetry and is a member of Aosdána. His most recent book of poems is *The Next Life* (Dedalus 2012).

Louis Brennan, an engineer, worked for a Waterford company that exported high-voltage equipment. He still collects first editions and rejection slips.

Lynn Cahill co-founded (with Richard Cook) the Cat Laughs Comedy Festival in Kilkenny, and was Festival Producer from 1994–2008. She is still happily living in Waterford, where she is the Marketing Manager for the Waterford Museum of Treasures in The Viking Triangle.

Tim Carey is Heritage Officer for Dún Laoghaire–Rathdown County Council. He has written a number of books, including *Mountjoy – the Story of a Prison, Hanged for Ireland* and *Croke Park: A History*, and co-authored *The Martello Towers of Dublin*.

Maurice Cashell was born in Ballymahon, County Longford, and has lived and worked in France, Switzerland and Belgium as well as in Ireland. He has been involved with writing groups in the People's College and the Irish Writers' Centre, and has published short stories, travel features and books and articles on Irish labour law and industrial relations.

Pat Coleman is a retired primary school principal who has been passionately involved in the GAA all his life. The big Sunday championship matches, with all their colour and excitement, are the highlights of his summer.

John Conroy was born in a village straddling the townlands of Abbeyknockmoy and Skehanagh in County Galway, but now lives in Maynooth, County Kildare. He is married with two children, and has been a contributor to *Sunday Miscellany* as well as other broadcasts over a number of years.

Leo Cullen is a novelist, poet and broadcaster (with BBC 4 and RTÉ Radio). Publications include a book of short stories *Clocking Ninety on the Road to Cloughjordan* (Blackstaff), a novel *Let's Twist Again* (Blackstaff) and poetry and short stories in many publications including the *Sunday Independent*.

Martina Devlin was born in Omagh, County Tyrone. She is an author and columnist for the *Irish Independent*. She has written a number of novels, non-fiction books and short stories, and awards include the Royal Society of Literature's V.S. Pritchett Prize, a Hennessy Literary Award and the National Newspapers of Ireland's 'Columnist of the Year' Award.

Theo Dorgan is a poet, novelist, prose writer, editor, translator and broadcaster. His most recent publications are *Greek*, a

313

collection of poems from Dedalus Press, and *Making Way*, a novel from New Island Books.

John Downing has long ago given up believing in miracles, but he still believes that the Limerick hurlers will raise the Liam McCarthy Cup at least once more in his lifetime. Meanwhile, he pursues another passion, as he observes and writes about politics, which also helps to pay the bills.

Noel Duffy's début collection *In the Library of Lost Objects* was short-listed for the 2012 Strong Award for best first collection by an Irish poet. His second, *On Light & Carbon*, is forthcoming from Ward Wood Publishing.

Noel Ellis is a primary school teacher working in Lucan and living in Beaumont, but originally hails from Carlow town. He has been involved in the GAA all his life, with his home team, Éire Óg, his school team, ScoilMhuire and his current club, Whitehall Colmcille.

Peter Fallon's most recent collection of poems is *The Company of Horses*. He held the Burns Library Chair at Boston College last year.

Theresa Farrell was born in County Galway in 1963, and was educated in Athenry. She moved to Dublin in the 1980s, married Richard, and has two grown-up children. She works in St Patrick's College, Drumcondra, and writes short stories in her spare time.

Mary Folan is from Galway, and is the Abbey Theatre Press Officer.

Catherine Foley is an award-winning writer and a former journalist with *The Irish Times*. Her novella *An Cailín Rua* won first prize at the Oireachtas Literary Awards in 2004. She has presented, co-scripted and co-produced television documentaries on well-known individuals such as the writer Molly Keane, the singer Tom Clancy and the journalist Donal Foley.

Norman Freeman grew up in Tipperary, and it gave him a lifelong absorption with the game of hurling. A seafarer in his early years, he later published two companion books about famous matches. His humorous treatment of the world of hurling featured on a Gaelic games website for several years, and is now appearing in the *Munster Express* newspaper.

Liam Horan is a native of Ballinrobe, County Mayo, where he lives with his wife Noreen. He is a former Gaelic games correspondent of the *Irish Independent*, and created the 'Championship Man' essay series on RTÉ Radio One. Along with writing colleague John Corless, he runs the theatre production company Half Solid Productions (www.halfsolid. com), and in 2012 John and Liam toured their first play *The Pull*.

Joe Kane, a native of Dublin, spent his adult years in Donegal, a county and a life that he loved. He worked primarily with infused glass and ceramics, later gaining an MA in Poetry from Lancaster University at fifty years of age. Two of his poetry books: *The Boy Who Nearly Won the Texaco Art Competition* and *Lazarus on the Backstrand* were published by New Island Books. He died in 2012, after many years of ill health.

Colbert Kearney is a retired academic, whose early induction into the mysteries of Hill 16 resulted in a passion for sport and an unhealthy respect for Kerry football.

Joe Kearney grew up near Callan in County Kilkenny. After a lifetime in the oil industry, he has reinvented himself as a documentary-maker and writer.

Cyril Kelly, a native of Listowel, spent many years teaching in Dublin, and is now retired. His writing has featured on RTÉ Radio One and Lyric FM. Broadcasts include contributions to *A Living Word*, *Sunday Miscellany*, *The Quiet Quarter* and *Fiction Fifteen*.

Mary Ledwidge is originally from Kilkenny, and now lives in County Laois.

Mae Leonard, a native of Limerick, now lives with her family in Naas, County Kildare. Her husband Joe was a member the All-Ireland Limerick Minor Hurling Team in 1958.

John MacKenna is the author of seventeen books of fiction, memoir and poetry. He is also a playwright. His novel *Clare* will be republished next year in New Island's *Modern Irish Classics* series, and his latest novel *Joseph* will follow in the autumn.

Josephine McArdle is a Westmeath woman, and daughter of the lifelong GAA enthusiast Paddy Murphy. She grew up in awe of this organisation, and writes in his memory.

Larry McCluskey is a Community Theatre actor, director and adjudicator, and is the current Chairman of Cootehill Celtic GAA Club. Now retired, he taught in Ireland and Ghana and was CEO of Wicklow and Monaghan VECs, as well as formerly being a member of the boards of An Chomhairle Ealaion and the Tyrone Guthrie Centre.

Pádraig McGinn is a retired school principal, living in Carrick-on-Shannon, County Leitrim. His stories have been published in the *Leitrim Guardian* and *First Cut*. He has been short-listed in a number of writing competitions, including The Bard of Armagh and the Strokestown Poetry Award.

Theresa McKenna is a proud Tipperary woman, born in Borrisokane, County Tipperary. She teaches in Eureka Secondary School, County Meath. Her writing reflects her interest in culture, language, history and nature. Some of her favourite writers include John Keats, William Wordsworth, John McGahern and John O'Donohue.

Tommy McKearney is an organiser with the Independent Workers Union, and lives with his wife Patricia in Monaghan. In his youth he played football for his local club in the Moy, County Tyrone, and also with that county's minor team.

Gerry Moran is from Kilkenny, and is a former principal of St Patrick's De La Salle Boys School in the city. He is the author of *Kilkenny City & County*.

Bernie Ní Fhlatharta is a journalist with the *Connacht Tribune*, and an occasional contributor to RTÉ's Raidió na Gaeltachta, which has broadcast her escapades for the past three decades.

William Nolan is a publisher and historical geographer. He played some hurling with Thurles CBS and Knocknagow (South Tipperary), and was a committee member and player with the now defunct Young Ireland Hurling Club in Dublin.

Conor O'Callaghan is originally from Dundalk, and now lives in Manchester. His memoir *Red Mist – Roy Keane and Ireland's World Cup Civil War* was published by Bloomsbury in 2004. He has also written four collections of poetry, published by The Gallery Press.

John O'Donnell's work has received various awards, including the Irish National Poetry Prize, the Ireland Funds Prize, the Hennessy Award for Poetry and, most recently, the Hennessy Award for Fiction. A barrister living and working in Dublin, he has published two collections of poetry; a third collection is forthcoming.

Bairbre O'Hogan was born in Dublin. She has worked in education and in tourism, and is now a State-accredited translator to and from Irish. Her main writing focus is on memoir, hoping that the material will give her sons access to their family stories.

Mary O'Malley has written seven books of poetry, and is working on poems, essays and a prose book. She is the recipient of various awards and a member of Aosdána.

Joe Ó Muircheartaigh is Dublin-born and Clare-based, but calls himself a Kerryman. He is Deputy Editor / Sports Editor of the *Clare People* in Ennis, and the author of four books.

Dan O'Neill is from Castlebar, County Mayo. His first assignment as a newly trained garda was in County Louth. Subsequently, he worked in business, and the tourism industry. He played football for Mayo and later for County Louth, for which he won an All-Ireland Senior Football medal.

Art Ó Súilleabháin is a children's writer, a writer of poetry and a contributor to new writing as Gaeilge and in English, living in Corrna Móna, at the northern end of Lough Corrib.

Eamon O'Shea is a Professor of Economics at the National University of Ireland, Galway. His primary research interests are the economics of ageing, dementia and rural gerontology. He was coach to the Tipperary Senior Hurling Team, which won the All-Ireland final in 2010, and is currently the manger of that team.

Joe O'Toole, a Dingle man, was an elected Independent Senator for twenty-four years, and was General Secretary of the Irish National Teachers Organisation. He was a member of the GAA Coiste Bainistíochta, and is a former President of ICTU.

Cathy Power has been a contributor to *Sunday Miscellany* for a decade, many of her pieces relating to her status as an avid fan of Kilkenny hurling, while being a proud Dubliner. Having spent twelve years living in Kilkenny, she now lives in the capital.

Paul Rouse is a lecturer in the School of History and Archives at University College Dublin. He has written extensively about the history of sport in Ireland, particularly about the history of the GAA.

Tom Rowley is a native of County Mayo, Dublin-based freelance writer and public-relations consultant. He is a former senior journalist with the *Irish Independent*, and Government media advisor. He is a regular contributor to a number of national publications.

Tommy Sands is a singer, songwriter and social activist from County Down. As part of the acclaimed Sands Family, one of the most important traditional groups in the early years of Ireland's folk revival, Tommy has worked to add beauty to the world and to point out where it still needs improvement.

Tom Seaver is a retired secondary school teacher, and a long-time follower of the GAA. He played for Peadar Macken's GFC in Dublin in the 1950s.

William J. Smyth played minor, under-21, intermediate and senior hurling with Tipperary and was a member of the first under-21 All-Ireland winning team. He lectured in historical and social geography in the USA and Canada before returning to UCD, Maynooth and, since 1977, is a Professor (now Emeritus) of Geography at UCC.

Alan Titley is the author of six novels, three collections of stories and one book of poetry. He has also written for stage and screen, and presented radio and television documentaries. He was formerly Head of the Irish Department in St Patrick's College, DCU, and is an Emeritus Professor of Modern Irish at UCC.

Patrick E. Walsh is a proud Thomastown man, but an even prouder son of a Rower Inistioge man.

Bert Wright entered the book trade in the 1980s, and in 1987 he moved to Dublin to open the first Irish Waterstone's shop on Dawson Street. Since then, he's been a bookstore manager; marketing manager with Waterstone's USA; book festival director and freelance bookselling consultant. He is an administrator of the Bord Gais Energy Irish Book Awards and Events Curator for several literary festivals. Married with two children, he lives in Dalkey, County Dublin.

Photograph and illustration details and credits

(p10) Official Programme of the All-Ireland Hurling Final 1964 © GAA Museum

(p16) Referee Damien Eagers removes a dog from the pitch, Croke Park, 2005. Photographer Gerry Kinneavy © Sportsfile

(p18) The Gates of Croke Park. Date and Photographer unknown © RTÉ Stills Library

(p31) Croke Park from Hill 16, 1963. Photographer Roy Bedell © RTÉ Stills Library

(p44) Official Programme of the All-Ireland Football Final 1947 © GAA Museum

(p55) Official Programme of the All-Ireland Football Final 1943 © GAA Museum

(p60) Tim Kennelly holding the Sam Maguire Cup after Kerry's victory over Dublin in the All-Ireland Football Senior Final, 1979. Photographer Tom Holton © RTÉ Stills Library

(p76) RTÉ Outside Unit. Date and Photographer unknown © RTÉ Stills Library

(p81) Phil Mulally with radio camera, RTÉ television outside broadcast unit, Croke Park, 1969. Photographer unknown © RTÉ Stills Library

(p93)Official Programme of the All-Ireland Hurling Final 1958 © GAA Museum

(p103) Official Programme of the All-Ireland Football Final 1957 © GAA Museum

(p104) Listening to the 1933 All-Ireland Hurling Final, 1933. Photographer Christy Riordan © RTÉ Stills Library

(p113) The Sunday Game studio, 2012. Photographer John Cooney © RTÉ Stills Library

(p132) The Artane Boys' Band, 1984. Photographer Tom Holton © RTÉ Stills Library

(p136) Official Programme of the All-Ireland Football Final 1939 © GAA Museum

*(p149) Kilkenny Hurlers © GAA Museum

(p159) Official Programme of the All-Ireland Football Final 1959 © GAA Museum

(p178) Martin Comerford and Michael Cahill leap for the sliotar during the All-Ireland Senior Hurling Final, 2010 © GAA Museum

(p191) Paul McComiskey sidesteps Eoin McCadagon during the 2010 All-Ireland Senior Football Final © GAA Museum

(p198) Micheál Ó Muircheartaigh, commenting on the Munster Hurling Final, 1987. Photographer Peter Harding © RTÉ Stills Library

(p204) Kilkenny Hurler Ollie Walsh © GAA Museum

(p210)Frank Hogan holds his banner, John 3:7, Croke Park, 2013 © Brian Fay

(p213) Nancy Cunningham, colours seller, 1975. Photographer Eve Holmes © RTÉ Stills Library

(p218) Fruit sellers outside Croke Park, 1977. Photographer Bill St Leger © RTÉ Stills Library (p229) Three Dublin supporters, Croke Park, 2013 © Brian Fay

(p237) George Cunningham, colours seller, 1975. Photographer Eve Holmes © RTÉ Stills Library

(p249) Rower-Inistioge team of 1968 with Michael Walsh (captain) front row, fifth from left © The Rower-Inistioge GAA Club

(p259) The Mayo team parade in Croke Park prior to the 2012 All-Ireland Senior Football Final © GAA Museum

(p262) Con Houlihan, 2004. Photographer John Cooney © RTÉ Stills Library

(p265) Jim McGuinness, manager of the winning Donegal team at the end of the All-Ireland Football Senior Final in Croke Park in 2013 © GAA Museum

(p268) The Wellington Monument, Phoenix Park, Dublin, 1966. Photographer Phil Dowling © RTÉ Stills Library

(p271) Kevin Heffernan in conversation with his team during a training session, 1983. Photographer John Cooney © RTÉ Stills Library

(p279) Official Programme of the All-Ireland Hurling Final 1938 © GAA Museum

(p289) Seamus Darby scoring the winning Goal for Offaly in the 1982 All-Ireland Senior Football Final against Kerry © Sportsfile

(p293) Steven Cluxton takes the final and winning point for Dublin, All-Ireland Senior Football Final 2011 © GAA Museum

(p309))Breandán Ó hEithir, 1980. Photographer Peter Harding © RTÉ Stills Library

(p311) Croke Park seats, 2013. Photographer Brian Fay.

Acknowledgements

This book and the regular *Sunday Miscellany* radio programme depend on the work, co-operation and support of many. Firstly, I would like to sincerely thank all those who have contributed to the programme over the years by sending open submissions or by accepting an invitation to contribute. You are the essential ingredient to making the programme the success it is. Every thanks to the sound engineers, programme planning and control, library and archive staff, the RTÉ Stills Library and the communications office. Particular thanks to my colleagues and former colleagues Pearl Quinn, Philippa Gee, Claire Martin, Robert Canning, Jack Smith, Brian Rice, James Moynes, Sarah Neville, Maureen Catterson, Emer Beasley, Peter Windle, John Bates, Peter Cheevers, Sarah Blake, Lisa O'Brien, Geralyn Aspil, Joan Ryan, Caroline O'Flanagan, Fionnuala Hayes, Liz Sweeney, Jarlath Holland, Brian Carthy, John Kenney, Des Cahill, Margaret Newport, Aidan Butler, Kay Sheehy, Eileen Heron, Marion Richardson, Ger Philpot, Kevin Brew, Bernadette Comerford, Aoife Nic Cormaic and Siobhan Mannion for their invaluably practical and good-humoured support.

Thank you Paul Waldron and everyone at All Write Media, as well as Gar Duffy, for providing the accompanying CD. Thanks also to Mark Reynolds at the GAA Museum, Tim Carey, Liam Horan and Lisa Grace at Sportsfile.

I would like to thank Lorelei Harris, RTÉ Editor, Drama Documentaries and Features for her continued support of my work on *Sunday Miscellany* and on this project in particular, which

Clíodhna Ní Anluain

has made all the difference. Also, former RTÉ Radio Managing Director, Clare Duignan, such a supporter of the programme, and Jim Jennings, acting RTÉ Radio Managing Director.

Thanks to my brothers Colm and Billy, my sisters Éilis and Máire and my mother Bernie who agreed to the inclusion of the lines of my father's poem in the book.

New Island Books has been the publisher of a number of *Sunday Miscellany* anthologies I have edited. They have always delivered such a beautiful production, and embraced the spirit and possibilities of bringing *Sunday Miscellany* collections to readers. It has been a pleasure and privilege to work with editor Justin Corfield, who so cheerfully and humorously kept me focused on the editing involved in this book. I am extremely grateful to Mariel Deegan, Aisling Glynn and Eoin Purcell, who saw the potential in gathering this material together as a book in the first place, and who were so open to the suggestions to include photography and a sample sound from the programme archive relating to this book, and whose texts are also included here.

The present GAA hurlers and footballers continue to provide unforgettable moments of inspiration to me, and contribute such a vital part in animating the conversation about this book and related matters around our kitchen table. Above all, however, it is my good fortune that my husband Brian Fay and our children Nóra and Eoghan share my passion for its subject. For their wonderful company and encouragement throughout this project, I am sincerely thankful.

324